Communications
in Computer and Information Science   1821

Rationale

The CCIS series is devoted to the publication of proceedings of computer science conferences. Its aim is to efficiently disseminate original research results in informatics in printed and electronic form. While the focus is on publication of peer-reviewed full papers presenting mature work, inclusion of reviewed short papers reporting on work in progress is welcome, too. Besides globally relevant meetings with internationally representative program committees guaranteeing a strict peer-reviewing and paper selection process, conferences run by societies or of high regional or national relevance are also considered for publication.

Topics

The topical scope of CCIS spans the entire spectrum of informatics ranging from foundational topics in the theory of computing to information and communications science and technology and a broad variety of interdisciplinary application fields.

Information for Volume Editors and Authors

Publication in CCIS is free of charge. No royalties are paid, however, we offer registered conference participants temporary free access to the online version of the conference proceedings on SpringerLink (http://link.springer.com) by means of an http referrer from the conference website and/or a number of complimentary printed copies, as specified in the official acceptance email of the event.

CCIS proceedings can be published in time for distribution at conferences or as post-proceedings, and delivered in the form of printed books and/or electronically as USBs and/or e-content licenses for accessing proceedings at SpringerLink. Furthermore, CCIS proceedings are included in the CCIS electronic book series hosted in the SpringerLink digital library at http://link.springer.com/bookseries/7899. Conferences publishing in CCIS are allowed to use Online Conference Service (OCS) for managing the whole proceedings lifecycle (from submission and reviewing to preparing for publication) free of charge.

Publication process

The language of publication is exclusively English. Authors publishing in CCIS have to sign the Springer CCIS copyright transfer form, however, they are free to use their material published in CCIS for substantially changed, more elaborate subsequent publications elsewhere. For the preparation of the camera-ready papers/files, authors have to strictly adhere to the Springer CCIS Authors' Instructions and are strongly encouraged to use the CCIS LaTeX style files or templates.

Abstracting/Indexing

CCIS is abstracted/indexed in DBLP, Google Scholar, EI-Compendex, Mathematical Reviews, SCImago, Scopus. CCIS volumes are also submitted for the inclusion in ISI Proceedings.

How to start

To start the evaluation of your proposal for inclusion in the CCIS series, please send an e-mail to ccis@springer.com.

Arthur Gibadullin

Editor

Information Technologies and Intelligent Decision Making Systems

Second International Conference, ITIDMS 2022
Virtual Event, December 12–14, 2022
Revised Selected Papers

Springer

Editor
Arthur Gibadullin
National Research University "MPEI"
Moscow, Russia

ISSN 1865-0929   ISSN 1865-0937 (electronic)
Communications in Computer and Information Science
ISBN 978-3-031-31352-3   ISBN 978-3-031-31353-0 (eBook)
https://doi.org/10.1007/978-3-031-31353-0

This Springer imprint is published by the registered company Springer Nature Switzerland AG
The registered company address is: Gewerbestrasse 11, 6330 Cham, Switzerland

Preface

The international scientific and practical conference "Information Technologies and Intelligent Decision Making Systems" (ITIDMS 2022) was held on December 12–14, 2022, on the Microsoft Teams platform due to COVID-19.

The conference was held with the aim of developing and exchanging international experience in the field of information, digital and intellectual technologies, within the framework of which proposals were formulated for digital, intellectual and information transformation, the development of computer models and the improvement of automated and computing processes.

A distinctive feature of the conference is that it presented reports of authors from USA, Canada, Bangladesh, Uzbekistan and Russia. Researchers from different countries addressed the process of transition on the path of information and digital development, and presented the main directions and developments that can improve efficiency and development.

The conference sessions were moderated by Artur Gibadullin of the National Research University "MPEI", Moscow, Russia.

Thus, the conference facilitated scientific recommendations on the use of information, computer, digital and intellectual technologies in industry and fields of activity that can be useful to state and regional authorities, international and supranational organizations, and the scientific and professional community.

Each presented paper was reviewed by at least three members of the Program Committee in a double-blind manner. As a result of the work of all reviewers, 14 papers were accepted for publication out of the 38 received submissions. The reviews were based on the assessment of the topic of the submitted materials, the relevance of the study, the scientific significance and novelty, the quality of the materials, and the originality of the work. Authors could revise their paper and submit it again for review. Reviewers, Program Committee members, and Organizing Committee members did not enter into discussions with the authors of the articles.

The Organizing Committee of the conference expresses its gratitude to the staff at Springer who supported the publication of these proceedings. In addition, the Organizing Committee would like to thank the conference participants, reviewers and everyone who helped organize this conference and shape the present volume for publication in the Springer CCIS series.

December 2022   Arthur Gibadullin

Organization

Program Committee Chairs

Yuri Vasilievich Gulyaev	Institute of Radio-engineering and Electronics, RAS, Russia
Vladimir Alekseevich Zernov	Russian New University, Russia
Andrey Sergeevich Kryukovskiy	Russian New University, Russia
Evgeny Alekseevich Palkin	Russian New University, Russia
Artur Arturovich Gibadullin	National Research University "Moscow Power Engineering Institute", Russia

Program Committee

Alexander Stepanovich Bugaev	Institute of Radio-engineering and Electronics RAS, Russia
Sergey Apollonovich Nikitiov	Institute of Radio-engineering and Electronics RAS, Russia
Oleg Vasilievich Zolotarev	Russian New University, Russia
Leonid Vitalievich Labunets	Russian New University, Russia
Maurizio Palesi	University of Catania, Italy
Yixuan Wang	Northwestern University, USA
Afroz Shah	Columbia University, USA
Ghali Naami	Sidi Mohamed Ben Abdellah University, Morocco
Jencia J.	Karunya Institute of Science and Technology, India
Pratap Sekhar Puhan	Sreenidhi Institute of Science and Technology, India
Priscilla Joy	Noorul Islam University, India
Meng Wei	Lanzhou Jiaotong University, China
Hymlin Rose S. G.	RMD College of Engineering, India
Ke Wang	University of North Carolina at Charlotte, USA
Rajanarayan Prusty	Alliance University, India
Kamal Saluja	Chitkara University Institute of Engineering and Technology, India
Dmitry Evgenievich Morkovkin	Financial University under the Government of the Russian Federation, Russia
Dmitry Vladimirovich Rastyagaev	Russian New University, Russia

Organizing Committee

Artur Arturovich Gibadullin	National Research University "Moscow Power Engineering Institute", Russia
Elena Vladislavovna Bovtrikova	Russian New University, Russia
Olga Evgenievna Matyunina	Russian New University, Russia
Dmitry Evgenievich Morkovkin	Financial University under the Government of the Russian Federation, Russia
Dmitry Vladimirovich Rastyagaev	Russian New University, Russia

Organizer

Russian New University, Russia

Contents

Algorithm for Solving the Problem of Multi-criteria Optimization of Poorly Formed Processes Based on the Construction of a Fuzzy Logic Model

D. T. Muhamediyeva[1(✉)] and U. U. Khasanov[2]

[1] "Tashkent Institute of Irrigation and Agricultural Mechanization Engineers", National Research University, Tashkent, Uzbekistan
dilnoz134@rambler.ru

[2] Urgench Branch of Tashkent University of Information Technologies Named After Muhammad Al Kharezmy, Urgench, Uzbekistan

Abstract. The purpose of the research is to develop fuzzy logical models and algorithms and a software complex of fire safety on the basis of an intellectual approach. The task of the research is to develop an algorithm for solving the problem of multi-criteria optimization of poorly formed processes based on the construction of a fuzzy logic model. In this case, the mathematical model of calculating the reasonable number of operational fire-rescue units, fire extinguishing equipment and assigning them to extinguishing areas, that is, the optimization of the composition of forces and equipment in the fire, is formalized in the form of interacting objects.

Keywords: Algorithm · Fuzzy Logic Models · Fire Safety · Mathematical Model

1 Introduction

Systematic analysis of complex processes and objects, research of their modeling processes in order to optimize their parameters and manage them showed that there is an inverse relationship between the "complexity" and "accuracy" of solving the above-mentioned problems. According to this law, as the complexity of the researched objects increases, deterministic, including purely probabilistic (stochastic) methods do not provide accurate, object-friendly models of processes and, accordingly, optimization, decision-making and control models [1, 2].

This determined the relevance of working with uncertainties, including those of a subjective nature, developing new directions in mathematics: the development and formation of interval fuzzy sets and lines of possibilities [3–5].

The need for scientific research works on the development of traditional and modern methods of intellectual processing of the system is emerging due to the increase in the emergency situations occurring in the world and the material and moral damage seen in them. In this regard, scientific research is being carried out in the world aimed at the joint

A. Gibadullin (Ed.): ITIDMS 2022, CCIS 1821, pp. 1–9, 2023.
https://doi.org/10.1007/978-3-031-31353-0_1

development of fuzzy logic, neural networks and evolutionary algorithms, as well as the creation of calculation algorithms, including the development of fuzzy logic models, algorithms and programs of weakly formed processes based on intellectual analysis of data [6–8].

2 Materials and Methods

The problem of multi-criteria optimization of the effective placement of firefighting units in given positions is written in the form (1) and (2):

$$z_1\left(x_{ij}^*\right) = \max_{x_{ij} \in D}\left(\sum_{i=1}^{m}\sum_{j=1}^{n} c_{ij}^1 x_{ij}\right),$$

$$z_2\left(x_{ij}^*\right) = \min_{x_{ij} \in D}\left(\sum_{i=1}^{m}\sum_{j=1}^{n} c_{ij}^2 x_{ij}\right),$$

$$\dots\dots\dots\dots\dots$$

$$z_s\left(x_{ij}^*\right) = \min_{x_{ij} \in D}\left(\sum_{i=1}^{m}\sum_{j=1}^{n} c_{ij}^s x_{ij}\right),$$
(1)

$$D = \left\{ x_{ij} \Big| \sum_{i=1}^{m} x_{ij} \le Q_{1j}, \ \sum_{j=1}^{n} x_{ij} \le Q_{2i}, \ x_{ij} > 0, \ i = \overline{1, m}, \ j = \overline{1, n} \right\},$$
(2)

Here:

n – number of objects on fire;

m – number of emergency departments;

S – number of criteria;

x_{ij} – j-resource directed from the emergency department to the i-facility; Q_{1j} – j-fire facility resource requirements;

Q_{2i} – Resources available in the i-Emergency Unit (EU).;

c_{ij}^s – i-s-cost (time, road, water, etc.) per unit of resources directed from the emergency department to j-fire facility.

In most cases, the limitations of parametric models consist of the mathematical description and quantitative expression of very different conditions on which a certain technical or production process depends. This diversity can be seen, in particular, in the fact that the causes influencing the changes in the quantities that help to express the corresponding changes should be viewed as independent but acting simultaneously. It is natural to represent problems of this type using several parameters. Often, only "fuzzy" information about the coefficients of a parametric model is available. The theory of fuzzy sets is used in the work as a mathematical apparatus that allows to formalize fuzzy data. S independent parameters $\lambda_1, \dots, \lambda_S$ parametric model or S parametric problem with, is written in matrix form as follows:

$$z(x_{ij}^*) = \min_{x_{ij} \in D}\left(\sum_{i=1}^{m}\sum_{j=1}^{n} (\lambda_1 c_{ij}^1 + \lambda_2 c_{ij}^2 + \dots + \lambda_S c_{ij}^S) x_{ij}\right),$$
(3)

$$D = \left\{ x_{ij} \,\middle|\, \sum_{i=1}^{m} x_{ij} \le Q_{1j}, \ \sum_{j=1}^{n} x_{ij} \le Q_{2i}, \ x_{ij} \ge 0, \ i = \overline{1,m}, \ j = \overline{1,n} \right\} \tag{4}$$

Here: λ_s- s-parameter of the multicriteria objective function.

In the case of multi-criteria optimization, it is difficult to evaluate the optimal solution of the problem according to the set of criteria. As the most common methods in this regard, we can take the additive check and the methods evaluated by the decision maker (VAT) [9]. An algorithm for solving the problem of multi-criteria optimization of poorly formed processes was developed based on the construction of a fuzzy logic model [10, 11].

We will consider a fuzzy method to identify alternative solutions. Solving the multi-criteria optimization problem consists of the following steps [12]:

– Formation of the objective function in an ambiguous environment.
– Determining the values of the boundary conditions in an ambiguous form.
– Develop relevance function for criteria.
– Defining a "preference" base and/or rule base for criteria.
– Calculation of the value of the objective function.
– Defuzzification of the objective function.

This $\Lambda \in D_A$ are found using the following fuzzy rule inferences:

$$\bigcup_{p=1}^{k_i} \left(\bigcap_{i=1}^{S} \lambda_i = \psi_{i,jp} \ - \ \text{with weight} \right) \rightarrow z_s(\lambda*) = z_s(\lambda*). \tag{5}$$

Here $\Psi_{i,jp}$ - jp in the numbered line λ_i a linguistic term that gives the value of a variable; w_{jp} rule weight coefficient with order number jp;
$z_s(\lambda) = z_s(\lambda*)$- fuzzy rule inference.

Ψ we consider size to be a linguistic variable that can take values ranging from "Very-Very Low" to "High". Kernel of the fuzzy variable Ψ denote as Ψ, therefore Ψ the value of the variable is "Very-Very Bad"corresponds to $\Psi = 1$, and the "Excellent" value is $\Psi = l$.

The result is a multi-criteria optimization problem $\Psi(\Lambda)$ which provides the maximum value of the discrete function $\Lambda \in D_A$ comes down to the problem of finding a vector:

$$\max_{\Lambda \atop \Lambda \in D_\Lambda} \Psi(\Lambda) = \Psi(\Lambda) = \Psi \tag{6}$$

Every incoming variable Ψ_{jp} will have its own relevance function with a fuzzy term. Ψ_{jp} having term λ_i relevance function of the element is as follows:

$$\mu^{jp}(\lambda_i) = \frac{1}{1 + \left(\dfrac{\lambda_i - b_i^{jp}}{c_i^{jp}} \right)^2}, \tag{7}$$

Here b_i^{jp}, c_i^{jp} - parameters of relevance functions.

Sugeno model of multicriteria optimization problem.

If $\lambda_1^1 = L$ and $\lambda_2^1 = L$ and $\lambda_3^1 = H$ or $\lambda_1^1 = L$ and $\lambda_2^1 = BA$ and $\lambda_3^1 = H$ or $\lambda_1^1 = L$ and $\lambda_2^1 = A$ and $\lambda_3^1 = A$ or $\lambda_1^1 = L$ and $\lambda_2^1 = H$ and $\lambda_3^1 = BA$ or $\lambda_1^1 = L$ and $\lambda_2^1 = H$ and $\lambda_3^1 = L$ if, then:

$$z = 14,06 + 0,0001 \frac{\sum\limits_{j=1}^{n} \mu(\lambda_1^{1j})\lambda_1^{1j}}{\sum\limits_{j=1}^{n} \mu(\lambda_1^{1j})} - 2,9 \frac{\sum\limits_{j=1}^{n} \mu(\lambda_2^{1j})\lambda_2^{1j}}{\sum\limits_{j=1}^{n} \mu(\lambda_2^{1j})} + 0,0001 \frac{\sum\limits_{j=1}^{n} \mu(\lambda_3^{1j})\lambda_3^{1j}}{\sum\limits_{j=1}^{n} \mu(\lambda_3^{1j})}. \quad (8)$$

If $\lambda_1^1 = BA$ and $\lambda_2^1 = L$ and $\lambda_3^1 = H$ or $\lambda_1^1 = BA$ and $\lambda_2^1 = BA$ and $\lambda_3^1 = A$ or $\lambda_1^1 = BA$ and $\lambda_2^1 = A$ and $\lambda_3^1 = BA$ or $\lambda_1^1 = BA$ and $\lambda_2^1 = H$ and $\lambda_3^1 = L$ if, then:

$$z = 21,25 + 0,0001 \frac{\sum\limits_{j=1}^{n} \mu(\lambda_1^{1j})\lambda_1^{1j}}{\sum\limits_{j=1}^{n} \mu(\lambda_1^{1j})} - 4,0001 \frac{\sum\limits_{j=1}^{n} \mu(\lambda_2^{1j})\lambda_2^{1j}}{\sum\limits_{j=1}^{n} \mu(\lambda_2^{1j})} + 0,0001 \frac{\sum\limits_{j=1}^{n} \mu(\lambda_3^{1j})\lambda_3^{1j}}{\sum\limits_{j=1}^{n} \mu(\lambda_3^{1j})}.$$

$$(9)$$

If $\lambda_1^1 = A$ and $\lambda_2^1 = L$ and $\lambda_3^1 = A$ or $\lambda_1^1 = A$ and $\lambda_2^1 = A$ and $\lambda_3^1 = L$ or $\lambda_1^1 = H$ and $\lambda_2^1 = L$ and $\lambda_3^1 = BA$ or $\lambda_1^1 = H$ and $\lambda_2^1 = BA$ and $\lambda_3^1 = L$ or $\lambda_1^1 = H$ and $\lambda_2^1 = L$ and $\lambda_3^1 = L$ if, then:

$$z = -14.0 + 70,5 \frac{\sum\limits_{j=1}^{n} \mu(\lambda_1^{1j})\lambda_1^{1j}}{\sum\limits_{j=1}^{n} \mu(\lambda_1^{1j})} - 4,0 \frac{\sum\limits_{j=1}^{n} \mu(\lambda_2^{1j})\lambda_2^{1j}}{\sum\limits_{j=1}^{n} \mu(\lambda_2^{1j})} + 0,0001 \left[\frac{\sum\limits_{j=1}^{n} \mu(\lambda_3^{1j})\lambda_3^{1j}}{\sum\limits_{j=1}^{n} \mu(\lambda_3^{1j})} \right]^2.$$

$$(10)$$

Here:

L – Low,

BA – Below average,

A – Average,

AA – Above average,

H – High.

The problem of multi-criteria optimization of weakly formed processes can be solved based on the construction of Sugeno's fuzzy logic model.

3 Results

The above-mentioned multi-criteria optimization model was solved for the case of m = 3, n = 4 and S = 3 based on the data presented in the following Table 1.

Table 1. Objective function coefficients and resources.

	Object1	Object 2	Object 3	Object 4	Available resources (Q_{2i})
EI 1	0.6	0.7	0.3	0.8	40
	0.1	0.2	0.3	0.1	
	0.2	0.1	0.1	0.1	
EI 2	0.5	0.4	0.5	0.3	15
	0.2	0.1	0.3	0.3	
	0.3	0.1	0.1	0.2	
EI 3	0.4	0.3	0.6	0.7	30
	0.3	0.2	0.3	0.3	
	0.2	0.2	0.1	0.2	
Required resources (Q_{1j})	20	20	10	35	

Using the information in the table above, the optimization problem is solved using three different objective functions for the optimization model.

Maximization objective function with respect to water volume:

$$Z_1 = 0.6x_{11} + 0.7x_{12} + 0.3x_{13} + 0.8x_{14} +$$
$$+0.5x_{21} + 0.4x_{22} + 0.5x_{23} + 0.3x_{24} + \quad (11)$$
$$+0.4x_{31} + 0.3x_{32} + 0.6x_{33} + 0.7x_{34}.$$

Minimization objective function with respect to time:

$$Z_2 = 0.1x_{11} + 0.2x_{12} + 0.3x_{13} + 0.1x_{14} +$$
$$+0.2x_{21} + 0.1x_{22} + 0.3x_{23} + 0.3x_{24} + \quad (12)$$
$$+0.3x_{31} + 0.2x_{32} + 0.3x_{33} + 0.3x_{34}.$$

Minimization objective function with respect to path:

$$Z_3 = 0.2x_{11} + 0.1x_{12} + 0.1x_{13} + 0.1x_{14} +$$
$$+0.3x_{21} + 0.1x_{22} + 0.1x_{23} + 0.2x_{24} + \quad (13)$$
$$+0.2x_{31} + 0.2x_{32} + 0.1x_{33} + 0.2x_{34}.$$

General objective function $Z = -\lambda_1 z_1 + \lambda_2 z_2 + \lambda_3 z_3$ will be in the form of.

When a multi-criteria optimization problem is solved considering a single objective function, for a chosen objective function λ_S the appropriate parameters of the vector are taken as 1 and the others are ignored, i.e. taken as $0.\lambda_S$ the sum of the values of the parameters of the vector is required to be equal to 1 based on the rule of the weight coefficient. In this case $\lambda_1,...,\lambda_S$ vector value is defined as:

$$\lambda_1 = 1, \ \lambda_2 = 0, \ \lambda_3 = 0, \quad (14)$$

For the paramaeters value of optimization is equal to $z_2 = 56.5$ for this case values of x_{ij}-are given in the Table 2.

Table 2. Values of x_{ij} for the parameters $\lambda_1 = 1,\ \lambda_2 = 0,\ \lambda_3 = 0$

	Object1	Object 2	Object 3	Object 4	Available resources (Q_{2i})
EI 1	5	20	0	15	40
EI 2	15	0	0	0	15
EI 3	0	0	10	20	30
Required resources (Q_{1j})	20	20	10	35	

For the second target function $z_2\ \lambda_S$ the values of the vector are defined as follows:

$$\lambda_1 = 0,\ \lambda_2 = 1,\ \lambda_3 = 0, \tag{15}$$

Value of the optimization model for the parameters is equal to, for this case x_{ij}-values of are given in Table 3.

Table 3. Values of x_{ij} for the parameters $\lambda_1 = 0,\ \lambda_2 = 1,\ \lambda_3 = 0$

	Object1	Object 2	Object 3	Object 4	Available resources (Q_{2i})
EI 1	5	0	0	35	40
EI 2	0	15	0	0	15
EI 3	15	5	10	0	30
Required resources (Q_{1j})	20	20	10	35	

For the third target function $z_3\ \lambda_S$ the values of the vector are defined as follows:

$$\lambda_1 = 0,\ \lambda_2 = 0,\ \lambda_3 = 1, \tag{16}$$

The value of the optimization model for the parameters is equal to $z_3 = 10.5$, for this casevalues of x_{ij}-are given in Table 4.

Table 4. Values of x_{ij} for the parameters $\lambda_1 = 0,\ \lambda_2 = 0,\ \lambda_3 = 1$

	Object1	Object 2	Object 3	Object 4	Available resources (Q_{2i})
EI 1	0	5	0	35	40
EI 2	0	15	0	0	15
EI 3	20	0	10	0	30
Required resources (Q_{1j})	20	20	10	35	

For the general target function Z the values of the vector λ_S are defined as follows:

$$\lambda_1 = 0.5,\ \lambda_2 = 0.2,\ \lambda_3 = 0.3, \tag{17}$$

General purpose function $Z = -\lambda_1 z_1 + \lambda_2 z_2 + \lambda_3 z_3$ will look like this:

$$Z = 0.22x_{11} + 0.28x_{12} + 0.06x_{13} + 0.35x_{14} +$$
$$+0.12x_{21} + 0.15x_{22} + 0.16x_{23} + 0.03x_{24} + \tag{18}$$
$$+0.08x_{31} + 0.05x_{32} + 0.21x_{33} + 0.23x_{34},$$

The value of the optimization model for these coefficients is equal to, for this case the values of x_{ij}-are given in Table 5.

Table 5. x_{ij} values of for the parameters $\lambda_1 = 0.5$, $\lambda_2 = 0.2$, $\lambda_3 = 0.3$

	Object1	Object 2	Object 3	Object 4	Available resources (Q_{2i})
EI 1	5	20	0	15	40
EI 2	15	0	0	0	15
EI 3	0	0	10	20	30
Required resources (Q_{1j})	20	20	10	35	

Table 6. x_{ij} values for the parameters $\lambda_1 = 0.8$, $\lambda_2 = 0.1$, $\lambda_3 = 0.1$

	Object1	Object 2	Object 3	Object 4	Available resources (Q_{2i})
EI 1	5	20	0	15	40
EI 2	15	0	0	0	15
EI 3	0	0	10	20	30
Required resources (Q_{1j})	20	20	10	35	

λ_S when other values of the vector are specified:

$$\lambda_1 = 0.8, \lambda_2 = 0.1, \lambda_3 = 0.1, \tag{19}$$

General objective function $Z = -\lambda_1 z_1 + \lambda_2 z_2 + \lambda_3 z_3$ will look like this:

$$Z = 0.45x_{11} + 0.53x_{12} + 0.20x_{13} + 0.62x_{14} +$$
$$+0.35x_{21} + 0.30x_{22} + 0.36x_{23} + 0.19x_{24} + \tag{20}$$
$$+0.27x_{31} + 0.20x_{32} + 0.44x_{33} + 0.51x_{34},$$

The value of the optimization model for the coefficients is equal to, for this case x_{ij}-the values of are given in Table 6.

This sequence is continued, the values of the objective function are found for the remaining parameters of the vector λ_S, and the training sample presented in Table 7 for the fuzzy logic model is generated as follows.

Table 7. Fuzzy knowledge base of multi-criteria optimization problem.

λ_1	λ_2	λ_3	Z
1.00	0.00	0.00	56.50
0.00	1.00	0.00	14.00
0.00	0.00	1.00	10.50
0.50	0.20	0.30	28.00
0.80	0.10	0.10	42.00
0.34	0.01	0.65	10.53
0.64	0.02	0.34	31.04
0.85	0.07	0.08	45.65
...	...	...	...

4   Conclusion

The scientific significance of the research results is based on the improvement of the classification model algorithm based on the matrix representation of Sugeno and Mamdani. Explained by application. An algorithm for solving the problem of multi-criteria optimization of poorly formed processes was developed based on the construction of a fuzzy logic model. This made it possible to solve the problem of multi-criteria optimization of effective placement of fire rescue units in given positions.

References

1. Bellman, R., Gierts, M.: On the analytic formalism on the theory of fuzzy Sets. Inf. Sci. **5**, 149–156 (1973)
2. Dubois, D., Prade, H.: Fuzzy Sets and Systems: Theory and Applications, p. 394. Acad. Press, New York (1980)
3. Zadeh, L.A.: Fuzzy Sets. Inf. Control **8**(3), 338–353 (1965)
4. Zadeh, L.A.: From computing with numbers to computing with words. In: Proceedings of Third ICAFS, pp. 1–2. Weisbaden, Germany (1998)
5. Zagidullin, B.I., Nagaev, I.A., Zagidullin, N., Zagidullin, S.: A neural network model for the diagnosis of myocardial infarction. Russ. J. Cardiol. **6**, 51–54 (2012)
6. Aliev, R.A., Aliev, R.R.: Theory of Intelligent Systems and Its Application, p. 720. Chashyoglu Publishing House, Baku (2001)
7. Arifzhanov, A., Mukhamedieand, D.K., Khasanov, U.U.: Modeling the processes of optimizing the structure of forces and means in a fire using parallel computing. High-Perform. Comput. Syst. Technol. **5**(2), 35–42 (2021)
8. Bekmuratov, T.F.: Acceptance of weakly structured decisions in logistics systems. J. "Probl. Informat. Energy", 6–11. UZB (2009)
9. Chernorutsky, I.G.: Methods of Optimization and Decision Making (St. Petersburg: Lan), p. 384 (2001)
10. Muhamediyeva, D.T., Mirzaraxmedova, A.X., Khasanov, U.U.: Development of a model for determining the optimal number of urban passenger transport. In: IOP Conference Series: Journal of Physics: Conference Series, vol. 2182, p. 012025 (2022)

11. Muhammediyeva, D.T., Khasanov, U.U.: Yield in the cultivation of cotton by sowing seeds under the pellicle. In: IOP Conference Series: Earth and Environmental Science, vol. 1076, p. 012015 (2022)
12. Fidler. M., Nedoma, J., Ramik, Y., Ron, I., Zimmermann, K.: Linear Optimization Problems with Inaccurate Data (M.; Izhevsk: Institute of Computer Research). Regular and Chaos Dynamics, p. 286 (2008)
13. Belomutenko, D.V., Istochkina, M.V., Belomutenko, S.V.: Analysis of the influence of natural conditions on the burning of forest plantations and their protection from fires on the example of the Volgograd region. In: Science and Practice in Solving Strategic and Tactical Problems of Sustainable Development of Russia: Collection of Scientific Articles Based on the Results of the National Scientific and Practical Conference, pp 109–110 (2019)
14. Muhamediyeva, D.T.: Building and training a fuzzy neural model of data mining tasks. In: IOP Conference Series: Journal of Physics: Conference Series, vol. 2182, p. 012024 (2022)

PACTDet - An Artificially Intelligent Approach to Detect Pulmonary Illnesses: Pneumonia, Asthma, COVID-19, and Tuberculosis

Sidratul Tanzila Tasmi[1]([📧]) [iD], Md. Mohsin Sarker Raihan[2] [iD], Atahar Imtiaz Nasif[3], and Abdullah Bin Shams[4] [iD]

[1] Department of Computer Science and Engineering, Islamic University of Technology, Dhaka 1704, Bangladesh
sidratultanzila@iut-dhaka.edu
[2] Department of Computer Science and Engineering, University of Science and Technology Chattogram (USTC), Chattogram, Bangladesh
[3] Department of Computer Science, Faculty of Science, University of British Columbia, 3333 University Way, Kelowna, BC V1V 1V7, Canada
[4] The Edward S. Rogers Sr., Department of Electrical Computer Engineering, University of Toronto, Toronto, ON M5S 3G4, Canada

Abstract. Pulmonary Illness has become very common due to different emerging viruses, bacteria, pollution, and lifestyle. If these diseases are not diagnosed in a patient, they may have a severe impact and fatal conditions in a patient's life. In this paper, we propose a methodology for the diagnosis of common pulmonary diseases: Pneumonia, Bronchial Asthma, COVID-19, and Tuberculosis based on symptoms. Our research paper functions as a technological doctor, which can detect the probability of a person having a certain category of pulmonary disease. The patient can then take necessary precautions and treatment for an early cure and minimize the severity of the disease. In this research, common classification-based machine learning algorithms: Random Forest, Decision Tree, Support Vector Machine, and Gradient Boosting algorithms were used after preprocessing the dataset from 2 sources. We have developed an Artificial Neural Network (ANN) model that can successfully detect the type of pulmonary disease with an accuracy of 99%. This application can help medical workers in their decision-making process regarding a patient, and the widespread, inexpensive application of this can help save people's lives globally.

Keywords: Pulmonary Disease · COVID-19 · Artificial Neural Network (ANN) · Machine Learning

1 Introduction

In recent decades, pulmonary diseases and infection has been very common, and through the effects of the ongoing global pandemic caused by the SARS-Cov-2 virus, people around the world globally are now very concerned about these conditions. Pulmonary

A. Gibadullin (Ed.): ITIDMS 2022, CCIS 1821, pp. 10–22, 2023.
https://doi.org/10.1007/978-3-031-31353-0_2

diseases are categories of illness and infections, that cause obstruction in the passage of airflow in the lung [1]. Today, Chronic Obstructive Pulmonary Disease (COPD) is the third leading cause of death worldwide, affecting an estimated 384 Million People, and causing the death of 3 Million worldwide [2]. Some of these pulmonary diseases may be present from childhood, e.g.: Asthma, and some of them could be contagious: COVID-19 and Tuberculosis. Asthma, one of the most common respiratory diseases affects an estimated 14% of children worldwide [3]. The common cause of asthma includes: having a genetic history of a parent having asthma, some allergic reactions, or chemical substances triggering. Pneumonia, another lung disease inflames the lungs by producing fluid inside it, making it very difficult to breathe for an infected person [4]. Tuberculosis [5], caused by pathogenic bacteria, not only affects the respiratory system, but also the nervous system, bones, and abdomen. It is also an infectious lung disease, that has affected at least 632 million [6] people worldwide, causing a global pandemic that has immensely hampered medical and financial sectors. An infected person can have symptoms of multiple pulmonary diseases, but taking each and every diagnostic test to discover his condition is not only time-consuming and expensive but also creates a possibility of improper utilization of medical resources. The applied machine learning algorithms in the research were: Random Forest, Decision Trees, Gradient Boosting, Support Vector Machine, and deep learning model, Artificial Neural Network. After collection of the data based on symptoms and intuitive statistical analysis, the models have given significant output results with a mean accuracy of 97%, precision of 98%, recall of 97%, and an f1Score of 97%. The Artificial Neural Network (ANN) model has performed with an outstanding accuracy of 99%. The application of this research can have a significant impact on the medical field. As machine learning algorithms are inexpensive and fast, the appropriate outcome of diagnosis can be provided within a few seconds. We have been actively working on pulmonary diseases, such as COVID-19, ever since the pandemic and developed different algorithms for its detection [7], alongside working on the prediction of mortality caused by pulmonary diseases such as COVID-19 [8–10].

This research paper application performs as a technological doctor, that can identify the probability of the type of pulmonary disease that the patient may have based on the symptoms. In this age of digitization, as more people are focusing on working from home, an easily available diagnostic method has become a need for everyone. This research application can also be accessed anytime, anywhere in this case. In addition to that, the diagnostic method is cost-free. Through proper diagnosis, a patient can take the necessary steps and precautions for early treatment. This would significantly reduce the pressure in the Intensive Care Unit (ICU) and access mechanical ventilation.

2 Literature Review

In the present world, Chronic Obstructive Pulmonary Disease (COPD) and asthma are major health complications. The numbers keep rising day by day, but due to misdiagnosis or doctors ignoring it, it remains unchecked. In the paper [11], they talked about the inhalation of corticosteroids as a treatment for asthma and COPD. But as it doesn't have as good of an effect on COPD as it has on asthma. Presently, the most effective treatment is seen to be the termination of smoking for COPD patients. These patients would be more motivated to give up smoking and subsequently reduce the risk of this disease. As a result, this practice is being carried out by practitioners in the medical world now. The significance of machine learning knows no bounds in the detection of Chronic Obstructive Pulmonary Diseases. In the paper [12], a convoluted neural network has been applied for the detection of such diseases through respiratory sounds. The deep learning technique applied in the paper has an accuracy of 93%. The next paper [13] played a significant role in diagnosis by detecting Chronic Obstructive Pulmonary Disease and Asthma using Machine Learning. Random Forest is a notable machine learning algorithm used in the case, that detected COPD with a precision of 97.7% and in the case of asthma with a precision of 83.3%. The deep learning approach was used in another paper [14], where through an X-ray dataset of infected people, the breathing problems have been identified with an accuracy of 89.77%. COPD was also diagnosed in the paper [15] through 10 predictors such as smoking status, cough, allergic symptoms, and so on using machine learning algorithms Gradient Boosting as primary and logistic regression as a secondary method. The areas under ROC curve for both models were under 0.956 and 0.943 respectively. The next paper [16] addresses better diagnosis using said radiological imaging and evaluating the detection of the disease from said medical imaging (X-rays). They used transfer learning which is a deep learning method that in turn is a subset of machine learning. Adoption of deep learning detects the presence of COVID-19 by exploiting transfer learning by showing network activation layers i.e., the areas in the chest X-ray considered generating the prediction. Three methods are adopted, to detect from a chest X-ray related to a healthy patient or a patient with the pulmonary disease to differentiate between generic pulmonary disease and COVID-19 which in turn highlights symptomatic of the COVID-19 disease. The model for discriminating between healthy and generic pulmonary diseases obtains a sensitivity of 96% and specificity of 98%. The applied models have received incredible performance metrics, with the first model reaching an accuracy of 94% and the second model reaching 98%.

3   Methods and Materials

Figure 1 provides the overall steps followed in the application of the research paper.

3.1   Collection of the Data Set and Statistical Analysis

The data sets used in the research paper have been collected from [17] and [18]. A pre-processed version of the data set has been collected from the link [19]. After statistical analysis, the 720 rows of data were balanced for each category of the target value, therefore not requiring data augmentation.

3.2   Correlation Matrix

It is an NxN matrix built to understand the correlation between all the attributes of the data set to each other. The correlation matrix used here is the Pearson Correlation matrix [20].

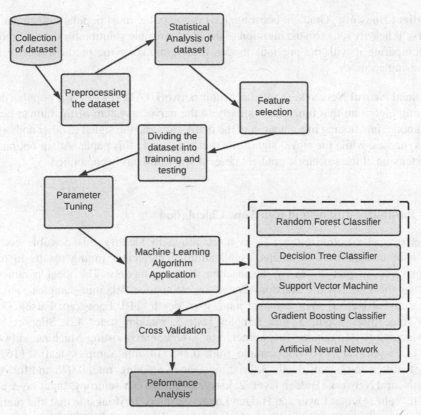

Fig. 1. Flowchart of the methodology of the research.

3.3 KNN Imputation

Machine learning models cannot automatically deal with missing values and input. To deal with the missing values of the data set, K Nearest Neighbor Impute [21] finds the mean of nearest neighbors and replaces the missing values of the data set using it.

3.4 Machine Learning Algorithms

Random Forest. Random Forest [22] is a popular machine learning model used not only for classification but also for regression types of problems. The model is built on multiple decision trees that take samples and find out the final outcome based on the majority vote.

Decision Tree Classifier. A decision tree [23] is one of the simplest machine learning algorithms widely used for classification problems. The model is built upon a tree-like structure, where each branch from a node represents a decision.

Support Vector Machine. In machine learning, support vector machine [24] is one of the most popular supervised models. This model is ideal for classification related problems but can also be used for regression.

Gradient Boosting. Gradient boosting, [25] is one of the most popular boosting algorithms. It heavily relies on the intuition of the ideal probable solution for the next model by comparing it with the previous model, thus minimizing the prediction error and increasing accuracy.

Artificial Neural Network. Artificial neural network (ANN) [26] is a popular deep learning algorithm that functions similarly to the nervous system of the human brain. Each node, functioning like a neuron of the brain, can send the signal to other nodes just like synapses, while the signal signifies a real number. In this paper, Adam optimizer, an extension of the stochastic gradient descent algorithm has been applied.

3.5 Parameter Tuning and Run Time Calculation

Hyperparameter optimization [27] is a technique to identify this possible combination of the optimum parameter. Application of parameter tuning results in minimum errors in predictions by the machine learning models. The ideal parameters used in the research are Random Forest (n_estimators: 50, min_samples_split: 6, min_samples_leaf: 1, max_features: auto, max_depth: 110, bootstrap: False), Decision Treee (max_depth: 5, min_samples_leaf: 5, random_state: 42), Support Vector Machine (C: 1, gamma: 0.1, kernel: 'rbf'), Gradient Boosting Machine: subsample: 1.0, n_estimator: 10, min_sample_split: 0.385714, min_samples_leaf: 0.116726, max_features: log2, max_depth: 3, loss: 'deviance', learning_rate: 0.075 and for Artificial Neural Network (Hidden layer: 2, loss:'categorical crossentropy, Input layer activation: 'relu', Output Layer and Hidden Layer: 'softmax'). Alongside that, the runtime for the overall process is calculated which is within the range 3.010099-05.

3.6 Cross Validation

Cross-validation [28] is an ideal technique to validate the performance of machine learning models. In this paper, the whole data set has been divided into 10 folds for cross-validation.

3.7 Performance Metrics

The performances of the machine learning algorithms can be determined by 4 metrics: accuracy, precision, recall, and f1score. To understand these metrics, understanding the confusion matrix is crucial. A confusion matrix [29] is a 4×4 matrix containing 4 important parameters: True Positive, True Negative, False Positive, and False Negative. True Positive defines the number of correctly predicted positive values while True Negative defines the number of correctly predicted negative values. On the other hand, False Positive define a number of incorrectly predicted positive value, and False negative define a number of incorrectly predicted negative value.

4 Result

The research has been performed based on two data sets. Initially, required target features: Bronchial Asthma, Pneumonia, and Tuberculosis have been collected. As the research paper identifies pulmonary disease based on classification, it is necessary that the machine learning algorithms don't confuse regular colds/coughs with these pulmonary diseases. Therefore, a category for the common cold and allergic reactions has also been kept. Through data distribution, 9 features with strong correlations with attributes have been taken to perform the machine learning analysis.

Afterward, the distribution of the multi-categorical target values was checked. For each category in the given data set, the number of rows has been 120. In the second data set, we collected data on patients who have been positive for COVID-19 based on certain symptoms. Although the first data set worked with 9 attributes, in the second data set, there were 5 common attributes. Working with only 5 attributes significantly reduced the performance of the machine learning models, and therefore, 9 attributes have been used. In order to make up for the missing attributes in the second data set, which merged the detection of pulmonary illness for Asthma, Tuberculosis, and Pneumonia along with COVID-19, the missing attributes were filled using KNN Imputer. In order to ensure that the K-NN impute is not biased to produce similar output, the rows from the second data set have been shuffled in the original data set. The correlation matrix after merging the data set can be seen in Fig. 2.

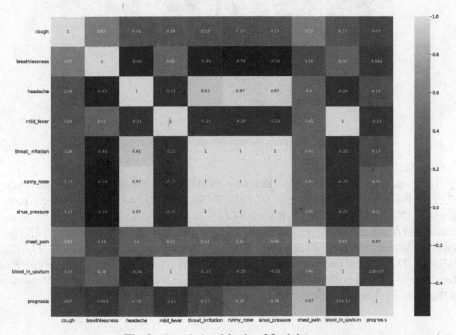

Fig. 2. Correlation Matrix of final data set.

The data set was then split into training and testing portions. The data set was divided into 10 folds using cross-validation so that all folds of the data set are equally tested and trained. Afterward, to ensure that machine learning algorithms do not only work on the given data set but also in real-life data, the parameters of the machine learning algorithms were optimized and tuned using Random Search. The parameters found through tuning the algorithms have been passed on to the 5 machine learning models, Random Forest, Decision Tree, Support Vector Machine, Gradient Boosting Classifier, and Artificial Neural Network, and their performance metrics were analyzed. For Artificial Neural Network, hidden layers were added with the necessary optimizer and activation function to analyze the performance. The ANN architecture has been given in Fig. 3.

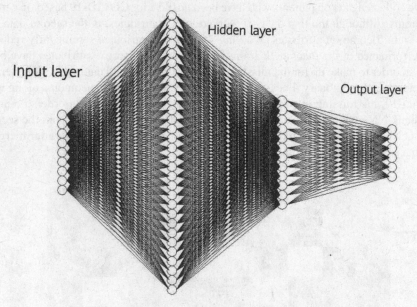

Fig. 3. Artificial Neural Network Architecture.

The outcome of the machine learning models are: Random Forest (Accuracy: 97.22%, Precision: 98.68%, Recall: 97.61%, F1Score: 97.53%), Decision Tree (Accuracy: 97.22%, Precision: 97.82%, Recall: 97.61%, F1Score: 97.53%), Gradient Boosting Classifier (Accuracy: 97.22%, Precision: 98.16%, Recall: 97.61%, F1Score: 97.53%), Support Vector Machine (Accuracy: 97.22%, Precision: 97.16%, Recall: 97.61%, F1Score: 97.53%) and finally Artificial Neural network (Accuracy: 99%, Precision: 99%, Recall: 99%, F1Score: 99%). A detailed comparative analysis of the overall performance of the machine learning models can be seen in Fig. 4.

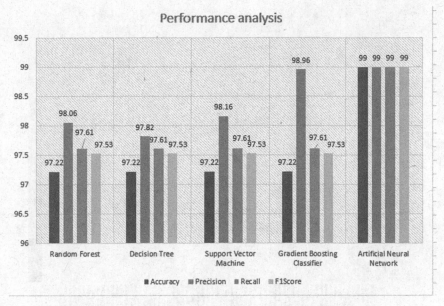

Fig. 4. Performance Comparison of the machine learning algorithms.

5 Discussion

5.1 Enhancing the Existing Work

The first portion of our work from which the symptoms of pulmonary diseases (Asthma, Tuberculosis, and Pneumonia) have been collected from the data set [17] and then pre-processed by [19] In this data set, the number of diseases has been diagnosed and the prognosis of a possible disease has been done through 132 columns. The collection of the target columns has been analyzed by plotting and understanding the relationship of the columns with the correlation matrix in Fig. 5.

The target columns were selected based on the relationship of target columns with features. The prognosis has been done accurately with an accuracy of 100%. This is a remarkable achievement. However, the drawbacks of working with 132 attributes are, first of all, it is time-consuming and straining for patients to answer their diseased condition just based on symptoms like that. Secondly, patients, answering questions regarding these many symptoms are prone to make mistakes regarding their health case. Finally, the calculation of a disease prognosis with so many columns is computationally expensive. After statistical review and analysis, we have narrowed down the symptoms from 132 columns to 9 specific columns from which the machine learning models have given the maximum performance result. Afterward, the application of the research paper was enhanced by the addition of the second data set. In the following data set, [18], the prognosis of a patient for being infected by COVID-19 has been studied based on symptoms. The data set contained 5 common attributes that matched with 5 of the attributes required to identify pulmonary diseases. However, the performances of the machine learning algorithms decreased significantly with the removal of the rest 4 attributes. In

Fig. 5. Correlation Matrix before column selection.

order to deal with this condition, we randomized the data collected from the second data set and shuffled them with the first data set. Afterward, KNN input was applied which dealt with the missing values of the rest 4 columns. This significantly increased the performances of the machine learning models. Since Artificial Neural Network (ANN) has given a nearly full accuracy with 99% we can conclude that it cannot only correctly identify the pulmonary diseases from the first data set, but also COVID-19 detection which was integrated along with it. The working procedure of the building up of the final dataset is shown in Fig. 6.

The final data set found through the analysis is available in [30] and the explanation of the multi-categorical target attribute is given in Table 1.

5.2 Analysis of the Research Architecture

After building up the dataset, the correlation matrix was plotted to ensure that our target attribute (Prognosis), prognosis has a correlation with the rest of the attributes. The correlation matrix is plotted within a range from -1 to $+1$, the magnitude towards $+$ 1 implies a strong correlation among each attribute, and towards -1 implies a weak correlation among attributes. "Chest Pain" a very common symptom in most people is strongly correlated with the prognosis column. Other columns include: Having a runny nose and pressure in the sinus. After analysis, the data set was divided into training and testing sections and the parameters passed to each machine learning algorithm have

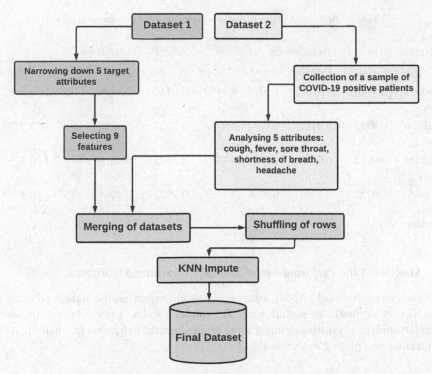

Fig. 6. Overall Explanation of final dataset preparation

Table 1. Integer representation of prognosis in the dataset.

Prognosis	Multicategory representation in the target column
Allergy	0
Bronchial Asthma	1
Common Cold	2
Pneumonia	3
Tuberculosis	4
COVID-19	5

been carefully tuned using Random Search. After finding the best parameters as seen in Table 1, the parameters were passed to the machine learning algorithms and through the performance metrics, the final outcomes of the machine learning algorithms were analyzed. A detailed comparison of the performance of the machine learning algorithms before and after applying to tune is given in Table 2.

Table 2. Performance Comparison before and after parameter tuning

Algorithm	Before Parameter Tuning				After Parameter Tuning			
	Accuracy	Precision	Recall	F1Score	Accuracy	Precision	Recall	F1Score
Random Forrest	0.9722	0.9753	0.9761	0.9753	0.9722	0.9806	0.9761	0.9753
Decision Tree	0.9722	0.9753	0.9761	0.9753	0.9722	0.9782	0.9761	0.9753
Gradient Boost	0.9722	0.9753	0.9761	0.9753	0.9722	0.9816	0.9761	0.9753
Support Vector Machine	0.9722	0.9753	0.9761	0.9753	0.9722	0.9796	0.9761	0.9753

5.3 Analysis of the Performances of Machine Learning Algorithms

Artificial Neural Network (ANN), a deep learning algorithm has the highest accuracy of 99%. This is a remarkable performance. The model also has a perfect precision score. To understand the overfitting or underfitting of the data, the validation graph of the ANN architecture was plotted as seen in Fig. 7.

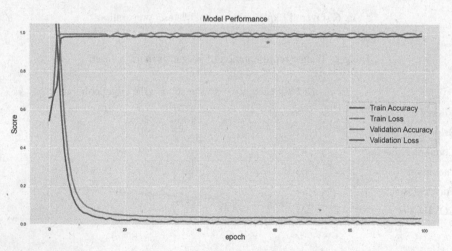

Fig. 7. Validation Graph of ANN.

On the other hand, the rest of the applied machine learning algorithms have a good performance of 97%. Most of the applied algorithms have a similar accuracy level, with only differentiating in the precision score. Among the rest of the algorithms, Random Forest and Gradient Boosting which are the ensemble learning methods have higher performance rates. The machine learning algorithms have a nearly accurate accuracy, indicating that, the probability of diagnosing a pulmonary disease by using machine learning and Artificial Intelligence is very high. This research can be further extended by scientists to further utilize machine learning in disease diagnosis and making crucial decision-making processes.

6 Conclusion

In the medical field, the application of machine learning models can help make crucial medical decisions that can not only aid medical workers but save the patient's life from the deterioration the disease may cause in the patient's life. In this research paper, common pulmonary diseases: Asthma, Tuberculosis, COVID- 19, and Pneumonia can be detected based on just 9 symptoms using an Artificial Neural Network with an accuracy of 99%. With near-perfect accuracy, pulmonary diseases can be detected without any external costs as the implementation of machine learning algorithms doesn't require additional costs. Furthermore, machine learning algorithms are quick to respond and don't deteriorate in functionality due to stress and load. The application of this paper can assist medical workers in making crucial medical decisions and recommending appropriate diagnoses to a suspected patient. In terms of medical facilities, a patient does not require to perform multiple diagnostic tests, which saves patients money, as well as makes proper utilization of medical resources. Finally, through this application, anyone can have access to the primary diagnosis of pulmonary diseases anytime, anywhere without providing any additional costs, which could save millions of lives globally.

References

1. Incalzi, R.A., Gemma, A., Marra, C., Muuolon, R.: Chronic obstrudive pulmonary disease. Am. Rev. Respir. Dis. **148**, 418–424 (1993)
2. Senior, R.M., Anthonisen, N.R.: Chronic obstructive pulmonary disease (COPD). Am. J. Respir. Crit. Care Med. **157**(4), S139–S147 (1998)
3. Dharmage, S.C., Perret, J.L., Custovic, A.: Epidemiology of asthma in children and adults. Front. Pediatr. **7**, 246 (2019)
4. Gereige, R.S., Laufer, P.M.: Pneumonia. Pediatr. Rev. **34**, 438–456 (2013)
5. Miller, L.G., Asch, S.M., Yu, E.I., Knowles, L., Gelberg, L., Davidson, P.: A population-based survey of tuberculosis symptoms: how atypical are atypical presentations? Clin. Infect. Dis. **30**, 293–299 (2000)
6. Worldometers, C.: COVID Live—Coronavirus Statistics-Worldometer (2022)
7. Shams, A.B., et al.: Telehealthcare and telepathology in pandemic: a noninvasive, low-cost micro-invasive and multimodal real-time online application for early diagnosis of COVID-19 infection. arXiv preprint arXiv:2109.07846 (2021)
8. Tasmi, S.T., Raihan, M.M.S., Shams, A.B.: Obstructive sleep apnea (OSA) and COVID-19: mortality prediction of COVID-19-infected patients with OSA using machine learning approaches. COVID **2**, 877–894 (2022)
9. Adib, Q.A.R., Tasmi, S.T., Bhuiyan, S.I., Raihan, M.S., Shams, A.B.: Prediction model for mortality analysis of pregnant women affected with COVID-19. In: 2021 24th International Conference on Computer and Information Technology (ICCIT), pp. 1–6. IEEE (2021)
10. Monjur, O., Preo, R.B., Shams, A.B., Raihan, M., Sarker, M., Fairoz, F.: COVID-19 prognosis and mortality risk predictions from symptoms: a cloud-based smartphone application. BioMed **1**, 114–125 (2021)

11. Van Schayck, C., Chavannes, N.: Detection of asthma and chronic obstructive pulmonary disease in primary care. Eur. Respir. J. **21**, 16s–22s (2003)
12. Srivastava, A., Jain, S., Miranda, R., Patil, S., Pandya, S., Kotecha, K.: Deep learning based respiratory sound analysis for detection of chronic obstructive pulmonary disease. PeerJ Comput. Sci. **7**, e369 (2021)
13. Spathis, D., Vlamos, P.: Diagnosing asthma and chronic obstructive pulmonary disease with machine learning. Health Inform. J. **25**, 811–827 (2019)
14. Tripathi, S., Shetty, S., Jain, S., Sharma, V.: Lung disease detection using deep learning. Int. J. Innov. Technol. Exploring Eng. **10**(8), 8 (2021)
15. Muro, S., et al.: Machine learning methods for the diagnosis of chronic obstructive pulmonary disease in healthy subjects: retrospective observational cohort study. JMIR Med. Inform. **9**, e24796 (2021)
16. Brunese, L., Mercaldo, F., Reginelli, A., Santone, A.: Explainable deep learning for pulmonary disease and coronavirus COVID-19 detection from X-rays. Comput. Methods Programs Biomed. **196**, 105608 (2020)
17. Chauhan, R.H., Naik, D.N., Halpati, R.A., Patel, S.J., Prajapati, M.: Disease prediction using machine learning. Clin. Rep., 783–787 (2008)
18. Zoabi, Y., Deri-Rozov, S., Shomron, N.: Machine learning-based prediction of COVID-19 diagnosis based on symptoms. NPJ Digit. Med. **4**, 3 (2021)
19. M. Gandhi, Disease Prediction from Symptoms. https://github.com/mihir-m-gandhi/Disease-Prediction-from-Symptoms/blob/d6a3fc2dc29941004f420caeda6951a236720ffd/Datasets/Training.csv. Accessed 19 Oct 2022
20. Cohen, I., et al.: Pearson correlation coefficient. In: Noise Reduction in Speech Processing. Springer Topics in Signal Processing, vol. 2, pp. 1–4. Springer, Berlin (2009). https://doi.org/10.1007/978-3-642-00296-0_5
21. Malarvizhi, R., Thanamani, A.S.: K-nearest neighbor in missing data imputation. Int. J. Eng. Res. Dev. **5**, 5–7 (2012)
22. Rigatti, S.J.: Random forest. J. Insur. Med. **47**, 31–39 (2017)
23. Myles, A.J., Feudale, R.N., Liu, Y., Woody, N.A., Brown, S.D.: An introduction to decision tree modeling. J. Chemometr.: J. Chemometr. Soc. **18**, 275–285 (2004)
24. Suthaharan, Shan: Support vector machine. In: Machine Learning Models and Algorithms for Big Data Classification. ISIS, vol. 36, pp. 207–235. Springer, Boston, MA (2016). https://doi.org/10.1007/978-1-4899-7641-3_9
25. Natekin, A., Knoll, A.: Gradient boosting machines, a tutorial. Front. Neurorobot. **7**, 21 (2013)
26. Yegnanarayana, B.: Artificial Neural Networks. PHI Learning Pvt. Ltd., New Delhi (2009)
27. Yu, T., Zhu, H.: Hyper-parameter optimization: a review of algorithms and applications. arXiv preprint arXiv:2003.05689 (2020)
28. Refaeilzadeh, P., Tang, L., Liu, H.: Cross-validation. In: LIU, L., ÖZSU, M.T. (eds.) Encyclopedia of database systems, vol. 5, pp. 532–538. Springer, Boston (2009). https://doi.org/10.1007/978-0-387-39940-9_565
29. Visa, S., Ramsay, B., Ralescu, A.L., Van Der Knaap, E.: Confusion matrix-based feature selection. MAICS **710**, 120–127 (2011)

Detection of Video Image Modification Using a Classifier Based on Adaptive Resonance Theory

Dmitriy Buhanov⬭, Sergey Chernikov⬭, Vladimir Polyakov⬭, and Maxim Panchenko^(✉)⬭

Belgorod State Technological University named after V.G. Shouhov, Belgorod, Russia
panchenko.mv@bstu.ru

Abstract. The paper proposes an approach to determine the intentional change of video stream data. It includes the following steps: data preparation using an error level analysis algorithm and the formation of compression noise histograms, the construction of concatenated noise vectors, and data classification. As a noise histogram classifier, it is proposed to use artificial neural networks of adaptive resonance theory with a hierarchical memory structure. This allows you to classify data with different similarity thresholds and obtain additional information when analyzing video data. The proposed approach allows you to perform both deferred and real-time analysis. When working in real time, the network allows you to unambiguously classify the received images, but in some cases there is uncertainty. In this case, it is required to carry out an additional analysis of the classifier memory structure, performed in manual mode. In the work, experiments were carried out in determining distortions in video data based on the dataset for detecting video inter-frame forgeries (VIFFD). Experiments have shown that the highest quality results were obtained when detecting copying as a way of distorting video data.

Keywords: Video Data Distortion · Error-Level Analysis · Adaptive Resonance Theory

1 Introduction

The modern development of information and telecommunication systems has led to the general spread of various data transmission systems. The most famous and widespread such system is the Internet. Its development and widespread distribution have led to an increase in the availability and increase in the volume of various kinds of content. The most common type of content is media data represented by digital images, photo, audio and video data [2].

The behavior of modern society is directly related to the influence of media content on a person, a group of people, communities, or entire nations [3, 4]. This raises questions about the quality and authenticity of such content. Distortions in it can appear both for natural, random reasons associated with the imperfection of data transmission systems, as well as based on targeted impact by interested people.

© The Author(s), under exclusive license to Springer Nature Switzerland AG 2023
A. Gibadullin (Ed.): ITIDMS 2022, CCIS 1821, pp. 23–32, 2023.
https://doi.org/10.1007/978-3-031-31353-0_3

The main source of media content is video data, in [5] it is shown that more than 90% of respondents use social networks as video services. Thus, the distortion of video content makes it easy to manipulate the population of entire countries.

There are many ways to change video data. In [6], a classification is presented according to the method of interaction with a sequence of frames. The types considered in the article include inserting a frame, deleting a frame, duplicating a frame, or mixing frames.

Determining the modification of a particular class can be done in various ways. In [7], the authors determine modifications by analyzing such an indicator of video image characteristics as P-frame error prediction. But determining whether all classes have been modified is a more difficult task. To solve this problem, the following approaches can be used: an optical flow approach [8], an approach based on Zernike opposite chromaticity moments [9], or an approach based on an error level analysis algorithm [10]. The optical flow approach has a lower accuracy in detecting deletion of frames than in detecting insertion and duplication of frames and shows poor results in the presence of a complex background in the video image, frequent object movements, and with a high degree of compression of the video file. The approach based on Zernike's opposite chromaticity moments also shows unsatisfactory results when working with a video image that has a dynamically changing background. The approach based on the error level analysis (ELA) algorithm contains a limitation of the analyzed video image file formats and shows the average classification completeness indicators [11].

The use of existing approaches does not allow to fully determine the modifications of video images with a dynamic background or have insufficient classification indicators. The paper proposes to improve classification performance by using artificial neural networks (ANNs) of adaptive resonance theory to analyze noise vectors obtained using the ELA algorithm.

2   An Approach to Determining the Fact of Video Data Modification Based on Frame Vectorization and the Use of the ART-2m Artificial Neural Network

The approach to determining the fact of video data modification consists of two parts, construction of the frame sequence noise vector and classification of these vectors (Fig. 1).

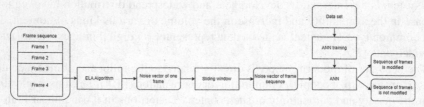

Fig. 1. Block diagram of the approach to determining the fact of modification of video data.

The construction of the frame sequence noise vector is based on the application of the ELA algorithm to a digital image. The ELA algorithm allows you to extract high-frequency compression noise from an image, which in general is a map of high-frequency image noise. This noise map is reduced to a monochrome form, and a histogram of monochrome noise is built on the basis of the monochrome noise map. The resulting histogram contains 256 values indicating the number of pixels of the corresponding value on the monochrome noise map. Next, the histogram is fed into a sliding window, whose task is to delay histograms of n frames for subsequent concatenation. When n histograms are collected in the sliding window, they are concatenated, the oldest histogram is removed from the sliding window, and the result of the concatenation is considered to be the noise vector of the frame sequence. The sliding window size is a configurable parameter that is responsible for the number of frames in a sequence whose histograms are analyzed in the data classification block. The frame sequence noise vector consists of 256 * n values, where 256 is the size of the single frame noise histogram and n is the size of the sliding window.

The algorithm for constructing the noise vector of a sequence of frames consists of the following steps:

1. Take a frame from the sequence;
2. Build a frame noise histogram:

    a. Apply the ELA algorithm to a single frame;
    b. Extract the high-frequency noise map from the results of the ELA algorithm;
    c. Convert the noise map to monochrome;

3. Add the constructed histogram to the current sliding window;
4. Get the noise vector of the sequence of frames.

The noise vector of a sequence of frames allows you to identify breakpoints in the video image. A break point is a place in a frame sequence where one of two adjacent frames is not part of the original frame sequence, or is not in its position [12]. The sliding window size was set to 4. Thus, each noise vector is represented by 1024 parameters and contains information about 4 consecutive frames, which allows you to accurately determine the presence of a break point.

Figure 2 shows examples of noise vectors in a sequence of frames, where the highest peak can be used to determine the point of contact between frames, and by counting them, you can make sure that the size of the sliding window was equal to 4 when the vector was composed. In the presented examples, the noise vector with the deleted frame has the most similar values with the noise vector of the sequence of frames without modification.

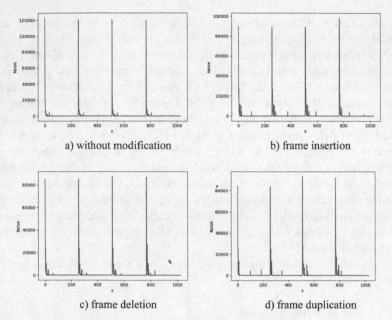

a) without modification   b) frame insertion

c) frame deletion   d) frame duplication

Fig. 2. Noise vectors in a sequence of frames.

Next, the resulting set of vectors is transferred to the classifier based on INS ART-2m, where it is classified, and a decision is made on its modification.

The sliding window size is a config parameter, it was set to 4 to demonstrate how the approach works, but other values are also possible. However, setting it to a smaller value makes it difficult to determine the presence of a breakpoint, and setting it to a larger value increases the amount of classifier input and can create situations where multiple breakpoints are captured within a single frame sequence.

3   Test Dataset

The following types of video image modification were studied in the work: insertion, deletion and duplication of frames. A VIFFD data set was chosen as a test, which contains 30 original video images and 90 modified video images, 30 of which were modified by inserting foreign frames, 30 by deleting frames and 30 by duplicating frames of one video image. Video images from the data set contain many records with a variety of static and dynamic backgrounds containing dynamic objects.

To obtain test data, video images from the VIFFD dataset were converted into sets of frame sequence noise vectors. The resulting vectors were divided into training and test sets. Table 1 provides information on the amount of test dataset.

Table 1. Test dataset separation.

Modification	Number of modified vectors	Number of unmodified vectors
Insert	120	6417
Removal	125	3782
Duplication	225	4924
Without modification	0	5343

Further research was carried out with this dataset. The small number of vectors with modifications is explained by the fact that the original video sequence after modification usually contains only one break point. Each break point generates n vectors with modifications, where n is the size of the sliding window, in this work it is taken equal to 4. Thus, only 4 frame sequences from the total number obtained from the video sequence will contain a break point.

4 Application of a Classifier Based on ART-2m with a Hierarchical Memory Structure

As a classifier, it is proposed to use artificial neural networks of adaptive resonance theory (ART) with a hierarchical memory structure (ART-2m). Their description was presented in [13]. Unlike other types of ANNs, the theory of adaptive resonance, first proposed and presented in [14, 15], makes it possible to perform guaranteed retraining. Its modification, which allows to operate with real inputs, is called ART-2.

The structure of such a network consists of three fields: F1, F2, and G. Figure 3 shows the interaction of fields in the ART network. Field F1 performs the function of preprocessing vectors of upstream signals $V = \{v1, v2, \ldots vn\}$, where n is the number of components. The F2 field searches for the received preprocessed vector from the F1 field in memory neurons Y and matches it with some neuron y_i (where i is the number of the active neuron). The G field is responsible for checking the compliance of the preprocessed vector from the F1 field with the data contained in the connection weights of the neuron y_i. Upon successful verification, it transmits a control signal to the F2 field for further retraining (training is understood as the modification of the corresponding weights of the connection of neurons Y).

The operation of the network allows you to determine whether the vector V belongs to one of the classes of images, information about which is stored in the corresponding weights of neurons Y.

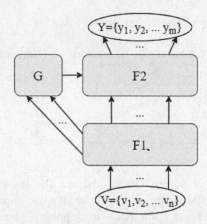

Fig. 3. Structure of the ART network

The network with a hierarchical memory structure proposed in [13] allows you to find a match to several classes at once, with different similarity parameters. The higher the Y-layer neurons are in the hierarchy, the more accurate the classification is. The organization of hierarchical memory makes it possible to find the similarity of objects with different similarity parameters in one training iteration. Figure 4 shows an example of the ART-2m memory structure when it is trained with data from two different types of images.

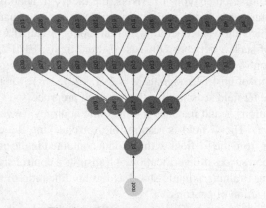

Fig. 4. ART-2m memory structure.

The figure shows a memory structure trained by two types of video images. Some contained modifications, others did not. The nodes (neurons) that exactly corresponded to the distorted video fragments are shown in red, the nodes without distortion are shown in green. The gray color marks the node that ambiguously identifies the image type. When training the network, this neuron characterized both modified videos and original ones. Root is a dummy node to represent memory as a tree, since there can be more than one neuron at the first level.

5 Results

When testing the developed system that implements the proposed approach to identify the fact of video image modification using a classifier based on the ART-2m ANN, experiments were carried out on data prepared based on the VIFFD sample.

In each experiment, the quality of the classification was examined in determining the modifications of various types. In Tables 2, 3, 4 and 5, the columns show the expected results, the rows show the actual classified results. Table 2 presents the matrix of errors in the detection of the "removal" modification.

Table 2. Detection of modification "removal".

	Without modification	With modifications
Without modification	3508	44
With modifications	391	85

To calculate the accuracy of the classifier, the following formula is used:

$$accuracy = \frac{TP + TN}{TP + TN + FP + FN} \tag{1}$$

where TP is correctly recognized video image data without modifications, TN is correctly recognized video image data with modifications, FP is incorrectly recognized data with modifications, FN is incorrectly recognized data without modifications.

So the accuracy will be equal to 0.883.

Table 3 presents the matrix of uncertainties in identifying the "insert" modification.

Table 3. Detection of modification "insert".

	Without modification	With modifications
Without modification	5894	28
With modifications	389	90

When determining the modification of the "insert", an accuracy of 0.935 was obtained. Table 4 presents the matrix of uncertainties in identifying the "copy" modification.

Table 4. Detection of modification "copy".

	Without modification	With modifications
Without modification	4803	108
With modifications	121	119

When determining the "copy" modification, an accuracy of 0.956 was obtained. Table 5 presents the matrix of uncertainties in identifying all three previously presented modifications of video images.

Table 5. Detection of modification of video images.

	Without modification	With modifications
Without modification	19441	180
With modifications	897	294

When determining the types of modifications under consideration, an accuracy of 0.948 was obtained. To evaluate the performance of the proposed approach, we determine the recall, precision, and *F-measure* using the following formulas:

$$precision = \frac{TP}{TP + FP} \tag{2}$$

$$recall = \frac{TP}{TP + FP} \tag{3}$$

$$F_\beta = (1 + \beta^2) \cdot \frac{precision \cdot recall}{(\beta^2 \cdot precision) + recall} \tag{4}$$

where β is the precision/completeness priority indicator, which is taken as 1 in this work, and therefore we can speak of a balanced F-measure, also called F1.

Table 6 presents the accuracy and recall values for various modification classes.

Table 6. ART-2m Performance Metrics

	Accuracy	Precision	Recall	F1 score
Removal	0.883	0.98	0.9	0.938298
Insert	0.935	0.995	0.938	0.96566
Copying	0.956	0.978	0.975	0.976498
All types	0.948	0.991	0.956	0.973185

The results of classification quality comparison are presented in Fig. 5.

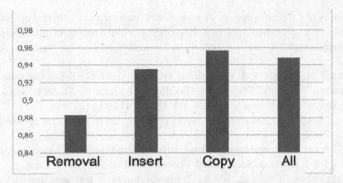

Fig. 5. Comparisons of the quality of classifications of various types of modifications.

It can be seen from the figure that the best result was obtained when determining the modification of the copy type, and the worst result was obtained when determining the deletion. This is because the noise vectors of the frame sequence from which the frame was removed are closest in value to the noise vectors of the frame sequence without modifications.

6 Conclusion

The paper proposes an approach to detect modification of a video image using a classifier based on an artificial neural network of adaptive resonance theory. This approach is based on the following steps: data preparation using the ELA algorithm, and the formation of concatenated compression noise histograms and classification of the resulting histograms using ART-2m.

The results of the experiments showed the possibility of using the developed approach in video data analysis systems. In the future, to test the approach, it is proposed to conduct studies on other data samples. To improve the accuracy of classification, it is proposed to conduct studies aimed at assessing the quality of classification with different sizes of the sliding window and functions for calculating the similarity parameter for different levels of ART-2m memory.

Acknowledgments. The work was supported by a grant from the Russian Foundation for Basic Research. Project number 19–29-09056mk.

References

1. Nguyen, X.H., Hu, Y.: VIFFD - A dataset for detecting video inter-frame forgeries. Mendeley Data, **6** (2020)
2. Wallach, O., Jamshed, P.: The World's Most Used Apps, by Downstream Traffic. https://www.visualcapitalist.com/the-worlds-most-used-apps-by-downstream-traffic. Accessed 08 Sept 2022

3. Shesterina, A.M.: Transformation of audiovisual content in a network environment: the possibilities of a contextual approach. https://cyberleninka.ru/article/n/transformatsiya-aud iovizualnogo-kontenta-v-setevoy-srede-vozmozhnosti-kontekstnogo-podhoda. Accessed 09 Sept 2022

4. Shagimulin, K.A., Melnikov, A.V.: The impact of video content on the mental state of a person. In: Psychology of Mental States: A Collection of Articles by Students, Undergraduates, Graduate Students and Young Scientists, vol. 13, pp. 411-415 (2019)

5. Shatunova, M.A.: The main trends of media consumption in the social networks of Runet. Young Sci. **21**(363), 349–352 (2021)

6. Mizher, M.A., et al.: A review of video falsifying techniques and video forgery detection techniques. Int. J. Electron. Secur. Digit. Forensics **9**, 191–208 (2017)

7. Stamm, M.C., Lin, W.S., Liu, K.J.R.: Temporal forensics and anti-forensics for motion compensated video. IEEE Trans. Inf. Forensics Secur. **7**, 1315–1329 (2017)

8. Wang, W., Jiang, X., Wang, S., Wan, M., Sun, T.: Identifying video forgery process using optical flow. In: Shi, Y.Q., Kim, H.J., Pérez-González, F. (eds.) IWDW 2013. LNCS, vol. 8389, pp. 244–257. Springer, Heidelberg (2014). https://doi.org/10.1007/978-3-662-43886-2_18

9. Liu, Y., Huang, T.: Exposing video inter-frame forgery by Zernike opponent chromaticity moments and coarseness analysis. Multimed. Syst. **23**(2), 223–238 (2015). https://doi.org/10.1007/s00530-015-0478-1

10. Wang, W., Dong, J., Tan, T.: Tampered region localization of digital color images based on JPEG compression noise. In: Kim, H.J., Shi, Y.Q., Barni, M. (eds.) IWDW 2010. LNCS, vol. 6526, pp. 120–133. Springer, Heidelberg (2011). https://doi.org/10.1007/978-3-642-18405-5_10

11. Bukhanov, D.G., Redkina, M.A., Chernikov, S.V.: Study of the ELA algorithm to detect the fact of editing in JPEG images. Math Methods Eng. Technol. **7**, 80–83 (2020)

12. Chernikov, S.V., Redkina, M.A.: Using the ELA algorithm to determine the fact of intentional distortion of a frame sequence in a video series. In: International Scientific and Technical Conference of Young Scientists, BSTU Named after V.G. Shouhov, pp. 3845–3849 (2021)

13. Bukhanov, D.G., Polyakov, V.M.: Network of adaptive resonance theory with multilevel memory. Economy. Inform. **45**(4), 713–721 (2018)

14. Carpenter, G.A., Grossberg, S., Rosen, D.B.: ART 2-A: an adaptive resonance algorithm for rapid category learning and recognition. Neural Netw. **4**, 493–504 (1991)

15. Carpenter, G.A., Grossberg, S.: ART 2: Stable self-organization of pattern recognition codes for analog input patterns. Appl. Opt. **26**, 4919–4930 (1987)

On the Reduction of Alternatives in the Process of Selecting Preferred Management Decisions

Igor S. Klimenko⬛ and Evgeny A. Palkin[✉]⬛

Russian New University, 22, Radio Str., Moscow 105005, Russia
palkin@rosnou.ru

Abstract. On the basis of N. Bohr's complementarity principle, a number of constructive analogies between measuring parameters of quantum objects and actions of persons making management decisions have been considered. In particular, an analogy between collapse of the wave function and reduction of alternatives at the moment of selection of a management decision has been established. Within the framework of the complementarity principle, a position has been formulated according to which the realization of a preferred alternative by an appropriate control action is analogous to the action of measurement on a quantum object. It is shown that by the time of implementation of the control action, the state of the decision-making situation can be formally represented as a superposition of alternatives, and the selected alternative acts as the measurement result. The features of the use of mutually complementary concepts in the choice of solutions associated with the presence of the decision maker's management goal are discussed.

Keywords: Reduction · Measurement · Choice on the Set of Alternatives · Decision-Making · Mutually Complementary Concepts

1 Introduction

In [1, 2] we derived three macroscopic uncertainty relations arising in the problem of managerial decision-making and showed their correspondence to the principle of complementarity extended to social systems by N. Bohr [3, 4]. In the general case, according to this principle, rational and irrational procedures performed by a decision maker (DM) are connected by uncertainty relations.

In particular, as applied to the decision-making task, it concerns such a pair of mutually complementary notions as reflection (analog of position) and action (analog of impulse). At the same time, within the framework of the complementarity principle, it is assumed that finding the verbal equivalent of this or that thought is analogous to the action of measurement on a quantum object.

The derived relations of uncertainties tie together all particular indicators of management efficiency as a complex operational property of a management process, determining its adaptability for achievement of management goals.

The information-time uncertainty relation according to [2] has the form:

$$H_D \, \Delta t_S \approx const \text{ with } \Delta t_S \leq t_L, \tag{1}$$

where H_D is residual information entropy (degree of decision uncertainty), Δt_S is time lapse of DM to make (synthesize) a decision. At the same time Δt_S value within its admissible value t_L is not a priori accurately determined for the DM.

In real control practice, the decision maker is often forced to find the best compromise between the time Δt_S and the consumption of other resources ΔR on the condition that the residual entropy of the solution H_D will not exceed some admissible value of H_L. Therefore, the resource-time uncertainty relation arises naturally:

$$\Delta R \, \Delta t_S \approx const \text{ with } H_D \leq H_L, \tag{2}$$

which can be interpreted as a ratio of uncertainties between expected expenditures of time and other resources.

Combining ΔR_Σ time t_L and other resources ΔR as aggregate management resources results in the information-resources uncertainty ratio:

$$H_D \, \Delta R_\Sigma \approx const; \quad \Delta R \leq \Delta R_L. \tag{3}$$

Correlation (3) means, that the less, total resources are spent during the process of the final decision preparation, the higher its residual entropy will be.

The above relations reflect the formulation and solution of optimization problems, which have to be solved by the DM in the choice of management decisions.

The decomposition of total management resources into three components: time resources, intellectual resources and financial (material) resources allows the DM to consider them as targets and formulate a three-parameter optimization problem, which consists in finding a solution in which the values of these targets will be acceptable to the DM.

2   Materials and Methods

The process of synthesizing the semantic information [5, 6], which constitutes the sense of a managerial decision, is a selection on the set of alternatives, which represent (model) the real situation of making a decision, accepted by the DM for consideration.

In practice, within the a priori limited period of time allotted for decision making, DM performs rational procedures of computational and logical nature, the purpose of which is to ensure the accuracy and completeness of the model of the decision situation. However, in the general case there is a residual entropy (uncertainty) of the decision [7].

Therefore, the DM is forced to perform, already at the heuristic level, also a subjective (irrational) assessment of the degree of risk characterizing the decision-making situation, as well as the degree of value of the acquired information, determined by the value of the probability of reaching the goal in each specific management cycle. As a consequence, the problem of choice is exacerbated by doubts about the readiness to take the decisive action - to bring the optimum control action to the control object (hereinafter referred to as CO).

Nevertheless, the time limit for making and implementing a decision, as it expires, forces the particular individual, acting as the DM, to cast aside doubts and perform, in fact, a heuristic thought procedure, namely, to decide to implement the most preferable of the available alternatives.

In the general case, the DM will seek to form sets of Pareto-optimal alternatives, i.e., to provide such a state of the decision-making situation, in which none of the target indicators can be improved without deterioration of the other. However, in real management practice, the selected indicators, as a rule, have different importance for the DM. In this case the optimality criterion is determined by lexicographic order - by the result of indicators ranking [8, 9].

The presence of hierarchy among the indicators (criteria), as we know, allows us to solve the lexicographic problems consistently, considering the optimal values of more significant indicators as constraints for the following ones.

In many practical cases, the duration of the time interval Δt_S is assumed to be the most significant indicator, since its elapse makes it completely impossible to achieve the goal. Regarding the choice of the information-resources ratio, depending on the specific situation, in some cases the DM will consider the amount of information received sufficient to implement the control action and save some resources, in other cases he will prefer to spend additional financial resources to further refine the decision within the allowable time interval.

Semantic information necessary to build an adequate model of the decision-making situation and the subsequent choice of the optimal decision, DM, in principle, can get three basic ways: generate independently, find in the information environment or purchase on the market conditions. In any case, it is necessary to have sufficient resources, including the resource of time.

As part of the statement of the general problem of decision-making it is advisable to consider intellectual resources, integrating the following components: human capital, intellectual property, information and innovation (knowledge), as well as business technology and organizational knowledge (corporate culture) as the most important for DM. As for material resources, the availability of financial resources adequate to the complexity of the task, which constitute the budget of any project, also remains fundamentally necessary.

Obviously, under the time limit, the DM has the opportunity to supplement its model of the decision-making situation, generated with the use of intellectual resources, with information obtained at the expense of the available financial (material) resources. Strictly speaking, both at the stage of synthesizing the model of the situation and at the stage of its refinement up to the development of a decision ready for implementation, the DM can rely only on available resources - at the first stage, as a rule, on intellectual resources, and at the second stage, on material (financial) resources. Thus, it can be a question of exchanging resources for the necessary information.

Ultimately, it is the qualitative indicators of the information used by the DM to synthesize a decision (primarily, its reliability, relevance, timeliness, completeness and accuracy) that determine the quality of the decision taken for implementation as the degree of its suitability for successful use as intended, that is, for timely and simultaneously confident implementation of the control action by moving the control object to the required state.

The quality of a decision (its adequacy to the real situation) is determined by the value of the semantic information used, measured, as an increase in the probability of achieving the target effect as a result of moving the control object to the next state. In turn, the value of information gives it a certain market value, which the DM is able to determine only subjectively - as the amount he is willing to pay of the available financial resources to acquire the missing information.

There are three main reasons for the economic value of information [10].

First, obtaining information reduces the uncertainty of a decision-making situation with economic consequences.

Secondly, the information circulating in the information field, including information of zero or negative value, affects people's behavior, which also has relevant economic consequences.

Finally, the information itself may have a market value, which is determined by the expected profit of the DM from its use in the interests of business.

We will focus on the task of reducing uncertainty, which seems to be the most difficult and at the same time the most relevant in relation to the usual conditions of management practice.

The subjective assessment on the part of different DMs of the decision-making situation in the real management practice is largely determined by their individual attitude to risk. This means that by a certain point in time within t_L under the same conditions different DMs will have opposite opinions about their readiness to move from reflection to decisive action. Some of them will consider the achieved accuracy of the decision to be sufficient to obtain a guaranteed target effect, others, on the contrary, will not risk to direct it to the CO.

This obvious circumstance, determining the uncertainty of the evaluation of the state of the real situation, for the doubting DM can be interpreted as a kind of superposition of two possible outcomes of the implementation of the decision. For optimists, who have assumed the risk of implementing a control action, the resolution of uncertainty will consist in observing (fixing) the outcome of the experience.

As for the cautious observers who have not ventured into the reduction of alternatives and refrained from implementing the decision, for them the spontaneous transition of the CO into the next state will cause either regret over the missed favorable opportunity, or an a posteriori statement that the prepared decision is erroneous.

3   Results

Let us return to the provision of the extended principle of additionality, according to which, finding a verbal equivalent of this or that thought is analogous to the action of measurement on a quantum object.

The question about influence of measurement on a quantum object is one of key ones in quantum physics, because at this level of structural organization of matter it is fundamentally necessary to consider interaction of an investigated object with an experimental setup. According to quantum theory it is considered that before a measurement a quantum system is in a superposition of admissible states. It is also assumed that after a measurement, which allows to determine some parameters of a system, a wave function changes by leaps and bounds, taking a form corresponding to the measured values of parameters.

One of ways to formally describe this transition is the notion of wave function reduction (von Neumann reduction) [11], defined as an instantaneous change in the description of the quantum state (wave function) of an object that occurs during a measurement. Since from the instantaneous change formally follows the propagation of interaction with the speed exceeding the speed of light, it is believed that this reduction is not a physical process, but a mathematical method of describing the observed result.

Without going into details of this problem on quantum level [12–14], we will focus on a number of constructive analogies, conditioned by the principle of additionality, between measuring parameters of quantum objects by means of wave function reduction and actions of conscious subject (DM) in the process of choosing a decision on set of alternatives.

The principle of complementarity (additionality) was formulated by Bohr as a tool for complete joint description of observed kinematic and dynamic parameters of quantum system. At the same time, it was accepted the key provision, according to which all empirical data should be described with the help of classical concepts, adequate to human consciousness and thinking.

In other words, the result of the experiment should in some form represent a verbal message that carries semantic information [5, 15–18], i.e., information that to a certain extent removes the a priori uncertainty about the outcome of the experience. Obviously, here we are talking about the reduction of alternatives of the formulated message in the classical sense of the term.

The formulation of the general problem of decision making traditionally implies the determination of the control goal T_C, as well as the time limit for decision making t_L, and the resources ΔR needed to synthesize a decision. Formally, the initial model of such a problem can be represented in the form of a tuple:

$$M_0 = <T_C, t_L, \Delta R, S_0>, \tag{4}$$

where S_0 - is the initial information for generating of variants of the decision, reflecting initial conditions of CO and situation, as well as an a priori estimate of the risk of the decision. In this case, at least two-factor risks are assessed: the risk of not making a decision when the decision in question is correct (first kind error) and the risk of making a decision when the decision was in fact incorrect (second kind error).

The task of the DM is to transform the initial information S_0 into the finite set of alternative models of the decision situation $\{M_S\}$:

$$G(S_0) \rightarrow \{M_S\}, \tag{5}$$

where G is a transformation operator.

At the next step, for each element of the set $\{M_S\}$ a specific decision on transfer of DM to the required state (set M_D) is put in a one-to-one correspondence (isomorphism):

$$F: \{M_S\} \rightarrow \{M_D\}, \tag{6}$$

where F is a transformation operator.

During DM's reflections on necessary and sufficient completeness of this set it can be supplemented and modified, but by the moment of decision making a fixed set of alternatives M_R is taken for consideration.

The decisive act of DM consists in choosing the only - in his opinion correct - decision $D_{opt} \in M_D$. Mutually additional constituents of DM actions are a process of thinking (performing computational, logical and heuristic procedures) and the volitional act of control action, determined by the chosen solution by its preference criterion. It is obvious that the semantics of the selected decision D_{opt} reflects the verbal equivalent of the DM's thought, finally stating the preference of a particular alternative for him.

Ultimately, the actions performed by the DM consist in the transformation of the initial information about the state of the decision-making situation S_0 into the final decision D_{opt}, selected on the set of alternatives taken for consideration by the preference criterion K:

$$D_{opt} : K\{G(S_0)\} \rightarrow (\exists i)\,(Di \in M_D). \tag{7}$$

In fact, the choice of this alternative is the result of measuring on an ordinal (ranking) scale obtained by the DM assessments of the probabilities of achieving the required target effect of each of the alternatives under consideration at an acceptable level of risk. This combination of requirements should reflect the criterion K.

The basis for establishing the order of preference of alternative solutions can be a heuristic determination of DM values of their residual entropy H_i, reflecting the degree of his uncertainty in the suitability of one or another model of the decision situation on the criterion K:

$$H_1 \prec H_2 \prec H_i \prec \dots H_{min}, \tag{8}$$

where H_{min} is the residual entropy of the model most preferred by the DM, given by his estimate of the goal attainability criterion when choosing a decision D_{opt}, and the sign $\prec$ means "the less preferred alternative".

Based on the ranking of alternative models of the situation, the DM establishes a strict order relation between the values of the goal attainability criterion for all alternatives taken into consideration:

$$K_1 \prec K_2 \prec K_i \prec \dots K_D, \tag{9}$$

where K_D is the a priori value of the goal attainability criterion when choosing a solution D_{opt}. For example, if the preference criterion is the probability P_i of achieving the goal, then the result of ranking the alternatives would look like:

$$P_1 \prec P_2 \prec P_i \prec \dots P_D, \tag{10}$$

If the result of decision can be defined in cost expression, that is the price of decision (C_{iD}) and the price of risk - the price of non-acceptance of decision (C_{iN}), then the combination can be taken as the preference criterion:

$$Ki = P_i\,C_{iD} - (1 - P_i)\,C_{iN} \tag{11}$$

In this case, the decision ranking problem (9) is determined by the residual entropy in the "price scale". Note that if the decision price and risk price are the same for all alternatives, then criterion (10) is equivalent to criterion (11).

4   Discussion

Thus, by the moment of conversion from reflection (comparative estimation of alternatives) to the action of choosing a concrete alternative, the state of decision-making situation S_{sit} can be formally presented as a superposition of all presented for choosing variants of decision, where the role of constants at decision function D_i is played by heuristically determined by DM values P_i of probability of achieving the goal of operation:

$$S_{sit} = \Sigma \, P_i \, D_i. \tag{12}$$

For transferring the control action to the object of control the DM prepares and sends a certain message S_C along the feedback loop, giving an instruction (command) on the transition of the CO to the required state taking into account the state of the environment.

It should be emphasized that the information synthesized by the DM in the process of analyzing the situation and generating decisions is not transmitted, because the content of the message S_C (the command information carried by it) is the result of choice as the quintessence of the DM's thoughts, and the CO receives only a certain command for its transition to the target state.

It can be assumed that at the moment of decision making, the DM, in fact, performs a measurement (assessment of the probability of achieving the required target effect) with the subsequent qualitative transition from thinking about the preference of alternatives to action - sending to the CO the control action, corresponding to the selected (taken) decision. The only alternative, defined by the DM as providing the highest probability of achieving the goal of the operation [15], serves as "measurable" here.

The result of choosing such a solution is a reduction of the set of alternatives to a single solution with specific observable consequences:

$$K\{\Sigma \, P_i \, D_i\} \rightarrow D_{opt}. \tag{13}$$

The formal analogy with the reduction of the wave function looks quite obvious. However, in contrast to von Neumann reduction (collapse of the wave function of a quantum system) the choice of the description (model) of a decision-making situation and the corresponding decision takes place in the mind of DM not instantly, but during a finite period of time. Therefore, it is possible to consider that a real process takes place here, and not only a mathematical method of phenomenon description is used.

The above stated allows us to formulate within the framework of extended Bohr additionality principle, according to which finding of a verbal equivalent of this or that thought is similar to a measurement action on a quantum object, may be supplemented as applied to management practice.

Valid, we can consider that finding of a preferred alternative by DM and its realization by means of corresponding control action is similar to the action of measurement on a quantum object. At that, DM actions (comparative estimation of a priori goal achievement probabilities) have necessary and sufficient signs of measuring procedure.

The role of measuring device is played by thinking apparatus of expert (DM), formulating in a finite time interval the decision on readiness to control action in a specific language. Nevertheless, the reduction of the decision appears only after the CO has worked out the control action. Obviously, such a definitely macroscopic process, in contrast to the reduction of the wave function, is objective in nature and, naturally, does not contradict the principle of causality.

Just as the reduction of the wave function allows us to determine the real probability density indicating the position of quantum system, the reduction of solutions makes it possible to identify the solution that has the maximum probability of achieving the control goal.

5 Conclusion

In conclusion, let us draw attention to the following circumstance.

The extension of the principle of additionality to the behavior of living organisms led to the adoption of the a priori statement on the purposefulness of the organic process as a heuristic principle. In accordance with the task of studying the phenomena peculiar to living organisms as empirical objects, the concept of purpose acquired a stable connection with the preservation and reproduction of living organisms, and the concept of expediency - with the regulatory mechanisms contributing to the achievement of these goals.

A special place in the course of the evolutionary process is occupied by man, who, on the one hand, is a participant in this process and, on the other hand, an observer of it. We therefore project our understanding of purpose associated with human activity onto the behavior of other living organisms, attributing to them the presence of conscious goals.

As a consequence, it is the manifestation of expediency in the process of the evolution of living nature that is generally regarded as an objectively existing goal in the first place. The evolutionary success of the individual is known to consist in the preservation and dissemination of its genetic information and, thereby, in the increase in the population and the species. This success is ensured by the action of two powerful instincts (nutrition and reproduction) and by the diversity of the gene pool in an uncertain natural environment.

Consequently, we can consider that the goal of any living organism is the maximum dissemination of information carried by it, and the real result of life activity consists in the optimization of the degree of achieving this goal (taking into account the natural limitations imposed by the biosphere).

This applies in full measure to our species as well. Today, as before, each individual of our species is undoubtedly focused on the pursuit of a conscious evolutionary goal of survival and reproduction through adaptation to the changing conditions of the global environment, which is the biosphere, of which our species remains an integral component.

Obviously, similar conscious evolutionary goals are characteristic of complex organizational-technical systems that conduct business under the statistical uncertainty of the world economic system. Here the evolutionary success consists in preserving the business itself as a system and in maximizing the distribution of its products, the structure of which incorporates valuable information synthesized in the process of creating these products.

It turns out that the goal of the DM, who manages the functioning, development and evolution of the organizational and technical system, is to spread the information generated in them, just as it happens in the course of the evolutionary process in living nature.

Obviously, the hierarchical structure of complex organizational-technical systems determines the existence of goals, formulated at the higher levels of the hierarchy, and the tasks (subgoals) assigned to the subordinate DM of the lower levels, the implementation of which ensures the achievement of these goals. Thus, at the social level, each human individual is oriented in his/her functioning to contribute to the fulfillment of the goals of economic and political systems of the higher levels of the hierarchy, thus providing himself/herself with resources to follow his/her evolutionary goals as a biological individual.

However, it is quite obvious that the current level of technological development of human society has opened before it the possibility of adapting to the conditions of the biosphere by influencing the processes taking place at the level of the biosphere itself.

The peculiarity of the modern stage of human and social evolution is that our species, being only one of a huge number of species constituting the biosphere, thanks to its technological evolution (i.e., essentially, the creation and distribution of non-biological information) has now practically equalized with the biosphere in terms of the possession of resources for the management of natural phenomena.

Humanity's departure from the biosphere obviously leads to increasing uncertainty in the dynamics of changes in the conditions of its biological evolution. In these conditions the purposeful choice of optimal managerial decisions for the achievement of the goals of strategic level and forecasting of the side effects of such decisions is put forward to the level of global problem of human civilization.

It can be assumed that the heuristic power of the principle of additionality will help to identify new means of describing, understanding and solving such problems.

References

1. Klimenko, I.S., Palkin, E.A., Sharapova, L.V.: Bohr's complementarity principle and management decision making. In: Gibadullin, A. (ed.) DITEM 2021. LNNS, vol. 432, pp. 181–189. Springer, Cham (2022). https://doi.org/10.1007/978-3-030-97730-6_16
2. Klimenko, I.S., Palkin, E.A.: On the uncertainty relations in the information-time-resources tryad arising in the decision-making process. Bull. Russian New Univ. Ser.: Complex Syst.: Models Anal. Control 2, 61–68 (2022)
3. Bohr, N.: Atomic Physics and Human Knowledge, p. 101. Science Edition, Inc. New York (1959)
4. Held, C.: The meaning of complementarity. Stud. Hist. Philos. Sci. 25, 871–893 (1994)
5. Floridi, L.: The philosophy of information. Metaphilos. Oxford 41(3), 420–442 (2010)
6. Floridi, L.: Semantic Conception of Information. The Stanford Enciclopedia of Philosophy (2005)
7. Brillouin, L.: Science and Information Theory, p. 351. Academic Press, New York (1962)
8. Rubinstein, A.: Lecture Notes in Microeconomics Theory, 2nd edn. Princeton University Press, Princeton (2013)
9. Harzheim, E.: Ordered Sets. Springer, Berlin (2006)
10. Hubbard, D.W.: How to Measure Anything, 3rd edn. Wiley, Hoboken (2014)

11. Von Neumann, J.: Mathematische Grundlagen der Quantenmechanik. Springer, Berlin (1932)
12. Penrose, R.: The Emperors New Mind. Oxford University Press, Oxford (1989)
13. Menskii, M.B.: Concept of consciousness in the context of quantum mechanics. Phys. Usp. **175**(4), 413–435 (2005)
14. Kadomtsev, B.D., Kadomtsev, M.B.: Wave function collapses. Phys. Usp. **166**, 651–659 (1996)
15. Kharkevich, A.A.: On the value of information. Probl. Cybern. **4**, 54–60 (1960)
16. Maralov, V.G., Gura, A., Tatlyev, R., Bukhtiyarova, I.N., Karavaev, D.M.: Influence of the sex and age on people's attitude toward hazards. Astra Salvensis **7**(13), 343–352 (2019)
17. Lukyanova, M., Kovshov, V., Zalilova, Z., Faizov, N.: Modeling the expansion of agricultural markets. Montenegrin J. Econ. **18**(2), 127–141 (2022)
18. Panchenko, A., Voloshina, A., Sadullozoda, S.S., Boltyansky, O., Panina, V.: Influence of the design features of orbital hydraulic motors on the change in the dynamic characteristics of hydraulic drives. In: Ivanov, V., Pavlenko, I., Liaposhchenko, O., Machado, J., Edl, M. (eds.) DSMIE 2022. LNME, pp. 101–111. Springer, Cham (2022). https://doi.org/10.1007/978-3-031-06044-1_10

Performance Analysis of Machine Learning Algorithm on Cloud Platforms: AWS vs Azure vs GCP

Suhaima Jamal[✉] and Hayden Wimmer

Georgia Southern University, Statesboro, GA 30458, USA
sj14077@georgiasouthern.edu

Abstract. The significance of adopting cloud technology in enterprises is accelerating and becoming ubiquitous in business and industry. Due to migrating the on-premises servers and services into cloud, companies can leverage several advantages such as cost optimization, high performance, and flexible system maintenance, to name a few. As the data volume, variety, veracity, and velocity are rising tremendously, adopting machine learning (ML) solutions in the cloud platform bring benefits from ML model building through model evaluation more efficiently and accurately. This study will provide a comparative performance analysis of the three big cloud vendors: Amazon Web Service (AWS), Microsoft Azure and Google Cloud Platform (GCP) by building regression models in each of the platforms. For validation purposes, i.e., training and testing the models, five different standard datasets from the UCI machine learning repository have been employed. This work utilizes the ML services of AWS Sage maker, Azure ML Studio and Google Big Query for conducting the experiments. Model evaluation criteria here include measuring R-squared values for each platform, calculating the error metrics (Mean Squared Error, Mean Absolute Error, Root Mean Squared Error etc.) and comparing the results to determine the best performing cloud provider in terms of ML service. The study concludes with presenting a comparative taxonomy of regression models across the three platforms.

Keywords: Cloud Computing · Machine Learning · Supervised Machine Learning · Regression · AWS · Azure · GCP

1 Introduction

In the technological revolution, cloud computing has been the biggest buzz nowadays impacting business and industry from every conceivable angle. The tendency to migrate to the cloud from local data centers, also known as on premise [1] is quite a common scenario in almost every institution. For managing complex and sophisticated IT infrastructure, scaling up and down required resources, focusing more on business operations, cloud computing is playing significant roles. For working in the cloud platforms, migrating all on-premises data or applications to cloud, managing the virtualized resources efficiently [2], and optimizing the cloud computing, it is an intelligent way to work with

A. Gibadullin (Ed.): ITIDMS 2022, CCIS 1821, pp. 43–60, 2023.
https://doi.org/10.1007/978-3-031-31353-0_5

one of the cloud partners. In terms of big data and increased workloads, integrating machine learning solutions to the cloud and to deploy in enterprise applications have added many advantages including flexibility, cost effectiveness and efficiency. To build, train, deploy, and test ML models with low coding experience and less maintenance and required expertise companies increasingly rely on cloud vendors. Figure 1 represents the general ML service structure of cloud environment. Larger cloud computing service providers offer multiple options to implement the intelligent features in the enterprise applications which don't demand highly skilled professionals to work with AI or ML projects thereby offering cost savings.

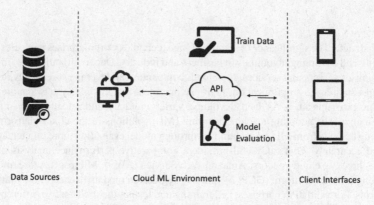

Fig. 1. ML Service Environment of Cloud Platform.

Enabling a computer system or machines to learn without explicit intervention or instruction of humans can be defined as Machine learning. Learning by the machine itself using algorithms or statistical approaches or models for analyzing data patterns and predicting outcomes is the basic idea behind this. ML and artificial intelligence are making a steady approach into every sector of industry such as enterprise, health care, education, and even non-profit organizations. Deployment of machine learning models in the cloud brings extended benefits by removing many technical hurdles. For handling resource management, scheduling tasks, and optimizing energy ML are algorithms are widely adopted [3]. Cloud providers like Azure, AWS, and GCP offer to work with a variety of machine learning algorithms, still there are significant differences in terms of front-end interface, background setup etc. AWS is called to be the most mature provider having a range of offers for small development companies, large enterprises and even for governments. They have the largest set of services. Microsoft Azure is popular for their drag and drop interface, which doesn't require prior coding experience. The geographic coverage of Azure appears broader than others. GCP on the other hand, is the smallest of the big three providers; however, it provides a robust set of solutions for any kind of applications.

Since our data is increasing in an enormous volume, the significance and dependency on machine learning is also escalating gradually. The greater the data volume, the more computational power is required, and machine learning is playing a vital role in this case. For machine learning workloads, cloud is providing a pay-per-use model which is very cost effective. To bring machine learning solutions to enterprise, therein lie certain barriers. To build, train and deploy models specialized skills are required. Apart from this, there is a high demand of computational power and special hardware adding up to high cost for development, labor, and infrastructure. All these barriers can be overcome with cloud computing solutions. Companies can leverage the highest speed and Graphical Processing Unit (GPU) power while training and experimenting machine learning models in cloud environment. Similarly, obstacles for storing high volume data are also overcome. Not only the large enterprises, but also small to medium companies are taking the advantages of this cloud computing technology [4]. While choosing cloud vendors for machine learning service, it is recommended to review the performance and offerings for each platform. During the collaboration with ML solutions, different cloud providers use different backend services, frameworks, and algorithms. Hence, performance of ML models might vary from platform to platform. It is strongly advised to understand and analyze the features and performance of the different cloud vendors while choosing one for machine learning implementation.

This study addresses this performance evaluation of ML models of different cloud platforms. At first, the relevant literatures to our work are summarized. Next, our method collected five standard datasets from the UCI machine learning data repository, examined the datasets and prepared data to input as for feeding into linear regression models, segregated the data for training and testing purposes, developed linear regression models in the three cloud platforms (Azure, AWS and GCP). Following the illustration of our methods, the results evaluate the models using the metrics like R Squared Value, Mean Squared Error (MSE), Root Mean Squared Error (RMSE) and Mean Absolute Error (MAE) on the three largest cloud platforms. Our research will assist enterprises in effective decision making to choose the suitable cloud vendor when they consider leveraging cloud technology infused with machine learning solutions.

2   Literature Review

There are many scholarly works on ML algorithms' comparisons specifically on supervised models, few are those noted in Sect. 2.1. Later, the papers on the performance analysis of ML models on several open-source data mining tools are summarized in Sect. 2.2. Furthermore, studies which focus on comparing different cloud vendors are summarized in Sect. 2.3.

2.1   Supervised ML Algorithms' Performance Comparison

Abdulqader et al. [5] presented several techniques of supervised machine learning algorithms for gene selection dataset. Various supervised algorithms: Support Vector Machine (SVM), Neural Network, K-nearest Neighbor, Naïve Bayes, Random Forest are elaborately discussed here. A survey has been conducted on gene selection methods using supervised machine learning algorithms. While using SVM technique on four sets of microarray data, the performance has been measured as highest. The lowest accuracy seems to be from Naïve Bayes which is 74.83% [5]. Similarly, from the experimental results of Meyer et al. [6] on four machine learning algorithm (Random Forest, Neural

Network, Averaged Neural Network and Support Vector Machine) on MSG SEVIRI data over Germany, SVM has relatively high error (123%) and its prediction rate is lower than other three. The R-squared values of each model increase significantly with the aggregation on to 24 h [6].

Likewise, another comparative study was conducted by Osisanwo et al. [7], where the classification indicates that SVM has the highest correctly classified instance (77.3021%). In another work, Maulud, Abdulazeez [8] described linear regression models elaborately and reviewed 23 papers on different types of linear regression: Simple, Polynomial and Multivariate Linear Regression (MLR) models. The paper discussed all the related equations for each of the models, and how least square method is utilized to find the best fit line or curve. The higher accuracy is 99.89% which is obtained by using MLRM technique on the Aero-Material dataset. The lowest accuracy (82.15) is found for the Pima Indian Diabetes dataset while using the same MLRM method [8]. Moreover, on the types, techniques and implementations of machine learning algorithms, Wang et al. [9] discussed in detail on linear regression models. It is noted that principal components analysis (PCA) has significance in reducing data dimensionality of unsupervised learning. Other important concepts like local representation, interpolation with kernel and smoothness prior also have impacts on predictive functions which are clearly demonstrated in this paper [9].

Again, Kolisetty, Rajput [10] aimed at facilitating the understanding of significance of ML for large data analysis. High volume data processing needs more computational power and increased hardware, it also becomes high in cost. Impact of these perspectives on real time data analysis is a major factor to be considered. This paper also suggests the opportunities from the encouraging features development in the field of machine learning with the use of big data [10]. On the other hand, Asim et al. [11] have adopted the three different machine learning approaches: lazy learning, decision tree with different variants and ensembling technique identifying professional bloggers. While working with D tree classifiers, famous algorithms of D tree: Random Tree, REP Tree, Random Forest, Simple Cart, NB Tree and AD Tree are used. Evaluating the results, it is found that the best correctly classifiers are Random Tree and Random Forest with 92% accuracy rate having only 8% error [11]. Moreover, Love [12] focused on the modes of unsupervised learning model: intentional and incidental, and their relationships with supervised classification learning. After running three algorithms on the collected data, four types were observed where type 2 supervised learning has the highest accuracy (95%). The overall work after result evaluation summarizes that there are no advantages of engaging intentional unsupervised learning over incidental except the target concept is low in dimension and non-linear [12].

2.2   ML Model Evaluation on Open-Source Data Mining Tools

There are numerous research works which has compared the performances of machine learning algorithms on open-source data mining tools. Like, Ratra, Gulia [13] 2020 aimed at analyzing data mining tools, Orange, and WEKA by implementing three classification algorithms: Naïve Bayes, K-nearest Neighbor and Random Forest. While comparing the precision metrics, the results show that WEKA has a higher percentage than Orange. Naïve Bayes performs the highest in both platforms which is 83.7% in WEKA and 82.4%

in Orange [13]. Similarly, Kodati, Vivekanandam [14] presented a comparative review on WEKA and Orange tools for mining and analyzing of Heart Disease Dataset from UCI data repository. Authors have conducted an analytical study on four machine learning algorithms: Naïve Bayes, SMO, Random Forest, and K-Nearest Neighbor. When the dimension of the inputs is high, Naïve Bayes has the highest performance in terms of Precision and Recall both in WEKA and Orange tools. The Precision and Recall values of K-Nearest Neighbor is 0.753 and 0.752 in WEKA, whereas in Orange it is consecutively 0.58 and 0.547. K-Nearest Neighbor has the lowest performance among the four [14].

In another study, Kavitha et al. [15] worked on regression models and compared two potential functions for linear regression algorithm: SMOReg function and Least-MedSq function. Open University Learning Analytics dataset has been used which is multivariate, time series and sequential. While comparing both models, it is obvious that the SMO regression function took 2.42 s which is less than the LeastMedSq function of linear regression (3.29 s). However, all the error metrics (mean absolute error, relative absolute error, root mean squared error) are less in LeastMedSq linear regression than SMO regression. The result concludes that the LeastMedSq function performs better for linear regression algorithm [15]. Moreover, another experiment conducted by Rajagopal et al. [16] on UNSW NB-15 dataset for intrusion detection. The experiment is conducted in Azure Machine Learning Studio for evaluating the models where 10-fold cross valida-tion technique has been applied. Four classification models (Random Forest, Decision Tree, Naïve Bayes and SVM) have been compared while Apache Spark is used as a processing paradigm. Result indicates that as a classifier, Decision Forest performs the highest. Moreover, the eight two class models took minimal time for training which ranged in 6 to 9 s. The study also emphasized that Microsoft Azure Machine Learning Studio (MAMLS) can be considered a potential Integrated Development Environment to handle large volume datasets [16].

2.3 Cloud Vendors' Comparison: Services and Design Taxonomies

Related to cloud platform comparison based on general services, Kaushik et al. [17] discussed and compared among three large cloud vendors: Amazon AWS, Microsoft Azure and Google Cloud Platform. It elaborated the different computing platforms of cloud as can be segmented into two elements front end and back end. Authors have tabulated all the prices of services that are provided by these three cloud vendors where it is obvious that Azure is the most expensive for general purpose instances. However, AWS has the cheapest options for choosing instances. For testing the performance, Phoronix Test Suite3 has been adopted on the Linux systems. The test processes were completed in Apache, RAM speed and Dbench benchmark. In the Apache measurement, it is seen that Azure handles more HTTP requests better than the two. Again, in the Dbench test, AWS and Azure differences are very negligible while GCP has lower performance than the two [17]. Similarly, in another survey by Alkhatib et al. [18], the finding shows that market shares of AWS (32%) is larger than Azure (19%) and GCP (7%). In terms of security, AWS has AWS Security Hub, Azure uses Azure Security Center and Google has their Cloud Security Command Center. While considering the weakness, Azure seems most expensive which can cut down their customers, AWS is sometimes considered as difficult to use and GCP has comparatively fewer features than others [18].

Another taxonomy of services is provided by Sikeridis et al. [19] on the four dominants in perspective of market share and the sub-services designating storage, data pipeline, analytics, databases, machine learning etc. While taking the cloud services, customers can choose to pay per usage models for billing. Major cloud vendors are providing a combination of low cost (Zero installation and maintenance cost) and high performance. Based on the service types of computer services and virtual machines, the offered services by Amazon, Microsoft, Google, and IBM have been tabulated where it is found that Max memory is used by Amazon (1952 GB: X1) and the lowest is IBM (242 GB). The virtualization of hypervisor based, and container based have been drawn as well. The serverless computing services for each provider are Amazon: AWS Lambda, Microsoft: Azure Function, Google: Cloud Functions and IBM: Open Whisk. All the four providers have no SQL, petabyte scale and relational databases [19].

So far, other studies focused on the comparisons of ML algorithms in open-source data mining tools or offline tools. However, the performance evaluation of these models in cloud platforms is yet to be measured. Hence, this study aims at building such an analysis among Azure, AWS and GCP by conducting experiments in the individual platform.

3   Methods

The overall flow diagram of the project has been presented in Fig. 2, where in the beginning of the process, a total of five datasets have been collected from UCI Machine Learning data repository. All these data are standard and publicly available. Data has been prepared to feed as inputs of the machine learning models using the WEKA tool. It has been ensured that there are no null or missing values in our data samples. After analyzing the data, linear regression models were built consecutively. At first ML model was built in Amazon AWS using the AWS Sage maker service. Then utilizing Azure ML studio, all the pipelines for ML models have been created. Later, taking the service of Google Big Query, model creation has been performed. Finally, all the models have been evaluated by calculating the metrics Mean Squared Error (MSE), Mean Absolute Error (MAE), Root Mean Squared Error (RMSE), Coefficient of determination or R-square etc.

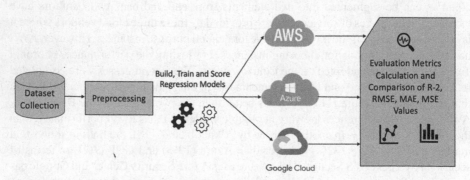

Fig. 2. Flow Diagram of Overall Project.

3.1 Datasets

All the datasets have been collected from UCI Machine Learning Data Repository which are standard for regression model analysis. Snapshots of the all the datasets are shown in Fig. 3 through 7. UCI machine learning repository has a large collection of datasets, data generators and domain theories which are widely used by scholars, students, and researchers as an authentic source of datasets.

Insurance Dataset. There are a total of 6 features (age, sex, bmi, children, smoker, and region) and one target variable, 'charges' in the data set. It has 1437 tuples in total. As sex, smoker and region attributes are non-numeric, numeric values have been assigned to these variables to make all data samples numeric [20]. For exploratory data analysis and hypothesis testing on specifically regression models, it is a widely used dataset available publicly.

	age	sex	bmi	children	smoker	region	charges
1	age	sex	bmi	children	smoker	region	charges
2	19	1	27.9	0	1	4	16884.924
3	18	0	33.77	1	0	3	1725.5523
4	28	0	33	3	0	3	4449.462
5	33	0	22.705	0	0	2	21984.4706
6	32	0	28.88	0	0	2	3866.8552
7	31	1	25.74	0	0	3	3756.6216
8	46	1	33.44	1	0	3	8240.5896
9	37	1	27.74	3	0	2	7281.5056
10	37	0	29.83	2	0	1	6406.4107

Fig. 3. A Snapshot of the Insurance Dataset.

Iris Dataset. This dataset contains a total of 4 independent variables (sepal width, petal length, and species) and one dependent variable, 'sepal length'. The dataset has a total 150 data samples. The species are of Iris-setosa, Iris-versicolor, and Iris-virginica. Based on these 4 features, the regression model will make the prediction on the sepal length variable [21] (Fig. 4).

Real Estate Home Price Prediction Dataset. Real estate house price prediction is also a standard dataset from UCI machine learning data repository. It has a total 6 feature variables and one target variable which is 'unit area price'. Depending on the 6 features, the model makes predictions of the house price on unit area. All the values of this dataset are numerical [22] (Fig. 5).

Wine Quality-Red Dataset. It has a total of 1598 data rows having twelve independent variables and one dependent variable, quality. As the dataset has all numeric variables, it has been kept unmodified while loading for further model build-up [23] (Fig. 6).

1	sepal width	petal length	petal width	species	sepal length
2	3.5	1.4	0.2	Iris-setosa	5.1
3	3	1.4	0.2	Iris-setosa	4.9
4	3.2	1.3	0.2	Iris-setosa	4.7
5	3.1	1.5	0.2	Iris-setosa	4.6
6	3.6	1.4	0.2	Iris-setosa	5
7	3.9	1.7	0.4	Iris-setosa	5.4
8	3.4	1.4	0.3	Iris-setosa	4.6
9	3.4	1.5	0.2	Iris-setosa	5
10	2.9	1.4	0.2	Iris-setosa	4.4

Fig. 4. A Snapshot of Iris Dataset.

1	x1	x2	x3	x4	x5	x6	Unit Area Price
2	2012.917	32	84.87882	10	24.98298	121.54024	37.9
3	2012.917	19.5	306.5947	9	24.98034	121.53951	42.2
4	2013.583	13.3	561.9845	5	24.98746	121.54391	47.3
5	2013.5	13.3	561.9845	5	24.98746	121.54391	54.8
6	2012.833	5	390.5684	5	24.97937	121.54245	43.1
7	2012.667	7.1	2175.03	3	24.96305	121.51254	32.1
8	2012.667	34.5	623.4731	7	24.97933	121.53642	40.3
9	2013.417	20.3	287.6025	6	24.98042	121.54228	46.7
10	2013.5	31.7	5512.038	1	24.95095	121.48458	18.8

Fig. 5. A Snapshot of Real State Home Price Prediction Dataset.

1	fixedAcidity	volatileAcidity	citricAcid	residualSugar	chlorides	freeSulfurDioxide	totalSulfurDioxide	density	pH	sulphates	alcohol	quality
2	7.4	0.7	0	1.9	0.076	11	34	0.9978	3.51	0.56	9.4	5
3	7.8	0.88	0	2.6	0.098	25	67	0.9968	3.2	0.68	9.8	5
4	7.8	0.76	0.04	2.3	0.092	15	54	0.997	3.26	0.65	9.8	5
5	11.2	0.28	0.56	1.9	0.075	17	60	0.998	3.16	0.58	9.8	6
6	7.4	0.7	0	1.9	0.076	11	34	0.9978	3.51	0.56	9.4	5
7	7.4	0.66	0	1.8	0.075	13	40	0.9978	3.51	0.56	9.4	5
8	7.9	0.6	0.06	1.6	0.069	15	59	0.9964	3.3	0.46	9.4	5
9	7.3	0.65	0	1.2	0.065	15	21	0.9946	3.39	0.47	10	7
10	7.8	0.58	0.02	2	0.073	9	18	0.9968	3.36	0.57	9.5	7

Fig. 6. A Snapshot of Wine Quality Red Dataset.

Wine Quality-White Dataset. This is also a standard dataset for working with regression models. The dataset contains a total of 13 attributes. Quality is the target or dependent variable here which is to predict using the 12 independent variables. The number of rows in the dataset is 4897. The values are all numeric and there are not any missing values. Hence, this dataset has been used without any modification [24].

	fixedAcidity	volatileAcidity	citricAcid	residualSugar	chlorides	freeSulfurDioxide	totalSulfurDioxide	density	pH	sulphates	alcohol	quality
2	7	0.27	0.36	20.7	0.045	45	170	1.001	3	0.45	8.8	6
3	6.3	0.3	0.34	1.6	0.049	14	132	0.994	3.3	0.49	9.5	6
4	8.1	0.28	0.4	6.9	0.05	30	97	0.9951	3.26	0.44	10.1	6
5	7.2	0.23	0.32	8.5	0.058	47	186	0.9956	3.19	0.4	9.9	6
6	7.2	0.23	0.32	8.5	0.058	47	186	0.9956	3.19	0.4	9.9	6
7	8.1	0.28	0.4	6.9	0.05	30	97	0.9951	3.26	0.44	10.1	6
8	6.2	0.32	0.16	7	0.045	30	136	0.9949	3.18	0.47	9.6	6
9	7	0.27	0.36	20.7	0.045	45	170	1.001	3	0.45	8.8	6
10	6.3	0.3	0.34	1.6	0.049	14	132	0.994	3.3	0.49	9.5	6
11	8.1	0.22	0.43	1.5	0.044	28	129	0.9938	3.22	0.45	11	6
12	8.1	0.27	0.41	1.45	0.033	11	63	0.9908	2.99	0.56	12	5

Fig. 7. A Snapshot of Wine Quality White Dataset.

3.2 Cloud Platforms

With the evolution of computing and technology, cloud computing has been a blessing for implementing and working with machine learning algorithms. However, different platforms have different orientation and interface for building models. For building and training cost-effective, memory efficient solutions with simple or complex machine learning algorithms, several cloud platforms like Azure, AWS and GCP have their different service levels. In this work, we will be implementing regression models using above five different datasets for running the experiment into three of the platforms (Azure, AWS and GCP).

3.3 Algorithm

Linear regression is one of the most famous supervised algorithms which is used for predictive analysis. It makes predictions for real or continuous or numeric values like age, salary, product price etc. The formula stands as:

$$Y = a + bX \tag{1}$$

where Y is the dependent or target variable, X is predictor or independent variable, and b is the slope of the line. This algorithm provides a straight line between these two variables X and Y as Fig. 8.

We will be working with a linear regression model and analyze the performance metrics in three cloud environments. This has been ensured that all the datasets were kept the same for all three platforms. Also, the procedures, data splitting process etc. were kept similar while building the models.

3.4 Procedure

Amazon AWS. In the AWS platform, the Sage maker service has been used which is a fully managed machine learning Amazon Elastic Compute Cloud (Amazon E2C) Compute Instance. With Sage Maker, different machine learning models can be easily and quickly built, trained, tested, and deployed in the production ready environment. The interface of AWS sage maker has been presented in Fig. 9. A Jupyter notebook instance has been created for building linear regression models. Initially the datasets have been loaded into Amazon S3 bucket which is the public cloud storage available in Amazon

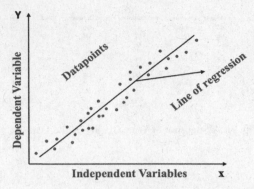

Fig. 8. Linear Regression Graph.

Web Service. The datasets have been split into 70%-30% ratio for training and testing using sk-learn functions. Using Sage maker boto3 services, the model has been trained and the model summary has been evaluated. A code snippet is attached in Fig. 10.

Fig. 9. Amazon AWS Sage Maker Interface.

Microsoft Azure. In our experiment, Azure Machine Learning Studio has been used for creating the machine learning pipelines in the designer and authoring section. Azure blob storage has been used for storing the datasets. The default computing instances of Azure have been utilized here. Randomization and splitting data ratio were kept as 70%-30%. Azure ML Studio interface and the flow of one of our pipeline creations is shown consecutively in Fig. 11 and Fig. 12.

```
In [5]:  from sklearn.model_selection import train_test_split
         training_data = df.sample(frac=0.7, random_state=25)
         testing_data= df.drop(training_data.index)

         print(f"No. of training examples: {training_data.shape[0]}")
         print(f"No. of testing examples: {testing_data.shape[0]}")

         No. of training examples: 937
         No. of testing examples: 401

In [6]:  import boto3
         import sagemaker
         from sagemaker import get_execution_role

         sagemaker_session = sagemaker.Session()
         role = sagemaker.get_execution_role()

In [9]:  import statsmodels.formula.api as smf

In [11]: model=smf.ols('charges ~ age + sex + bmi + children + smoker + region',data
```

Fig. 10. Code Snippet from AWS Sage Maker Jupyter Notebook.

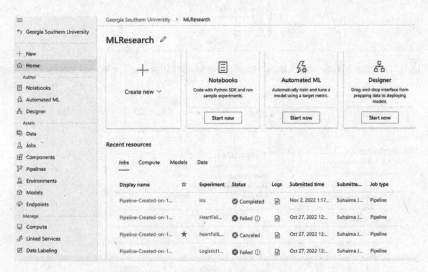

Fig. 11. Azure ML Studio Interface.

Google Cloud Big Query. Using Google Big Query, our linear regression model is built in Google Cloud. Google Big Query is a serverless and cost-effective warehouse to work with big data and get insights by extracting the features. After building the model, all the results have been evaluated for our five datasets. The snapshot of the evaluation criteria using insurance dataset has been attached in Fig. 13 where different error metrics like Mean Absolute Error, Mean Squared Error, Mean Squared Log Error etc. can be found.

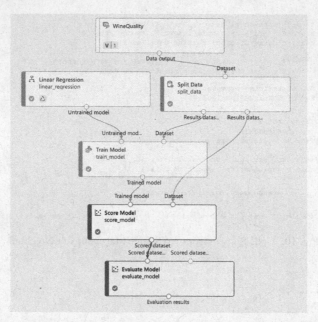

Fig. 12. Azure ML Studio: Linear Regression Model Pipeline for Wine Quality Dataset.

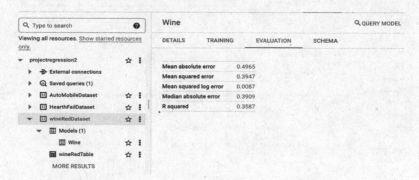

Fig. 13. Google Big Query Model Evaluation for Wine Quality Dataset.

4 Experimental Results

We have used five different datasets standard for regression models from UCI machine learning and run our experiments in three cloud platforms (Azure, AWS and GCP). First, linear regression models have been built using AWS Sage maker Jupyter Notebook instance. Then in Azure ML studio, the pipelines of the models have been created for all the five datasets and the evaluation results are recorded. All the results were collected from these two platforms. Later, we worked on Google Big Query for building and evaluating our model in Google Cloud Platform. Finally, the comparison of R squared values and different error metrics are calculated and compared among the three platforms' results.

4.1   R Squared Value or Coefficient of Determination

This statistical measure in the regression model determines the variance proportion of the dependent variable which can be explained by the independent variable. The fitness of the model can be determined by this value. The higher R-squared value is the better for the model fitness.

R-Squared Formula:

$$R_{Squared} = \frac{SS_{Regression}}{SS_{Total}} \tag{2}$$

$SS_{Regression}$ = Sum of squares due to regression.
SS_{Total} = Total sum of squares.

Interpretation of R-Squared Values. The higher the R-squared value, the better the regression models fit with the testing data. When R-squared = 1, all the variations of y values are accounted for by the values of x.

When R-squared = 0.5, 50% of the variations of y values are accounted for by the values of x. When R-squared = 0, None of the variation of y is accounted for by x.

Table 1. R squared value comparison.

Platform	Dataset Name					Average
	Insurance	Iris	Real Estate Home Price	Wine Quality Red	Wine Quality White	
Azure	0.745	0.870	0.594	0.296	0.281	0.557
AWS	0.751	0.868	0.582	0.361	0.261	0.565
GCP	0.784	0.868	0.582	0.359	0.261	0.571

From our experiments, obtained R-squared values from Azure, AWS and GCP have been tabulated in Table 1. At first R-squared values are calculated for each of the dataset and then the average is calculated to compare the results. The higher average R-squared value is obtained from GCP (0.571) and then AWS (0.565). However, Azure (0.557) has comparatively lower performance than the other two. The bar chart in Fig. 14 shows the performance comparison among these three cloud providers.

4.2   Error Metrics

Error metrics are used to quantify performance of models and provide ways for forecasting to compare different models quantitatively. These metrics give a precise gauge on the performance of the models. There are few common error metrics for reporting and evaluating linear regression model performance, these are: Mean Squared Error (MSE), Mean Absolute Error (MAE), Root Mean Squared Error (RMSE) and Mean Squared Log Error (MSLE).

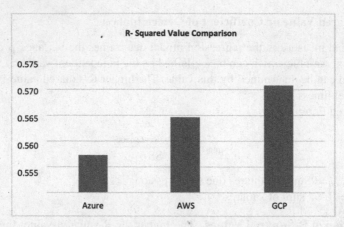

Fig. 14. Comparison Graph of R-Squared Value.

Root Mean Squared Error (RMSE). This calculates the square root of average squared distance which is the difference between the actual and the predicted value. This is a very popular evaluating metric for regression models as it calculates both how the prediction is close to the actual average and indicates the effects of large error. Large errors will always have a significant impact on the RMSE value. The formula for RMSE is as below:

$$RMSE = SD_y\sqrt{(1 - r^2)} \qquad (3)$$

SD is the standard deviation. The lower the RMSE value, the better the model fits to the dataset.

Mean Absolute Error (MAE). Mean Absolute Error is the loss function of a regression model. The loss denotes the mean of the absolute differences between actual and predicted values or, the deviation from the actual value. Less MAE value is better and if it tends to zero the model is more accurate. MAE formula is as follows:

$$MAE = \frac{1}{n}\sum_{1}^{n}|Y - \underline{Y}| \qquad (4)$$

Here Y is the output value.
$\underline{Y}$ is the predicted value.
n is the total data points.

Mean Squared Log Error (MSLE). The measurement of the ratio between log transformed actual and log transformed predicted value of a model can be noted by Mean Squared Log Error (MSLE).

$$MSLE = \frac{1}{N}\sum_{i}^{N}(log_e(1 + y_i) - log_e(1 + \underline{y_i}))^2 \qquad (5)$$

The error metrics from Azure and GCP are tabulated in Tables 2 and 3. For the five datasets Mean Absolute Error, Mean Squared Error, Mean Squared Log Error and Root

Table 2. Error metrics of Microsoft Azure Platform.

Datasets					
Error Metrics	Insurance	Iris	Real Estate Home Price	Wine Quality Red	Wine Quality White
Mean Absolute Error (MAE)	7197.14	0.213	6.273	0.554	0.596
Relative Absolute Error	0.4698	0.340	0.609	0.781	0.878
Relative Squared Error	0.255	0.130	0.406	0.704	0.719
Root Mean Squared Error (RMSE)	6217.802	0.276	8.371	0.719	0.770

Mean Squared Error are calculated here. Table 4 shows the average MAE and RMSE error rate between Azure and GCP where the error values are lowest for GCP which makes this platform better performing than the other. The comparison graph is presented in Fig. 15.

Table 3. Error metrics of Google Cloud Platform.

Datasets					
Error Metrics	Insurance	Iris	Real Estate Home Price	Wine Quality Red	Wine Quality White
Mean Absolute Error (MAE)	3820.149	0.242	6.131	0.497	0.585
Mean Squared Error	30712073	0.090	77.132	0.395	0.555
Mean Squared Log Error	0.528	0.002	0.064	0.009	0.012
Median Absolute Error	2143.254	0.209	4.97	0.391	0.496

5 Discussion

The evaluation criteria include calculating the R-Squared values and error metrics for understanding how well the ML models are performing across platforms. From our experimental results in the three platforms: Azure, AWS and GCP, the average R-Squared

Table 4. Average Error Metrics of Azure and GCP.

Platform	Average MAE	Average RMSE
Azure	1440.955	1245.587
GCP	765.521	1124.004

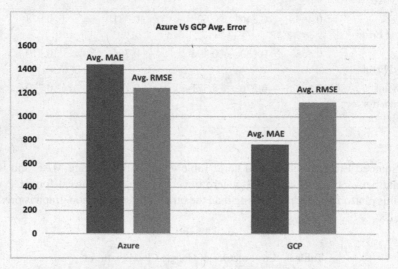

Fig. 15. Comparison Graph of Avg. Error between Azure and GCP.

value was found in GCP, 0.57, which is higher than the AWS and Azure. As the higher R-Squared values indicate better fitness of the ML models, hence, it can be said that the best performance of the regression model is obtained in GCP. AWS is in the second position having a R^2 value 0.565. On the other side, Azure has comparatively lower R^2 value (0.557) than the others which is open to interpretation. While comparing the error metrics among AWS and GCP, it is noticeable that the average record of error metrics in GCP (average MAE = 765.521, average RMSE = 1124.004) are comparatively lower than Azure (average MAE = 1440.955, average RMSE = 1245.5876) which denotes that linear regression model performance in GCP is better than Azure. As a continuation of the current study, we are keen to develop further analytical and comparative study on other ML models to scrutinize more on the performance of different cloud vendors in terms of Machine Learning collaboration.

6   Conclusion and Future Scope

Cloud technology is making the way for enterprises to perform their technological operations more efficiently and effectively. For working with ML models, cloud platforms are tremendously being utilized. However, the leadership is very competitive among the cloud vendors, i.e., Amazon Web Service (AWS), Microsoft Azure and Google Cloud

Platform (GCP). It is always hard to select the best performing provider, still, it is a strong recommendation to understand the machine learning algorithms' performance before choosing any cloud vendor to work with. From the experiment conducted in the three big cloud giants, we have a clear idea on regression model performance in these platforms, and it reveals that the performance variation is not much for the three, still, it is slightly higher in GCP than the other two. Our findings will assist enterprises in understanding the performance variations of machine learning services while selecting a cloud platform to work on. Further study on other models, like, classification can be conducted and compared among the cloud platforms to achieve more insights on machine learning model performance.

References

1. Townsend, M., Wimmer, H., Du, J.: Barriers and drivers to adoption of cloud infrastructure services: a security perspective. In: 2020 IEEE International IOT, Electronics and Mechatronics Conference (IEMTRONICS), pp. 1–7. IEEE (2020)
2. Parida, B.R., Rath, A.K., Mohapatra, H.: Binary self-adaptive salp swarm optimization-based dynamic load balancing in cloud computing. Int. J. Inf. Technol. Web Eng. (IJITWE) 17, 1–25 (2022)
3. Khan, T., Tian, W., Zhou, G., Ilager, S., Gong, M., Buyya, R.: Machine learning (ML)–centric resource management in cloud computing: a review and future directions. J. Netw. Comput. Appl. 103405 (2022)
4. Grigoriou, N.N., Fink, A.: Cloud computing: Key to enabling smart production and industry 4.0. In: Madsen, O., Berger, U., Møller, C., Heidemann Lassen, A., Vejrum Waehrens, B., Schou, C. (eds.) The Future of Smart Production for SMEs, pp. 315–322. Springer, Cham (2023). https://doi.org/10.1007/978-3-031-15428-7_26
5. Abdulqader, D.M., Abdulazeez, A.M., Zeebaree, D.Q.: Machine learning supervised algorithms of gene selection: a review. Mach. Learn. 62, 233–244 (2020)
6. Meyer, H., Kühnlein, M., Appelhans, T., Nauss, T.: Comparison of four machine learning algorithms for their applicability in satellite-based optical rainfall retrievals. Atmos. Res. 169, 424–433 (2016)
7. Osisanwo, F., Akinsola, J., Awodele, O., Hinmikaiye, J., Olakanmi, O., Akinjobi, J.: Supervised machine learning algorithms: classification and comparison. Int. J. Comput. Trends Technol. (IJCTT) 48, 128–138 (2017)
8. Maulud, D., Abdulazeez, A.M.: A review on linear regression comprehensive in machine learning. J. Appl. Sci. Technol. Trends 1, 140–147 (2020)
9. Wang, H., Lei, Z., Zhang, X., Zhou, B., Peng, J.: Machine learning basics. Deep Learn. 98–164 (2016)
10. Kolisetty, V.V., Rajput, D.S.: A review on the significance of machine learning for data analysis in big data. Jordan. J. Comput. Inf. Technol. (JJCIT) 6, 155–171 (2020)
11. Asim, Y., Shahid, A.R., Malik, A.K., Raza, B.: Significance of machine learning algorithms in professional blogger's classification. Comput. Electr. Eng. 65, 461–473 (2018)
12. Love, B.C.: Comparing supervised and unsupervised category learning. Psychon. Bull. Rev. 9, 829–835 (2002)
13. Ratra, R., Gulia, P.: Experimental evaluation of open source data mining tools (WEKA and Orange). Int. J. Eng. Trends Technol. 68, 30–35 (2020)
14. Kodati, S.: Analysis of heart disease using in data mining tools Orange and Weka. Global J. Comp. Sci. Technol. 18, 17–21 (2018)

15. Kavitha, S., Varuna, S., Ramya, R.: A comparative analysis on linear regression and support vector regression. In: 2016 Online International Conference on Green Engineering and Technologies (IC-GET), pp. 1–5. IEEE (2016)
16. Rajagopal, S., Hareesha, K.S., Kundapur, P.P.: Performance analysis of binary and multiclass models using azure machine learning. Int. J. Electr. Comput. Eng. (2088–8708) **10** (2020)
17. Kaushik, P., Rao, A.M., Singh, D.P., Vashisht, S., Gupta, S.: Cloud computing and comparison based on service and performance between Amazon AWS, Microsoft Azure, and Google Cloud. In: 2021 International Conference on Technological Advancements and Innovations (ICTAI), pp. 268–273. IEEE (2021)
18. Alkhatib, A., Al Sabbagh, A., Maraqa, R.: Public cloud computing: big three vendors. In: 2021 International Conference on Information Technology (ICIT), pp. 230–237. IEEE (2021)
19. Sikeridis, D., Papapanagiotou, I., Rimal, B.P., Devetsikiotis, M.: A comparative taxonomy and survey of public cloud infrastructure vendors. arXiv preprint arXiv:1710.01476 (2017)
20. Kaggle   Dataset.   https://www.kaggle.com/datasets/teertha/ushealthinsurancedataset. Accessed 23 Dec 2022
21. Kaggle Dataset. https://www.kaggle.com/datasets/arshid/iris-flower-dataset. Accessed 24 Dec 2022
22. Kaggle Dataset. https://www.kaggle.com/datasets/quantbruce/real-estate-price-prediction. Accessed 24 Dec 2022
23. Kaggle Dataset. https://www.kaggle.com/datasets/uciml/red-wine-quality-cortez-et-al-2009. Accessed 26 Dec 2022
24. Kaggle   Dataset.   https://www.kaggle.com/datasets/piyushagni5/white-wine-quality. Accessed 26 Dec 2022

Mathematical Modeling of the Translation Process and Its Optimization by the Criterion of Quality Maximization

Alena A. Zhivotova(✉) (iD), Victor D. Berdonosov(iD), and Sergey A. Gordin(iD)

Komsomolsk-na-Amure State University, Komsomolsk-na-Amure, Russia
zhivotova.aa@gmail.com

Abstract. The paper substantiates the relevance of the issue of source texts optimizational pre-editing to improve machine translation quality. The paper provides in-depth research of applied linguistics fundamental concepts and describes a mathematical model of the translation process basing on set theory; a model for assessing translation task complexity and a strategy for source texts optimizational pre-editing are proposed; problem statement for further research is formulated.

Keywords: Machine Translation · Mathematical Modeling · Translation Quality · Optimizational Pre-Editing · Computational Linguistics

1 Introduction

Neural and hybrid machine translation (MT) systems increase accuracy and quality every year, but paradoxically, with the increase in MT quality, the level of MT user competence required for translation evaluation and editing also increases. Due to the overall smoothness of the translation, a user without proper qualifications may not pay attention to gross lexical and syntactic errors that significantly distort source text meaning. This is especially true for the translation of highly specialized texts, because not such large training corpora are collected as for texts of general topics.

Most studies consider MT systems to be automatic, which is incorrect. For the correct use of MT systems requires direct human participation at all stages of system work from downloading a source text and collecting relevant training data to evaluating the translation quality. The rule is true that to achieve an optimal result, MT user must know at least one language from the translation language pair, and the better the user knows the translation language, the more accurate translation and its post-editing will be. Final translation quality is improved if MT user is a native speaker of the target language.

Thus, despite the increased efficiency of MT, its use is significantly limited for users without knowledge and skills in translation language.

Considering MT as a mean of automated support providing a translator with models and algorithms to support decision-making regarding translation, we can conclude that by providing the user with text processing tools in the language of which he is a native speaker at any stage of translation, it is possible to improve translation quality.

This hypothesis is confirmed by studies on interactive MT. The most studies are devoted to MT post-editing, including the automation of post-editing [1–4]. Less researches are devoted to pre-editing, but existing practical papers indicate the effectiveness of this approach to improving MT quality [5–7].

It is relevant to conduct in-depth study of translation quality dependence on source text parameters and source text processing strategies to maximize MT quality. The relevance of the task was also demonstrated in the study on the analysis of promising areas for MT systems development [8]. First of all, it is necessary to develop a generalized mathematical and process model of translation to identify the possibility of processing the source text to maximize the translation quality.

2 Materials and Methods

The solution to the problem of developing models, methods and a set of programs for text optimizational pre-editing for further translation lies in the field of applied computational linguistics.

Main task of computational linguistics (CL) is to develop methods and means of creating linguistic processors for applied tasks of automatic text processing in natural language [9]. The development of a linguistic processor for some applied tasks involves a formal description of linguistic properties of a text being processed that can be considered as a text model or a language model.

MT is the earliest application of CL along with which this knowledge field itself arose and developed. The first MT tools were based on the simplest strategy of word-by-word translation, but it quickly became clear that MT requires a much more complete linguistic model. We have previously studied such models and systems in detail [8].

CL is closely related to AI [10] that develops software models of individual intellectual processes. Despite the obvious intersection of researches in CL and AI (as language proficiency refers to intellectual processes), AI does not include the entire CL, since it has its own theoretical basis and methodology. Common to these sciences are computer modeling as the main method and the final study goal; and the heuristic nature of many methods used.

Machine learning in CL is used to process collections of text documents using a text feature model in which features are defined for each document separately. Features can be various text informational properties: linguistic, statistical and structural. For example, the frequency of certain words (or their classes) in a document, the frequency of special signs use, the ratio of words classes, the use of certain syntactic structure or text parts, creation date and others [11].

To formulate and formalize the task of this study, let's analyze the process of translating a text from one natural language to another with decomposition into stages and describe a generalized mathematical model. We use set theory as the main methodology for describing a mathematical model.

3 Model Terms and Definitions

Definitions of model main parts are formulated based on analysing the subject area and fundamental researches in CL [12].

Language is a complex sign system, naturally or artificially created and correlating conceptual content and typical sound (spelling).

Set of existing languages: $lng \in LNG : LNG = \{lng_0, lng_1, \ldots lng_{nLNG}\}$.

The conceptual content is determined by semantic units.

Semantic unit means an abstract entity that is not limited by a specific language or other means of expression (for example, the language of mathematical logic) that provides identification of certain objects, phenomena, and properties of an application domain.

Example: The semantic unit is rain. Ways of expression: rain; precipitation in the form of water droplets; a natural phenomenon when water drops fall from the sky; дождь(in Russian); regen (in German); etc.

Set of semantic units: $su \in SU : SU = \{su_0, su_1, \ldots su_{nSU}\}$.

Let U_{su} be the universal set of all possible expressions of all possible semantic units in all possible languages.

I_{su} is the set of indexes numbering semantic units: $isu \in Isu : Isu = \{0, 1, \ldots, nSU\}$.

In this case, sets SU and Isu are bijective, i.e. $Isu \leftrightarrow SU$.

Each element $isu \in Isu$ is uniquely assigned with subset of semantic unit's expressions $E_{isu} \subseteq U_{su}$. Then $fsSU = (E_{isu})_{isu \in Isu}$ is a countable family of sets of semantic unit expressions.

$$fsSU = (E_{isu})_{isu \in Isu} = \bigcup_{isu \in Isu} E_{isu} = \{x : \exists\, isu\, x \in E_{isu}\} \qquad (1)$$

Application domain or **subject area** is an abstract concept that defines a set of objects within a common context.

Set of application domains (subject areas): $ad \in AD : AD = \{ad_0, ad_1, \ldots ad_{nAD}\}$.

One of the ways to express semantic units and communicate within a certain application domain is text.

Text is a written message objectified in the form of a written document consisting of a number of statements united by different types of lexical, grammatical and logical connections, having a certain moral nature, pragmatic rationale and, accordingly, literarily processed. A text of any size is a relatively autonomous (complete) expression. Set of texts: $txt \in TXT : TXT = \{txt_0, txt_1, \ldots txt_{nTXT}\}$.

Levels of text segmentation: Symbol $\rightarrow$ Morpheme (root, suffix, etc.) $\rightarrow$ Lemma $\rightarrow$ Word Form $\rightarrow$ Lexeme $\rightarrow$ Phrase $\rightarrow$ N-gram $\rightarrow$ Sentence $\rightarrow$ Paragraph $\rightarrow$ Section $\rightarrow$ Document (book) $\rightarrow$ Corpora.

The text as an object of analysis and research has a certain set of properties or features. Set of text properties or features: $tf \in TF : TF = \{tf_0, tf_1, \ldots tf_{nTF}\}$.

In natural language processing tasks, text properties can be conditionally divided into groups of features: *general* (number of characters/words/lines, etc., style, language, application domain and other), $GF \subset TF$; *lexical* (percentage of text coverage with lexical minima, frequency lists, etc.), $LF \subset TF$; *morphological* (number of various parts of speech or word classes and grammatical forms), $MF \subset TF$; *syntactic* (depth of verb and noun groups, connections between verbs in sentences), $SF \subset TF$; *features based on basic calculations* (average length of words and sentences, etc.), $BF \subset TF$.

$$TF = GF \cup LF \cup MF \cup SF \cup BF \tag{2}$$

The set of properties and attributes determines text main parameters including integrity, coherence, difficulty, readability, complexity, and others. Set of text main parameters: $mp \in MP : MP = \{mp_0, mp_1, \ldots mp_{nMP}\}$.

The main parameters of the text are readability and complexity.

Readability allows evaluating whether a text corresponds to the recipient's reading ability and at the level of its individual segments (for example, sentences) to identify parts that require simplification (special terms, abbreviations, lack of context (tables, invoices, pictures, etc.), too short or too long sentences, errors, and other). Various metrics have been developed to estimate readability: Flesch Index, Flesch–Kincaid readability tests, FOG, SMOG, Dale-Chale index, Coleman-Li index, Automated Readability Index (ARI).

Complexity of a text is determined by its morphological, lexical, syntactic features (objective estimation), as well as its informational (cognitive) difficulty (subjective estimation). The cognitive difficulty of a text is determined at the recipients level by its ability to identify semantic units in the text [13].

Translation is the activity of interpreting the conceptual content of a text in one language and creating a new text of equivalent conceptual content in another language.

Translation is performed by a translator from the set of translators, the competence of each of whom is determined by a set of knowledge, skills and expertise in in the field of language proficiency. Set of translators: $tr \in TR : TR = \{tr_0, tr_1, \ldots, tr_{nTR}\}$.

Language knowledge or **language proficiency** is the mastery of grammatical and vocabulary aspects of a language. Knowledge of languages can be characterized by the collection of sets of lexemes, grammatical rules, morphological rules, syntax and punctuation rules, frequency dictionaries.

Lexeme means an abstract two-sided unit of a language vocabulary in the totality of all its specific grammatical forms and inflections expressing them, as well as all possible meanings in all its uses and implementations.

The set of lexemes is defined by set of lemmas: $lm \in LM : LM = \{lm_0, lm_1, \ldots lm_{nLM}\}$, where lm_{iLM} is the initial dictionary form of a word or lemma. In Russian, for nouns and adjectives this is the nominative singular form, for verbs and verb forms this is the infinitive form.

Let U_{wf} be the universal set of all possible word forms of all possible lemmas in all possible languages, and Ilm be the set of indices numbering lemmas: $ilm \in Ilm : Ilm = \{0, 1, \ldots, nLM\}$, $Ilm \leftrightarrow LM$.

Each element $ilm \in Ilm$ is uniquely assigned with subset of lexemes $LXM_{ilm} \subseteq U_{wf}$. Then $fsLXM = (LXM_{ilm})_{ilm \in Ilm}$ is a countable family of sets of lexemes.

$$fsLXM = (LXM_{ilm})_{ilm \in Ilm} = \bigcup_{ilm \in Ilm} LXM_{ilm} = \{x : \exists ilmx \in LXM_{ilm}\} \tag{3}$$

The number of word uses of a lemma in all variants of its lexemes in a certain text (corpus, speech fragment) is called its frequency measured in lexical statistics and described in **frequency dictionaries.** Let U_{freq} be the universal set of all frequencies of all possible lemmas and collocations in all possible languages for all application domains. Each element $ilm \in Ilm$ is uniquely assigned with subset of frequencies $FREQ_{ilm} \subseteq U_{freq}$. Then $fsFREQ = (FREQ_{ilm})_{ilm \in Ilm}$ is a countable family of sets of lemma usage frequencies.

$$fsFREQ = (FREQ_{ilm})_{ilm \in Ilm} = \bigcup_{ilm \in Ilm} REQ_{ilm} = \{x : \exists\, ilm\, x \in FREQ_{ilm}\} \quad (4)$$

The interpretation and translation of words into other languages are described in dictionaries. **Dictionary** is a collection of words, fixed collocations with explanations, interpretations and/or with translation into another language and consisting of lexical entries.

Lexical entry is a tuple of word (word forms of individual lemmas) combinations of length m and n ($m, n \le 4$) in different languages, such that they describe one semantic unit as closely as possible to each other, that is

$$LE = \{(wrd.comb1;\ wrd.comb2) : su_{iSU}|wrd.comb\,1 \rightarrow su_{jSU}|wrd.comb2\} \quad (5)$$

$$wrd.comb\,1 = (wLNG1_{0wf}, wLNG1_{iwf}, \ldots, wLNG1_{mwf}) \quad (6)$$

$$wrd.comb\,2 = \big(wLNG2_{0wf}, wLNG2_{jwf}, \ldots, wLNG2_{nwf}\big) \quad (7)$$

$$wLNG1_{iwf}, wLNG2_{jwf} \in U_{wf} \quad (8)$$

$$su_{iSU}, su_{jSU} \in SU \quad (9)$$

Let U_{le} be the universal set of all possible lexical entries. Each element of the set of indices numbering semantic units $isu \in Isu$ is uniquely assigned with set of lexical entries $DIC_{isu} \subseteq U_{le}$, i.e. $fsDIC = (DIC_{isu})_{isu \in Isu}$ is a countable family of sets of dictionaries.

$$fsDIC = (DIC_{isu})_{isu \in Isu} = \bigcup_{isu \in Isu} DIC_{isu} = \{x : \exists\, isu\, x \in DIC_{isu}\} \quad (10)$$

The rules of using words are characterized by the following sets: set of grammatical rules $gr \in GR : GR = \{gr_0, gr_1, \ldots gr_{nGR}\}$; set of morphological rules $mr \in MR : MR = \{mr_0, mr_1, \ldots, mr_{nMR}\}$; set of syntactic and punctuation rules $spr \in SPR : SPR = \{spr_0, spr_1, \ldots spr_{nSPR}\}$.

Translator skills are translator's abilities that allow him to interpret semantic units expressed in a text in a source language and create an equivalent text in a target language in accordance with the requirements for translation. Set of skills: $skl \in SKL : SKL = \{skl_0, skl_1, \ldots skl_{nSKL}\}$, where skl_{iSKL} is a function of processing, converting or generating text in such a way that the created text express the meaning of a source text as accurately as possible, that is

$$skl_{iSKL}(txt_{iTXT}) = txt'_{iTXT} : MNG|txt'_{iTXT} \rightarrow MNG|txt_{iTXT}, \quad (11)$$

where MNG is a **meaning** or an ordered set of semantic units expressed by a text: $MNG = \{(su_0, su_1, \ldots, su_{nMNG}) : su_{iMNG} \in SU\}$.

Set of all meanings: $MNG \in sMNG : sMNG = \{MNG_0, MNG_1, \ldots MNG_{nMNG}\}$.

Skills are related to the ability to process text according to quality requirements. Set of requirements for translation quality: $req \in REQ : REQ = \{req_0, req_1, \ldots req_{nREQ}\}$, where req_{iREQ} is a certain linguistic requirement that the final result of the translation must meet written in the form of a condition or statement.

Requirements are defined by target language norm $LN \subset REQ$; recipient's cultural traditions $CT \subset REQ$; industry standards according to an application domain $IS|ad_{iAD} \subset REQ$; customer and/or recipient of the translation $CR \subset REQ$.

Set REQ includes all other requirements that are not included in other subsets of requirements. Subsets of requirements may intersect each other. Customer's and/or recipient's translation requirements are a set of collocations used to express semantic units in customer's texts. If there are customer's requirements from, the frequency of collocations defined by such requirements is taken as the maximum when translating customer's texts.

Translator expertise means the experience of using a language in solving translation tasks in various subject areas gained as a result of training or practical activity. Expertise is characterized by the accumulation of experience through the following concepts.

Set of **fixed n-grams** that is combinations of words of unlimited length that describe some meanings (tuple of semantic units). The relationships within semantic units tuples and their compositions as well as n-grams describing the compiled tuples generically called texts $txt \in TXT$ are determined/supplemented/corrected by the translator for various application domains in the process of learning and/or practical activity, i.e. $fngm \in FNGM : FNGM = \{fngm0, fngm1, \ldots, yfngm_{nFNGM}\}$, where $fngm_{nFNGM} = \{(txt, MNG) : txt \in TXT, MNG \in sMNG\}$.

Family of sets of the **frequencies of fixed n-grams usage** to express meanings in general and/or within a certain application domain. Let $Ifngm$ be the set of indices numbering fixed n-grams: $ifngm \in Ifngm : Ifngm = \{0, 1, \ldots, nFNGM\}$, $Ifngm \leftrightarrow FNGM$.

Each element $ifngm \in Ifngm$ is uniquely assigned with subset of frequencies $FNGMfreq_{ifngm} \subset U_{freq}$. Then $fsFNGMfreq = (FNGMfreq_{ifngm})_{ifngm \in Ifngm}$ is a countable family of sets of fixed n-grams usage frequencies.

$$fsFNGMfreq = (FNGMfreq_{ifngm})_{ifngm \in Ifngm}$$
$$= \bigcup_{ifngm \in Ifngm} FREQ_{ifngm} = \{x : \exists ifngm\, x \in FNGMfreq_{ifngm}\} \quad (12)$$

Competence of a translator tr_{iTR} is always evaluated within an applied task, the initial data of which are a source language $lng_{src} \in LNG$ and a target language $lng_{tgt} \in LNG$. Mathematically, we define the translator's competence within an applied task as a vector, coordinates of which are conditional subsets:

$$\overrightarrow{Ctr_{iTR}} = \{(fsSUE \mid lng_{src} \cup fsSUE \mid lng_{tgt})\mid tr_{iTR},$$
$$(fsLXM \mid lng_{src} \cup fsLXM \mid lng_{tgt})\mid tr_{iTR},$$
$$(fsFREQ \mid lng_{src} \cup fsFREQ \mid lng_{tgt})\mid tr_{iTR},$$
$$(fsDIC \mid lng_{src} \cup fsDIC \mid lng_{tgt})\mid tr_{iTR},$$
$$(GR \mid lng_{src} \cup GR \mid lng_{tgt})\mid tr_{iTR},$$
$$(MR \mid lng_{src} \cup MR \mid lng_{tgt})\mid tr_{iTR},$$
$$(SPR \mid lng_{src} \cup SPR \mid lng_{tgt})\mid tr_{iTR},$$
$$(SKL \mid lng_{src} \cup SKL \mid lng_{tgt})\mid tr_{iTR},$$
$$(FNGM \mid lng_{src} \cup FNGM \mid lng_{tgt})\mid tr_{iTR},$$
$$(fsFNGMfreq \mid lng_{src} \cup fsFNGMfreq \mid lng_{tgt})\mid tr_{iTR}\} \qquad (13)$$

Specialization of a translator tr_{iTR} *means* accumulated experience by expressing semantic units within a certain subject area ad_{iAD} and/or training. Mathematically, we define the translator's specialization within an applied task as a vector, coordinates of which are conditional subsets:

$$\overrightarrow{Str_{iTR}, ad_{iAD}} = \{(TT \mid ad_{iAD})\mid tr_{iTR}, (FNGM \ ad_{iAD}\mid)\mid tr_{iTR},$$
$$(fsFNGMfreq \mid ad_{iAD})tr_{iTR}\} \qquad (14)$$

Next, we will consider the application of described model terms in the translation process.

4 Staged Mathematical Model of Translation Process

4.1 Estimation of a Translation Task Complexity

Translator tr_{iTR} receives text txt_{iTXT} in language lng_{src} for translation into language lng_{tgt} and customer's translation requirements $CR \mid txt_{iTXT}$ (if any), and $CR \mid txt_{iTXT} \subset REQ \mid txt_{iTXT}$. Before the translation, the translator estimates the **translation task complexity**.

When estimating the translation task complexity, the translator pays attention to unknown words and collocations in lng_{src} for which he cannot identify the meaning of a semantic unit, or semantic units for which he cannot find an analogue in lng_{tgt} among words and collocations of words known to him. Set of features $TF \mid txt_{iTXT}$ and parameters $MP \mid txt_{iTXT}$ the source text and whether the translator has sufficient competence $\overrightarrow{Ctr_{iTR}}$ regarding languages lng_{src} and lng_{tgt} and specialization $\overrightarrow{Str_{iTR}, ad_{iAD}}$, i.e. expertise in describing semantic units in the target language within a given subject area of the source text, defines the probability of the translator creating a text in the target language meeting requirements $REQ \mid txt_{iTXT}$.

The algorithm for estimating the translation task complexity is as follows:

Step 1. Based on text's application domain ad_{iAD}, set of text features estimates $FE = TF \cup MP$ is stated.

Step 2. For each value tf_{iTF}, $mp_{iMP} \in FE$, based on translation requirements $REQ \mid txt_{iTXT}$, translator's competencies regarding language pair $\overrightarrow{Ctr_{iTR}}$ and translator's specialization regarding text's application domain $\overrightarrow{Str_{iTR}}$, $\overrightarrow{ad_{iAD}}$, significance weight w_{fek} is evaluated; and set of normalized values of significance weights w_{fek} form matrix of complexity estimates significance $\overline{W_{oy}}$ of $1 \times k$ dimension, where k is the total number of estimates, which are coefficients of equation for the theoretical evaluation of translation quality.

Step 3. For each i-th text segment at $i = \overline{1, N}$ we form estimates matrix of the source text segment C_{fei} of $1 \times k$ dimension, where k is the total number of features estimates.

Step 4. Based on features estimates C_{fei} and significance matrix $\overline{W_{oy}}$, we derive the equation for the theoretical evaluation of resultant factor, i.e. translation quality $\widehat{TQ}$:

$$\widehat{TQ}_i = w_0 + w_{1fe}\, C_{fei\,1} + w_{2fe} C_{fei\,2} + \cdots + w_{fek} C_{feik} \tag{15}$$

Step 5. For each i-th text segment, we calculate the probability of creating a translated text at a quality level determined by requirements $REQ|txt_{iTXT}$ by applying the logit transformation [14] to Eq. (15):

$$p_i = \frac{1}{1 + e^{-\widehat{TQ}_i}} \tag{16}$$

Step 6. The translation task complexity for translating i-th segment of a source text is estimated by the formula:

$$TTC_i = \frac{1}{p_i}, \tag{17}$$

where p_i *is* the probability of a translator creating a translation of a required quality, calculated by formula (16).

Step 7. The resulting translation task complexity for translating a source text is the highest value of translation task complexity TTC_i among N source text's segments, i.e.

$$TTTC_{txt_{iTXT}} = max\ TTC_i \tag{18}$$

Depending on value $TTC_{txt_{iTXT}}$, the translator chooses a strategy for further text processing. Possible options for manual translation and MT are given in Table 1.

Table 1. Translator's actions depending on translation task complexity.

Translation task complexity	Action for manual translation	Action for MT
low	translation	translation
average	preliminary editing/translation requirements approval with the customer	automatic pre-editing
high	refusal to translate/sending text back to the customer for revision	semi-automatic pre-editing with user involvement

The ranges of values $TTC_{txt_{iTXT}}$ corresponding to low, medium and high levels are determined based on a preliminary analysis of translation requirements and taking into account the method of translation(manual/machine). Function of estimating the translation task complexity F_{estm}:

$$F_{estm} : txt_{iTXT} \rightarrow TTC_{txt_{iTXT}} | (REQ|txt_{iTXT}, TF, MP, \overrightarrow{Ctr_{iTR}}, \overrightarrow{Str_{iTR}}, \overrightarrow{ad_{iAD}}). \quad (19)$$

4.2 Source Text Pre-editing

Pre-editing is the process of automatic/semi-automatic chaging features/parametrs of a source text to optimize the translation task complexity taking into account the impact of such a change on the translation quality.

Pre-editing is performed using a variety of algorithms when the translation task complexity is medium or high to meet the criteria of $TTC_{txt_{iTXT}}$ minimization, minimaximization of some source text's features/parametrs, or other.

The purpose of pre-editing is to reduce the translation task complexity $TTC_{txtiTXT}$ to a low one.

At the initial stage of pre-editing, we select text segments that correspond to high values of TTC_i, that is

$$txt_i^* \in txt_{iTXT} | TTC_i > TTC_{alw} \quad (20)$$

where TTC_{alw} is an acceptable value of the translation task complexity, i.e. low.

For text segments with medium or high translation task complexity, we determine coordinates of vector C_{fei}, the values of which increase the translation task complexity of this segment: $C_{fei} | TTC_i > TTC_{alw}$.

Let U_{TPA} be the universal set of all possible text processing algorithms. Ife is the set of indexes numbering estimates of features/parametrs of texts. At that, sets FE and Ife are bijective, i.e. $Ife \leftrightarrow FE$. Each element $ife \in Ife$ is uniquely assigned with a subset of optimizational algorithms $PA_{ife} \subseteq U_{TPA}$. Then $fsPA = (PA_{ife})_{ife \in Ife}$ is a countable family of sets of pre-editing algorithms for optimizing text features estimates.

$$fsPA = (PA_{ife})_{ife \in Ife} = \bigcup_{ife \in Ife} PA_{ife} = \{x : \exists ife \, x \in PA_{ife}\} \quad (21)$$

For each found element of matrix C_{fei} meeting condition $C_{fei} | TTC_i > TTC_{alw}$., depending on its value and limitations of pre-editing algorithms, a pre-editing strategy is determined (Table 2). The choice of an algorithm depends on the optimization criterion of a selected feature estimation value.

Next, we edit the source text in accordance with available methods and algorithms of pre-editing, get text txt'_{iTXT} and proceed to the stage of translation.

Pre-editing function F_{pre_ed}:

$$F_{pre\_ed}: txt_{iTXT}, TTC_{txt_{iTXT}}, C_{fe}, \overrightarrow{W_{ou}} \rightarrow$$
$$txt'_{iTXT} | (TTC \rightarrow min, fsPA, \overrightarrow{Ctr_{iTR}}, \overrightarrow{Str_{iTR}}, \overrightarrow{ad_{iAD}}) \quad (22)$$

Table 2. Pre-editing strategies.

Feature estimate	Action
Acceptable	automatic pre-editing using algorithms
unacceptable	semi-automatic pre-editing with user involvement

4.3 Translation

The purpose of this stage is to generate a quality translation of text txt'_{iTXT} from language lng_{src} into language lng_{tgt}. We will assume that a **quality translation** is the expression of the source text meaning in compliance with the linguistic and cultural traditions in target language according to the requirements of a final recipient.

The translation includes the following steps:

Step 1. Segmentation of the text into N segments. Text segmentation is the process of dividing a written text into significant parts sufficient to express its semantic content without distorting the general meaning.

Next, for each *i-th* segment, when $i = \overline{1, N}$:

Step 2. Analysis of the meaning of the source text in language lng_{src} based on translator's competence regarding language lng_{tgt} $(\overrightarrow{Ctr_{iTR}}|lng_{src})$ and translator's specialization in source text subject area ad_{iAD} $(\overrightarrow{Str_{iTR}, ad_{iAD}})$ to determine the set of semantic units that it describes:

$$f_a : (txt'_{iTXT}, \overrightarrow{Ctr_{iTR}}|lng_{src}, \overrightarrow{Str_{iTR}, ad_{iAD}}) \rightarrow MNG_i \qquad (23)$$

Step 3. Generation of a text that maximally recreates source text meaning MNG_i according to requirements $REQ|txt_{iTXT}$, but by means of language lng_{tgt} based on translator's competence regarding language lng_{tgt} $(\overrightarrow{Ctr_{iTR}}|lng_{tgt})$ and translator's specialization in the source text subject area $\overrightarrow{(Cnep_{iПЕР}, \partial n_{iДП})}$:

$$f_g : (MNG_i, \overrightarrow{Ctr_{iTR}}|lng_{tgt}, \overrightarrow{Str_{iTR}, ad_{iAD}} \rightarrow txt'_{iTXT}|(MNG_j \rightarrow MNG_i, REQ|txt_{iTXT}) \qquad (24)$$

Translation function F_{tr}:

$$F_{tr} : (txt'_{iTXT}, \overrightarrow{Ctr_{iTR}}, \overrightarrow{Ctr_{iTR}, ad_{iAD}}) \rightarrow txt_{jTXT}|(MNG_j \rightarrow MNG_i, REQ|txt_{iTXT}) \quad (25)$$

4.4 Translation Quality Assessment

Translation quality assessment is a complex task of estimating the optimality of expression of the meaning of source text txt_{iTXT} in language lng_{src} by means of language lng_{tgt} in the form of text txt_{jTXT}. The criteria of optimality are the criteria of translation quality: $qc \in QC : QC = \{qc_0, qc_1, \ldots, qc_{nQC}\}$.

Based on translation requirements $REQ|txt_{iTXT}$ and applicability within application domain ad_{iAD}, we define set of applicable quality criteria $AQC = QC|REQ|txt_{iTXT}$,

$AQC \subseteq QC$ and set of significance weights w_{iaqc} for applicable criteria, which state normalized matrix of quality criteria significance $\overline{W_{AQC}}$ of $1 \times M$ dimension, where M is the total number of applicable criteria.

The assessment is carried out by translation quality controller tr_{jTR} of appropriate competence $\overrightarrow{Ctr_{jTR}}$ and specialization $\overrightarrow{Str_{jTR}, ad_{iAD}}$. The translator translated the text can be the controller if translation self-check is performed, then it is considered that $tr_{jTR} = tr_{iTR}$, but it should be considered that in this case the assessment of translation quality will be influenced by competence $\overrightarrow{C'tr_{iTR}}$ and specialization $\overrightarrow{S'tr_{iTR}, ad_{iAD}}$, since the translator gains new experience in the process of translation and the values of his competence and specializations change.

Further, for each i-th pair of uniquely matched text segments txt_{iTXT} and txt_{jTXT} at $i = \overline{1, N}$ optimality is estimated according to each k-th applicable quality criterion $k = \overline{1, M}$ basing on MNG_i and text's features $TF|txt_{iTXT}$ and parameters $MP|txt_{iTXT}$. The accuracy of determining the optimality depends on quality controller's competence and specialization. Translation optimality estimation for i-th text segment according to k-th criterion:

$$f_{koe} : ((MNG_i)_i, (TF|txt_{iTXT}, MP|txt_{iTXT})_i) \rightarrow OS_{i,k}|(AQC_k, \overrightarrow{Ctr_{jTR}}, \overrightarrow{Str_{jTR}, ad_{iAD}})$$
$$(26)$$

Translation quality assessment for i-th text segment is the determinant of a matrix got by multiplying the matrix of optimality scores OS_i of translated text segment according to criteria AQC and transposed matrix of applicable quality criteria significance $\overline{W_{AQC}^T}$:

$$QS_i = \left| OS_i \times \overline{W_{AQC}^T} \right| \qquad (27)$$

The resulting score of translation quality of text txt_{iTXT} into language lng_{tgt} is the ratio of the sum of quality translation scores of text segments to their total number, that is

$$QS = \frac{\sum_N^i QS_i}{N} \qquad (28)$$

Translation quality score allows evaluating the effectiveness of the translator's work and determine a strategy for processing the translated text, if QS is unacceptable. Possible options for text post-processing are described in Table 3.

Ranges of QS corresponding to extremely low, low, medium and high levels are determined based on the analysis of applicable translation quality criteria, their significance, as well as target values according to translation requirements $REQ|txt_{iTXT}$.

Translation quality assessment function F_{qa}:

$$F_{qa} : (txt_{iTXT}, txt_{jTXT} \rightarrow QS|(REQ|txt_{iTXT}, \overrightarrow{Ctr_{jTR}}, \overrightarrow{Str_{jTR}, ad_{iAD}}) \qquad (29)$$

Table 3. Actions depending on translation quality score.

Quality score	Action
extremely low	translation by another translator
Low	post-editing with expert involvement
average	independent / automatic post-editing
High	–

4.5 Translated Text Post-editing

Post-editing is the process of automatic/semi-automatic changing features/parameters of a translated text to optimize the translation quality score. Post-editing is performed if the quality score of a completed translation is below acceptable target value QS_{tgt}.

The purpose of post-editing is to maximize translation quality score, i.e. $QS \rightarrow max||QS_{tgt}$.

For text segments with quality score QS_i lower than high or target QS, we determine the elements of matrix OS_i which lower the translation quality of the segment: $OS_i \mid QS_i$.

Let U_{TPA} be the universal set of all possible text processing algorithms. Iqc is the set of indexes numbering quality criteria. In this case, sets QC and Iqc are bijective, i.e. $Iqc \leftrightarrow QC$. Each element $iqc \in Iqc$ is uniquely assigned with subset of algorithms optimizing text features and parameters to meet criteria QC: $QOA_{iqc} \subseteq U_{TPA}$. Then $fsQOA = (QOA_{iqc})_{iqc \in Iqc}$ is a countable family of sets of post-editing algorithms for optimizing text features and parameters to meet the quality criteria.

$$fsQOA = (QOA_{iqc})_{iqc \in Iqc} = \bigcup_{iqc \in Iqc} QOA_{iqc} = \{x : \exists iqc \, x \in QOA_{iqc}\} \quad (30)$$

For each found element of matrix OS_i meeting condition $OS_i|QS_i < max||QS_{tgt}$, depending on its value and limitations of post-editing algorithms, a post-editing strategy is determined (Table 4). The choice of an algorithm depends on the optimization criterion of a selected feature estimation value.

Table 4. Post-editing strategies.

Feature estimate	Action
acceptable	Automatic post-editing using algorithms
unacceptable	semi-automatic post-editing with user involvement

Then each found segment is edited using post-editing algorithms until OS_i meet condition $OS_i|QS_i \rightarrow max||QS_{tgt}$. Re-estimation $of\ OS_i$ is carried out according to formula (26). At the output we get text txt_{finTXT}. The effectiveness of post-editing algorithms depends on specialization $\overrightarrow{Str_{jTR}}$, ad_{iAD} and competence $\overrightarrow{Ctr_{iTR}}$ of a translator performing post-editing. Post-editing function F_{post_ed}:

$$F_{post\_ed} : (txt_{iTXT}, txt_{jTXT}, QS, OS, \overline{W_{AQC}}) \rightarrow txt_{finTXT} \mid$$

$$(QS \rightarrow max\|QS_{tgt}, fsQOA, \overrightarrow{Ctr_{iTR}}, \overrightarrow{Str_{iTR}}, ad_{iAD}) \tag{31}$$

4.6 Translator Training

Translator training means obtaining and/or updating translator's competencies and specializations based on the study of training texts and/or a practical translation experience gained. It is important to note that the retraining occurs continuously in the process of translator's work.

Each translator has a variety of competencies and specializations, depending on languages $LNG|tr_{iTR}$ and application domains $AD|tr_{iTR}$ known to the translator. Set of translator competences: $cmpt \in C : C = \{cmpt_0, cmpt_1, \ldots cmpt_{nC}\}$, where $cmpt_{iC}$ is determined by formula (13) for some language pair (lng_{src}, lng_{tgt}).

Set of translator specializations: $spec \in S : S = \{spec_0, spec_1, \ldots spec_{nS}\}$, where $spec_{iS}$ is determined by formula (14) for application domain ad_{iAD}.

The training is conducted on real texts with following quality control and work on errors. Depending on the composition of training texts, a translator masters specialization in a subject area, for example, medicine or technical translation. The more a translator learns from special texts, the higher the translation quality of texts of the relevant subject area, and the translation quality in other subject areas increases due to better language acquisition. During training, the translator improves knowledge, develops skills and learns how individual words and their combinations are used in different domains to express semantic units.

Set of **training texts**: $tt \in TT : TT = \{tt_0, tt_1, \ldots tt_{nTT}\}$, where tt_{iTT} is a pair of values txt_{src} in source language lng_{src} and txt_{tgt} in target language lng_{tgt} uniquely matched to each other in meaning (set of expressed semantic units) taken as a reference, i.e.

$$tt_{iTT} = \{(txt_{ex}; txt_{ebix}): MNG| \, txt_{src} = MNG \mid txt_{tgt}\}. \tag{32}$$

Translator training function F_{train}:

$$F_{train} : (TT, C_{0,triTR}, S_{0,triTR}) \rightarrow C_{triTR}, S_{triTR}. \tag{33}$$

5 Results

Under the research, a generalized model of translation process based on set theory was first developed describing concepts of applied linguistics in MT field, including the formalization of such concepts as translator's experience, specialization and competence. The model can be widely used for further decomposition in tasks of MT and natural language processing.

The results of modelling show that already at the stage of source text evaluation, it is possible to predict the expected quality of translation based on source text's features and translator's competence and specialization.

6 Discussion

Further research suggests a deeper decomposition and modeling of stages 1 and 2, since in modern MT systems these stages are usually not implemented or partially implemented. It is proposed to use regression analysis for defining weights of features of a highly specialized text in Russian to estimate the complexity of translation task into English using MT. The following steps proposed:

Step 1. Determination of MT quality criterion (target variable), MT generation and its evaluation for a training set.
Step 2. Estimation of the values of Russian-language text features (model factors).
Step 3. Regression analysis to obtain a multivariate regression equation defining the dependence of the target variable on the model factors.
Step 4. Estimating for test set the probability of getting target variable value classified as "qualitative translation".
Step 5. Estimation of modeling accuracy.
Step 6. Analysis of the identified model factors and their significance weights in assessing translation quality.

Solving the optimization problem as per the criterion of maximizing the probability of getting target variable value classified as "qualitative translation" will allow us to identify the range of optimal factors' values of the model of a highly specialized text in Russian and propose strategies for optimizational pre-editing to improve the quality of MT into English.

7 Conclusion

During the modeling a methodology for estimating translation task complexity was first developed and its practicability was first substantiated. It can be used in the tasks of applied computational linguistics to improve MT systems. We also first proposed a strategy for preprocessing the source depending on the translation task complexity estimate.

Further analysis will reveal significant and nuisance features of the source text in Russian, as well as develop a set of algorithms for optimizational pre-editing, the use of which will make MT more accessible to a wide range of users without translation skills.

Acknowledgments. The study was conducted using a grant from the Russian Science Foundation No. 22-29-01232, https://rscf.ru/project/22-29-01232/.

References

1. Yamada, M.: The impact of Google neural machine translation on post-editing by student translators. J. Spec. Transl. **31**, 87–106 (2019)
2. Folaron, D., O'Brien, S., Winther Balling, L., Carl, M., Simard, M., Specia, L.: Post-editing of machine translation: processes and applications. Mach. Transl. **29**, 69–76 (2015)

3. Aziz, W., Castilho, S., Specia, L.: PET: a tool for post-editing and assessing machine translation. In: Proceedings of the 8th International Conference on Language Resources and Evaluation, pp. 3982–3987. ELRA, Istanbul (2012)

4. Toledo Báez, M.: Machine translation and post-editing: impact of training and direc-tionality on quality and productivity. Revista Tradumàtica. Tecnologies de la Traducció **16**, 24–34 (2018)

5. Taufik, A.: Pre-editing of Google neural machine translation. J. Engl. Lang. Cult. **10**(2), 64–74 (2020)

6. Mercader-Alarcón, J., Sánchez-Martínez, F.: Analysis of translation errors and evaluation of pre-editing rules for the translation of english news texts into spanish with lucy LT. Revista Tradumàtica. Tecnologies de la Traducció **14**, 172–186 (2016)

7. Hiraoka, Y., Yamada, M.: Pre-editing plus neural machine translation for subti-tling: effective pre-editing rules for subtitling of TED Talks. In: Forcada, M., Way, A. (eds.) Dublin MT Summit XVII, vol. 2, pp. 64–74. European Association for Machine Translation, Dublin (2019)

8. Zhivotova, A.A., Berdonosov, V.D., Redkolis, E.V.: Machine translation systems analysis and development prospects. In: 020 International Multi-Conference on Industrial Engineering and Modern Technologies (FarEastCon), pp. 1–7. IEEE, Vladivostok (2020)

9. Church, K., Liberman, M.: The future of computational linguistics: on beyond alchemy. Front. Artif. Intel. **4**, 625341 (2021)

10. Moore, J.D., Wiemer-Hastings, P.: Discourse in computational linguistics and artificial intelligence. In: Graesser, A.C., Gernsbacher, M.A., Goldman, S.R. (eds.) Handbook of discourse processes, pp. 439–485. Lawrence Erlbaum Associates Publishers (2003)

11. Dmitrieva, A.D., Laposhina, A.N., Lebedeva, M.Y.: A Quantitative study of simplification strategies in adapted texts for L2 learners of Russian. In: Computational Linguistics and Intelligent Technologies: Proceedings of Dialogue International Conference, pp. 191–204. The State University of Management, Moscow (2021)

12. Chernyavskaya, V.E.: Text Linguistics. Discourse Linguistics. LENAND, Moscow (2018)

13. Solnyshkina, M.I., Kazachkova, M.B., Kharkov, E.Q.: Tools for assessing text in English complexity. Foreign Lang. Sch. **3**, 15–21 (2020)

14. Hosmer, D.W., Lemeshow, S.: Applied Logistic Regression, 2nd edn. Wiley Chichester, New York (2000)

Optimization with Quantum Algorithm that is Based on Grover's Method

Sh. A. Toirov$^{(\boxtimes)}$ (ID), I. M. Boynazarov (ID), Sh. A. Abatov (ID), B. M. Mirsaidov, and Z. Ruziyeva (ID)

Samarkand Branch of Tashkent University of Information Technology, 2, Ibin Sino Str, Samarkand, Uzbekistan
`tashuxrat@mail.ru`

Abstract. This article reviews the processes of solving the global optimization problems by Grover's method of quantum algorithm, and presents all the solutions that are possible at the same time in solving global optimization problems by quantum algorithm and the methods of identifying the correct result. Searching for a solution to a global optimization task is typical for a systematic analysis. Adoption of optimal solutions and management of complex systems in information uncertainty and dangerous conditions have been developing for many years in various directions. In recent years, the solution to this problem is considered successful as a new form of intelligent computing. One of such intellectual computation is Grover's method of quantum algorithm. The software for solving the optimization problems based on the quantum algorithm is developed and the obtained results are analyzed.

Keywords: Quantum algorithm · Grover's Method · Global Optimization · Intellectual Management

1 Introduction

It is becoming more crucial in the world to learn quantum algorithm, and to improvise, develop and introduce the methods and algorithms of solving problems by these algorithms. Nowadays, the tasks solved by quantum algorithms are generating more efficient results than the problems that are solved using other algorithms [1]. At present, special attention is paid to the analytical analysis of mathematical models of these algorithms and the creation of quantum computers that run on the basis of quantum algorithms. In quantum computing (quantum algorithms) the quality (feature) of the process that is being studied is determined as a result of direct parallel calculations [2]. In addition, these algorithms may be applied to speed up the solution of the problems that are difficult to solve or for the ones that are not possible to be solved algorithmically by traditional (classic) methods.

A. Gibadullin (Ed.): ITIDMS 2022, CCIS 1821, pp. 76–86, 2023.
https://doi.org/10.1007/978-3-031-31353-0_7

2 Main Body

Searching for a solution to a global (multi-criteria, in general) optimization task is typical for a systematic analysis. Adoption of optimal solutions and management of complex systems in information uncertainty and dangerous (risky) conditions have been developing for many years in various directions. In recent years, the solution to this problem is considered successful as a new form of intelligent computing. One of such intellectual computation is Grover's method of quantum algorithm [3]. This algorithm searches through $N = 2^n$ an unordered set of elements in order to find the element that satisfies some conditions. Currently, while the best classical search algorithm on unstructured data takes time $O(N)$, Grover's algorithm allows for a quadratic speedup of search on a quantum computer in operations just $O\left(\sqrt{N}\right)$.

Grover's search algorithm is considered to be one of the best methods of quantum algorithms, and it shows that when the classical algorithms of quantum system is used, it depends on the slowness of operation time, and that it can be used in order to improve its quality. In this case, in order to reach a high speed, Grover's algorithm bases on the quantum super-position of the processes [7]. As numerous quantum algorithms, Grover's algorithm also sets off by putting n qubit registers of the machine into the super-position that is equal to all the possible 2^n cases [8]. It is important to remember that the amplitude associated with each possible configuration of each qubit is equal to $\frac{1}{\sqrt{2^n}}$ and the probability of being of the 2^n state of the system in any state is equal to $\frac{1}{2^n}$. All these possible states correspond to all possible entries in the database of Grover's algorithm, and therefore, starting with a given amplitude assigned to each element in the search space, each element is considered simultaneously in quantum superposition and amplitudes are controlled from there [9].

Along with the superposition of states, Grover's algorithm belongs, in general, to the family of quantum algorithms that use amplitude amplifiers, which take the advantage of quantum amplitudes that distinguish amplitudes from probabilities. The key to these algorithms is a selective displacement of one state of quantum system, of its space that satisfy some kind of condition in each iteration. These amplitude amplifier algorithms are so unique to quantum calculating that such feature of amplitudes has no parallel in classical probabilities [11].

3 Literature Survey

In the late 1980s, genetic algorithms [1] achieved enough popularity as a method of optimization and machine learning. In [2] genetic algorithms are search algorithms based on Darwinian natural selection and genetic mechanisms present in organisms. Once a new generation of offspring chromosomes is obtained, the algorithm simulates genetic mechanisms such as crossover and mutation. However, there are genetic algorithms based on other genetic mechanisms such is the case of bacterial conjugation [3]. In [4] this review classifies genetic-algorithm environments into application-oriented systems, algorithm-oriented systems, and toolkits. It also presents detailed case studies of leading environments. In [5] Richard Feynman was an extraordinary man by many measures, and it was very interesting to read his paper and some of his books. In this work he shows the ability to take new perspective at things that marked many of his accomplishments in life, and helps set the agenda for the research in quantum computing. Simulation by Monte Carlo [6] methods of the effect of selection against pheno-typic extremes has shown that selection can produce a degree of genetic canali zation which is more restrictive than that indicated by the limits of selection, showing that canalization of a rigid degree can be caused by loose selection. In [7] proposes a novel evolutionary algorithm inspired by quantum computing, called a quantum-inspired evolutionary algorithm (QEA), which is based on the concept and principles of quantum computing, such as a quantum bit and superposition of states. The main purpose is to examine some (potential) applications of quantum computation in AI and to review the interplay between quantum theory and AI [8]. In [9] are popular heuristic optimisation methods based on simulated genetic mechanisms, i.e., mutation, crossover, etc. and population dynamical processes such as reproduction, selection, etc. Over the last decade, the possibility to emulate a quantum computer (a computer using quantum-mechanical phenomena to perform operations on data) has led to a new class of GAs known as "Quantum Genetic Algorithms" (QGAs). Algorithms are described for efficiently simulating quantum mechanical systems on quantum computers. A class of algorithms for simulating the Schrödinger equation for interacting many-body systems are presented in some detail [10, 11]. Although experimental evidence suggests the influence of quantum effects in living organisms, one of the most critical problems in quantum biology is the explanation of how those effects that take place in a microscopic level can manifest in the macroscopic world of living beings [12].

4 Methods

Grover's algorithm begins with quantum register of the qubits n, here n - the number of qubits that are needed to represent a search space of size $2^n = N$, all starting from $|0\rangle$:

$$|0\rangle^{\otimes n} = |0\rangle \tag{1}$$

The first step is to place the process states in an equal superposition, which is done by using the Hadamard conversion $H^{\otimes n}$, where the operations $\Theta(\lg N) = \Theta(\lg 2^n) = \Theta(n)$, n practical initial Hadamard gate, i.e. it appears in the form of Eq. (2):

$$|\psi\rangle = H^{\otimes n}|0\rangle^{\otimes n} = \frac{1}{\sqrt{2^n}} \sum_{x=0}^{2^n-1} |x\rangle \tag{2}$$

The following series of transforms are usually called Grover's iteration and the above-mentioned amplitude amplifier carries out the main part of algorithm [4]. In Grover's algorithm the iteration iterates $\frac{\pi}{4}\sqrt{2^n}$ times. According to this algorithm, because the observed state is true, in order to reach an optimal probability the total rotation of the space $\frac{\pi}{4}$ happens after average $\frac{\pi}{4}\sqrt{2^n}$ rotation so that the former becomes radian [5]. The first step in Grover's iteration is an appeal to the quantum oracle O, which modifies the system depending on the configuration it is looking for.

An oracle is basically a black box function, and it's a quantum black box, which means it can observe and change the system without falling into a classical state that admits that the system is in the right state. If the system is indeed in the correct state, then the oracle rotates the space by radians π, otherwise it does not anything and effectively defines the correct state for further modification by subsequent processes. It is important to remember that such kind of a spatial shift conducts no changes in the correct state probability of the system leaving it the same, even though the amplitude is negated [6].

Oracle's quantum programs often use an extra drawing qubit, but this extra qubit is unnecessary, so the effect of the oracle on $|x\rangle$ can simply be written in the form of (3), i.e.:

$$|x\rangle \xrightarrow{o} (-1)^{f(x)}|x\rangle \tag{3}$$

Here, if x, then $f(x) = 1$, otherwise $f(x) = 0$. The exact implementation of $f(x)$ depends on a particular search problem.

The next part of Grover's iteration is called the diffusion conversion, which performs an average inversion, changing the amplitude of each state to a value lower than the average before the transformation, and vice versa.

$$D = \begin{pmatrix} \frac{2}{N} - 1 & \frac{2}{N} & \frac{2}{N} & \frac{2}{N} \\ \frac{2}{N} & \frac{2}{N} - 1 & \frac{2}{N} & \frac{2}{N} \\ \cdot & & \cdot & \cdot \\ \cdot & \cdot & \cdot & \\ \frac{2}{N} & \frac{2}{N} & \frac{2}{N} & \frac{2}{N} - 1 \end{pmatrix} \tag{4}$$

This diffusion conversion $H^{\otimes n}$ consists of another program of the Hadamard conversion, followed by a conditional transformation shift that shifts each state from $|0\rangle$ to -1, which is, in its own turn, followed by another Hadamard conversion.

Here, the unitary operator of the spatial shift is represented by $2|0\rangle\langle 0| - I$ and can be written in the following two ways.

$$[2|0\rangle\langle 0| - I]|0\rangle = 2|0\rangle\langle 0|0\rangle - I|0\rangle = |0\rangle$$
$$[2|0\rangle\langle 0| - I]|x\rangle = 2|0\rangle\langle 0|x\rangle - I|x\rangle = -|x\rangle \tag{5}$$

The Eq. (5) can be written in the form of Eq. (6) below, using the formula from Eq. (2). In that case, the universal diffusion conversion is expressed in the form of (6).

$$H^{\otimes n}[2|0\rangle\langle 0| - I]H^{\otimes n} = 2H^{\otimes n}|0\rangle\langle 0|H^{\otimes n} - I = 2|\psi\rangle\langle\psi| - I \tag{6}$$

and universal Grover's iteration gets in the form of (7).

$$[2|\psi\rangle\langle\psi| - I]O \tag{7}$$

When considering the running time of Grover's iteration, the exact running time of the oracle depends on the specific problem and the implementation of that problem, so the reference to O is treated as a single simple operation [4].

After a sufficient number of iterations of Grover's iteration are accomplished, a classical measurement is performed to determine the result, this completion of the algorithm continues until the probability $O(1)$ [11].

The steps of Grover's algorithm are implemented and summarized as the following [19]:

Input:

- $O|x\rangle = (-1)^{f(x)}|x\rangle$ is quantum oracle O, which performs the operation, where $f(x) = 0$ is $f(x_0) = 1$ for all the $0 \le x < 2^n$, except for $x \ne x_0$.

  - A qubit $|0\rangle$ initiated to state n

- Output: x_0

The running time: the operations $O(\sqrt{2^n})$, with the probability $O(1)$.

Process:

1. The initial state $|0\rangle^{\otimes n}$

2. Using Hadamard conversion for all the qubits

$$H^{\otimes n}|0\rangle^{\otimes n} = \frac{1}{\sqrt{2^n}} \sum_{x=0}^{2^n-1} |x\rangle = |\psi\rangle$$

3. Using Grover's iteration $R \approx \frac{\pi}{4}\sqrt{2^n}$ times

$$[2|\psi\rangle\langle\psi| - I]^R |\psi\rangle \approx |x_0\rangle$$

4. Measuring the register x_0

5 Results

The mathematical solutions of the information mentioned above through a specific example will be as following. Let's say, $f(x) = \frac{x+6}{2+cos(x)}$ is the form of the function, and the oracle receives values between 0 and 16. The next step is to consider the process consisting of states $N = 16 = 2^4$ and the state x_0 it is looking for is represented by 1011 bytes [19].

To describe this process, it is expressed as following, it consists of $n = 4$ qubits and $|x\rangle$ is written as following:

$$|x\rangle = \alpha_0|0000\rangle + \alpha_0|0001\rangle + \ldots\ldots\ldots + \alpha_{15}|1111\rangle \tag{8}$$

Here, a_i is the amplitude of the state $|i\rangle$. Grover's algorithm begins with $|0\rangle$ qubit. $1|0000\rangle$ and then, the Hadamard transform $\frac{1}{\sqrt{N}} = \frac{1}{\sqrt{16}} = \frac{1}{4}$ is applied to obtain an equal amplitude associated with each state, so that the solution to the problem is equal to the probability of being in one of the 16 possible states. It is written as following:

$$H^4|0000\rangle = \frac{1}{4}|0000\rangle + \frac{1}{4}|0001\rangle + \ldots + \frac{1}{4}|1111\rangle = \frac{1}{4}\sum_{x=0}^{15}|x\rangle = \psi \tag{9}$$

A geometric interpretation of the amplitudes of the states is an effective way to better visualize how this algorithm processes. Since amplitudes are conserved throughout the execution of Grover's algorithm, they can be visualized as axis-perpendicular lines whose length is proportional to the amplitude they represent [14]. The equal superposition of states resulting from the first Adamard conversation will be as following Fig. 1.

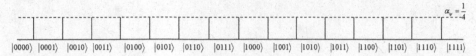

Fig. 1. The equal superposition of the states.

In order to find the solution Grover's iteration is implemented $\frac{\pi}{4}\sqrt{N} = \frac{\pi}{4}\sqrt{16} = \pi \approx 3, 14$ and it rotates up to 3 iterations [20].

In each iteration, the quantum O should be identified first, followed by an inversion through an average or diffusion conversion. The oracle query negates the amplitude of the state $|x_0\rangle$, in this case $|1011\rangle$ gives the following configuration:

$$|x\rangle = \frac{1}{4}|0000\rangle + \frac{1}{4}|0000\rangle + \ldots - \frac{1}{4}|1011\rangle + \ldots + \frac{1}{4}|1111\rangle \tag{10}$$

and its geometric picture is as following (Fig. 2):

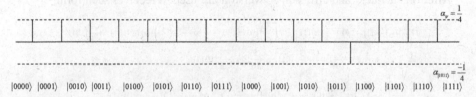

Fig. 2. The negated state of the amplitude.

The next process is the implementation of the diffusion conversion $2|\psi\rangle\langle\psi| - I$, it increases the amplitudes from the average value, but if the difference is negative, decreases them [16].

$$[2|\psi\rangle\langle\psi| - I]|x\rangle = [2|\psi\rangle\langle\psi| - I]\left[|\psi\rangle - \frac{2}{4}|1011\rangle\right] = 2|\psi\rangle\langle\psi|\psi\rangle - |\psi\rangle - |\psi\rangle\langle\psi|1011\rangle + \frac{1}{2}|1011\rangle$$

$$= 2|\psi\rangle - |\psi\rangle - \frac{1}{4}|\psi\rangle + \frac{1}{2}|1011\rangle = \frac{3}{4}|\psi\rangle + \frac{1}{2}|1011\rangle = \frac{3}{4}\left[\frac{1}{4}\sum_{x=0}^{15}|x\rangle\right] + \frac{1}{2}|1011\rangle$$

$$= \frac{3}{16}\sum_{\substack{x=0 \\ x\neq x_0}}^{15}|x\rangle + \frac{3}{16}|1011\rangle + \frac{1}{2}|1011\rangle = \frac{3}{16}\sum_{\substack{x=0 \\ x\neq x_0}}^{15}|x\rangle + \frac{11}{16}|1011\rangle \tag{11}$$

It is important to remember that $\langle\psi|\psi\rangle = 16\frac{1}{4}\left[\frac{1}{4}\right] = 1$. Moreover, because $|1011\rangle$ is one of the main vectors, it uses the identification $\langle\psi|1011\rangle = \langle1011|\psi\rangle = \frac{1}{4}$ and it gets possible to express the above-mentioned $|x\rangle$ as following:

$$|x\rangle = \frac{3}{16}|0000\rangle + \frac{3}{16}|0000\rangle + \ldots - \frac{11}{16}|1011\rangle + \ldots + \frac{3}{16}|1111\rangle \qquad (12)$$

Its geometric picture is as following (Fig. 3):

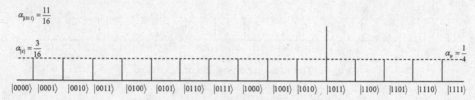

Fig. 3. The changing state of the amplitude.

This process finishes the first iteration. In the case, when the same two changes are used in the iteration, $|x\rangle$ gets as following:

$$|x\rangle = \frac{3}{16}|0000\rangle + \frac{3}{16}|0001\rangle + \frac{3}{16}|0010\rangle + \frac{3}{16}|0011\rangle + \ldots - \frac{11}{16}|1011\rangle + \ldots + \frac{3}{16}|1111\rangle$$

$$= \frac{3}{16}\sum_{\substack{x=0 \\ x\neq11}}^{15}|x\rangle - \frac{11}{16}|1011\rangle = \frac{3}{16}\sum_{\substack{x=0 \\ x\neq11}}^{15}|x\rangle - \frac{3}{16}|1011\rangle - \frac{11}{16}|1011\rangle = \frac{3}{16}\sum_{x=0}^{15}|x\rangle - \frac{7}{8}|1011\rangle \qquad (13)$$

After oracle query and diffusion conversion are used, it receives such form:

$$[2|\psi\rangle\langle\psi| - I]\left[\frac{3}{4}|\psi\rangle - \frac{7}{8}|1011\rangle\right] = 2\left(\frac{3}{4}\right)|\psi\rangle\langle\psi|\psi\rangle - \frac{3}{4}|\psi\rangle - 2\left(\frac{7}{8}\right)|\psi\rangle\langle\psi|1011\rangle + \frac{7}{8}|1011\rangle$$

$$= \frac{3}{2}|\psi\rangle - \frac{3}{4}|\psi\rangle - \frac{7}{16}|\psi\rangle + \frac{7}{8}|1011\rangle = \frac{5}{16}|\psi\rangle + \frac{7}{8}|1011\rangle$$

$$= \frac{5}{16}\left[\frac{1}{4}\sum_{\substack{x=0 \\ x\neq11}}^{15}|x\rangle + \frac{1}{4}|1011\rangle\right] + \frac{7}{8}|1011\rangle = \frac{5}{64}\sum_{\substack{x=0 \\ x\neq11}}^{15}|x\rangle + \frac{5}{64}|1011\rangle + \frac{7}{8}|1011\rangle$$

$$= \frac{5}{64}\sum_{\substack{x=0 \\ x\neq11}}^{15}|x\rangle + \frac{61}{64}|1011\rangle \qquad (14)$$

The success of the algorithm has an exact result in a geometric picture [18] (Fig. 4).

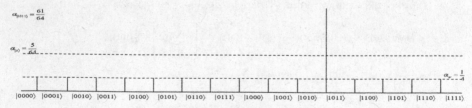

Fig. 4. The changing state of the amplitude.

Now, when the process is observed, the measurement probability of state's $|1011\rangle$ correct solution is equal to $\frac{61}{64} \approx 95, 3\%$ and the probability of the incorrect state is equal to $\frac{5}{64} \approx 0, 07\%$.

The results obtained after performing the above mathematical solutions in the quantum algorithm program are the followings [20]:

Firstly, the program develops the superposition state:

$$
\begin{aligned}
&[0.25]\\
&[0.25]\\
&[0.25]\\
&[0.25]\\
&[0.25]]
\end{aligned}
\tag{15}
$$

In the second place, the oracle O defines the maximum $|\psi\rangle$:

$$
\begin{aligned}
&[[\ 1.\ 0.\ 0.\ 0.\ 0.\ 0.\ 0.\ 0.\ 0.\ 0.\ 0.\ 0.\ 0.\ 0.\ 0.\ 0.]\\
&[0.\ 1.\ 0.\ 0.\ 0.\ 0.\ 0.\ 0.\ 0.\ 0.\ 0.\ 0.\ 0.\ 0.\ 0.\ 0.]\\
&[0.\ 0.\ 1.\ 0.\ 0.\ 0.\ 0.\ 0.\ 0.\ 0.\ 0.\ 0.\ 0.\ 0.\ 0.\ 0.]\\
&[0.\ 0.\ 0.\ 1.\ 0.\ 0.\ 0.\ 0.\ 0.\ 0.\ 0.\ 0.\ 0.\ 0.\ 0.\ 0.]\\
&[0.\ 0.\ 0.\ 0.\ 1.\ 0.\ 0.\ 0.\ 0.\ 0.\ 0.\ 0.\ 0.\ 0.\ 0.\ 0.]\\
&[0.\ 0.\ 0.\ 0.\ 0.\ 1.\ 0.\ 0.\ 0.\ 0.\ 0.\ 0.\ 0.\ 0.\ 0.\ 0.]\\
&[0.\ 0.\ 0.\ 0.\ 0.\ 0.\ 1.\ 0.\ 0.\ 0.\ 0.\ 0.\ 0.\ 0.\ 0.\ 0.]\\
&[0.\ 0.\ 0.\ 0.\ 0.\ 0.\ 0.\ 1.\ 0.\ 0.\ 0.\ 0.\ 0.\ 0.\ 0.\ 0.]\\
&[0.\ 0.\ 0.\ 0.\ 0.\ 0.\ 0.\ 0.\ 1.\ 0.\ 0.\ 0.\ 0.\ 0.\ 0.\ 0.]\\
&[0.\ 0.\ 0.\ 0.\ 0.\ 0.\ 0.\ 0.\ 0.\ 1.\ 0.\ 0.\ 0.\ 0.\ 0.\ 0.]\\
&[0.\ 0.\ 0.\ 0.\ 0.\ 0.\ 0.\ 0.\ 0.\ 0.\ 1.\ 0.\ 0.\ 0.\ 0.\ 0.]\\
&[0.\ 0.\ 0.\ 0.\ 0.\ 0.\ 0.\ 0.\ 0.\ 0.\ 0.\ -\mathbf{1}.\ 0.\ 0.\ 0.\ 0.]
\end{aligned}
\tag{16}
$$

By doing so, when $O|\psi\rangle^{Q(t)} = (-1)^{f(x)}|\psi\rangle^{Q(t)}$ is used, the following superposition is taken:

$$
\begin{aligned}
&[[\ 0.25]\\
&[\ 0.25]\\
&[\ 0.25]\\
&[\ 0.25]\\
&[\ 0.25]\\
&[\ 0.25]\\
&[\ 0.25]\\
&[\ 0.25]\\
&[\ 0.25]\\
&[\ 0.25]\\
&[\ 0.25]\\
&[-\mathbf{0.25}]]
\end{aligned}
\tag{17}
$$

This second step indicates the number of given iterations. The maximum number of Grover's iterations are calculated as following:

$$\frac{\pi}{4}\sqrt{2^n} \tag{18}$$

n is the number of the qubits or the length of the quantum chromosome, therefore, $n = 4$ in the example of the function described in the problem.

At the result of the iteration of the second step:

$$
\begin{aligned}
&[[\,1.\ 0.\ 0.\ 0.\ 0.\ 0.\ 0.\ 0.\ 0.\ 0.\ 0.\ 0.\ 0.\ 0.\ 0.\ 0.] \\
&[\,0.\ 1.\ 0.\ 0.\ 0.\ 0.\ 0.\ 0.\ 0.\ 0.\ 0.\ 0.\ 0.\ 0.\ 0.\ 0.] \\
&[\,0.\ 0.\ 1.\ 0.\ 0.\ 0.\ 0.\ 0.\ 0.\ 0.\ 0.\ 0.\ 0.\ 0.\ 0.\ 0.] \\
&[\,0.\ 0.\ 0.\ 1.\ 0.\ 0.\ 0.\ 0.\ 0.\ 0.\ 0.\ 0.\ 0.\ 0.\ 0.\ 0.] \\
&[\,0.\ 0.\ 0.\ 0.\ 1.\ 0.\ 0.\ 0.\ 0.\ 0.\ 0.\ 0.\ 0.\ 0.\ 0.\ 0.] \\
&[\,0.\ 0.\ 0.\ 0.\ 0.\ 1.\ 0.\ 0.\ 0.\ 0.\ 0.\ 0.\ 0.\ 0.\ 0.\ 0.] \\
&[\,0.\ 0.\ 0.\ 0.\ 0.\ 0.\ 1.\ 0.\ 0.\ 0.\ 0.\ 0.\ 0.\ 0.\ 0.\ 0.] \\
&[\,0.\ 0.\ 0.\ 0.\ 0.\ 0.\ 0.\ 1.\ 0.\ 0.\ 0.\ 0.\ 0.\ 0.\ 0.\ 0.] \\
&[\,0.\ 0.\ 0.\ 0.\ 0.\ 0.\ 0.\ 0.\ 1.\ 0.\ 0.\ 0.\ 0.\ 0.\ 0.\ 0.] \\
&[\,0.\ 0.\ 0.\ 0.\ 0.\ 0.\ 0.\ 0.\ 0.\ 1.\ 0.\ 0.\ 0.\ 0.\ 0.\ 0.] \\
&[\,0.\ 0.\ 0.\ 0.\ 0.\ 0.\ 0.\ 0.\ 0.\ 0.\ 1.\ 0.\ 0.\ 0.\ 0.\ 0.] \\
&[\,0.\ 0.\ 0.\ 0.\ 0.\ 0.\ 0.\ 0.\ 0.\ 0.\ 0.\ -1.\ 0.\ 0.\ 0.\ 0.]
\end{aligned} \tag{19}
$$

$$
\begin{aligned}
&[[\,0.187] \\
&[\,0.187] \\
&[\,0.187] \\
&[\,0.187] \\
&[\,0.187] \\
&[\,0.187] \\
&[\,0.187] \\
&[\,0.187] \\
&[\,0.187] \\
&[\,0.187] \\
&[\,0.187] \\
&[-0.687]]
\end{aligned} \tag{20}
$$

In the third and last places, Grover's diffusion operator G finds the chromosome with a specified state at $|\psi\rangle^{Q(t)}$[21]. Therefore, by implementing the following process

$|\psi\rangle^{Q(t)} = G|\psi\rangle^{Q(t)}$, the result is obtained:

$$
\begin{bmatrix}
[0.07812] \\
[0.07812] \\
[0.07812] \\
[0.07812] \\
[0.07812] \\
[0.07812] \\
[0.07812] \\
[0.07812] \\
[0.07812] \\
[0.07812] \\
[0.07812] \\
\mathbf{[0.95312]}
\end{bmatrix}
\tag{21}
$$

Finally, when $|\psi\rangle^{Q(t)}$ is implemented, the state indicated by the maximum chromosome is obtained. In other words, the quantum algorithm state is equal to $|11\rangle$, the chromosome is – to $|1011\rangle$ and the aim function is - to $|599\rangle$ (Fig. 5).

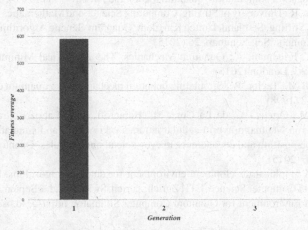

Fig. 5. The graph of the result of the optimization carried out by the quantum algorithm based on Grover's method.

6   Conclusion

In conclusion, it was considered to what extend given information about object of the research is used purposefully in the modeling process, as a result of mathematical analysis of Grover's method of the quantum algorithm, i.e. it is important to provide the adequacy of the model. The results of the optimization performed with the quantum algorithm based on Grover's method are presented. Grover's algorithm is more likely to get a correct answer than a wrong answer, when the input size is $N = 2^n$, the error only decreases with the input size. Even though Grover's algorithm is probabilistic, the error gets negligible as N gets larger.

References

1. Goldberg, D.E.: Genetic Algorithms in Search, Optimization, and Machine Learning, pp. 1–432. Addison-Wesley, Reading (1989)
2. Lahoz-Beltra, R.: Bioinformatica: simulacion, vida artificial e inteligencia artificial. Ediciones Diaz de Santos: A Coruna, Spain, pp. 237–323 (2004)
3. Perales-Gravan, C., Lahoz-Beltra, R.: An AM radioreceiver designed with a genetic algorithm based on a bacterial conjugation genetic operator. IEEE Trans. Evolut. Comput. **12**, 129–142 (2008)
4. Ribeiro Filho, J.L., Treleaven, P.C., Alippi, C.: Genetic-algorithm programming environments. IEEE Comput. **24**, 28–43 (1994)
5. Feynman, R.P.: Simulating physics with computers. Int. J. Theor. Phys. **21**, 467–488 (1982)
6. Fraser, A.S.: Simulation of genetic systems by automatic digital computers. Aust. J. Biol. Sci. **10**, 48491 (1957)
7. Han, K.-H., Kim, J.-H.: Quantum-inspired evolutionary algorithm for a class of combinatorial optimization. IEEE Trans. Evolut. Comput. **6**, 580–593 (2002)
8. Ying, M.: Quantum computation, quantum theory and AI. Artif. Intell. **174**, 162–176 (2010)
9. Lahoz-Beltra, R.: University of Stirling, Computing Science and Mathematics School of Natural Sciences, Stirling, Scotland, United Kingdom. Quantum Genetic Algorithms for Computer Scientists. Comput. Sci. Seminars **26** (2015)
10. Susskind, L., Friedman, A.: Quantum Mechanics: The Theoretical Minimum, pp. 1–364. Penguin Books, London (2015)
11. Boghosian, B.M., Taylor, W.: Simulating quantum mechanics on a quantum computer. Phys. D **120**, 30–42 (1998)
12. Alfonseca, M., Ortega, A., de La Cruz, M., Hameroff, S.R., Lahoz-Beltra, R.: A model of quantum-von Neumann hybrid cellular automata: Principles and simulation of quantum coherent superposition and decoherence in cytoskeletal microtubules. Quantum Inf. Comput. **15**, pp. 22-36 (2015)
13. Zeiter, D.: A graphical development environment for quantum algorithms. Master's thesis, Department of Computer Science, ETH Zurich, Zurich, Switzerland, 3 September 2008 (2008)
14. QCAD: GUI Environment for Quantum Computer Simulator. http://qcad.osdn.jp. Accessed 06 Sept 2022
15. Quantum-Quantum Computer Simulation Applet. http://jquantum.sourceforge.net/ QuantumApplet.html. Accessed 06 Sept 2022
16. Hayes, B.: Programming your quantum computer. Am. Sci. **102**, 22–25 (2014)
17. QCL-A Programming Language for Quantum Computers. http://tph.tuwien.ac.at/~oemer/qcl. html. Accessed 06 Sept 2022
18. Al Daoud, E.: Quantum computing for solving a system of nonlinear equations over GF(q). Int. Arab J. Inf. Technol. **4**, 201–205 (2007)
19. Lahoz-Beltra, R. Simple genetic algorithm (SGA). Figshare (2016)
20. Lahoz-Beltra, R., Perales-Gravan, C.: A survey of nonparametric tests for the statistical analysis of evolutionary computational experiments. Int. J. Inf. Theor. Appl. **17**, 49–61 (2010)
21. Toirov, Sh., Narmuradov, U.: Processes of applying of quantum genetic algorithm in function optimization. In: American Institute of Physics: Conference Proceedings, vol. 2365, pp. 1–6 (2021)

Evaluation of the Efficiency of Fault Tolerance Algorithms for Distributed Peer-To-Peer Worker Processes Connected Through a Key-Value Store

Teymur Zeynally[✉] [iD] and Dmitry Demidov [iD]

Moscow Polytechnic University, Moscow, Russia
z.teymur.e@gmail.com, d.g.demidov@mospolytech:ru

Abstract. In this paper, an experimental evaluation of algorithms that ensure the coordination and fault tolerance of distributed services that perform the payload (worker processes) is carried out. Worker processes coordinate their work through key-value stores. All worker processes are peer-to-peer, they can "negotiate" among themselves, and do not have a leader who coordinates the work of the others. During the experiment, various network destabilizing factors are emulated, such as: bandwidth limitations, packet delay, packet loss, packet duplication, packet corruption. The influence of the listed destabilizing factors on the operability of processes is evaluated and deviations of parameters from their control state are revealed. The analysis of the obtained results is carried out.

Keywords: Distributed System · Worker Process · Key-Value Storage · Prioritization · Fault Ttolerance

1 Introduction

Enterprise information systems and technologies make extensive use of services that iteratively execute payloads. The works of Teymur Zeynally, Dmitry Demidov, and Lubomir Dimitrov listed ways to organize the interaction of these services through a key-value store [1, 2]. The presented algorithms are designed to organize fault tolerance and coordinate the payload execution order with the node prioritization method. The type of payload is not specified but is characterized by iterative execution according to a certain schedule. Schedules can be quite flexible and depend on the current load on the system. The presented algorithms have two rules that characterize their behavior and are the reason for their appearance: the payload is executed once in the specified period, and the same payload is not executed in parallel. Both rules must be true regardless of the number of nodes, period, and duration of the payload. The presented algorithms do not imply the choice of a leader to coordinate actions; all nodes of the system are equal and can coordinate and prioritize their actions themselves. All interaction takes place between the nodes of the non-Byzantine system: the nodes will not intentionally distort information [8]. In the presented algorithms, the key-value storage, in particular etcd, is responsible for reaching consensus in distributed systems. The presented algorithms are algorithms for interacting with the storage to achieve the above behavior.

A. Gibadullin (Ed.): ITIDMS 2022, CCIS 1821, pp. 87–98, 2023.
https://doi.org/10.1007/978-3-031-31353-0_8

The current work is aimed at experimentally evaluating the practical effectiveness of the presented algorithms and identifying the thresholds at which a system built on the presented algorithms will stop working. Systems based on the presented algorithms are not specified to work in the absence of a connection to the storage. But the above rules should not be violated until the complete cessation of work. In addition to checking for violations of the two rules described above, it is interesting to get an answer to several questions. What is the minimum payload execution interval? How do network factors affect the duration of operations of interaction with the storage and the logic of the algorithm without a payload?

2   Materials and Methods

The methodological basis of the current study is an experiment with subsequent analysis of the data obtained.

The experiment is carried out on a single computing device, with a linux-based operating system and containerization support. Technical and software characteristics of the device: CPU: Intel i5-6200U (4) 2.8 GHz, RAM: 12 Gb, OS: Manjaro Linux x86_64, Kernel: 5.15.85–1. Docker version 20.10.22 was chosen as the containerizer.

The operating system was chosen based on linux. it is convenient to emulate in a virtual network from containerized applications. To emulate network destabilizing factors, was chosen Docker Traffic Control (docker image of docker-tc) from lukaszlach. It allows you to emulate bandwidth limitations, delays, packet loss, packet duplication, packet corruption on the network of specific containers.

However, docker-tc supports docker hosts only on linux. Etcd version 3.3.8 with docker image from quay.io was chosen as a key-value store. Interaction with etcd occurs via gRPC over an insecure channel (TLS is not used) [9]. The application itself that interacts with etcd is developed on net7.0. The application container image is based on the mcr.microsoft.com/dotnet/runtime:7.0 image. During the experiment, it was necessary to store, aggregate, analyze and visualize information. As a time series database for storing, aggregating and analyzing data, InfluxDb version 2.5.1 was used. Grafana version 9.3.2 was used for visualization. The visualization is based on the Plotly panel from nline-plotlyjs-panel version 1.1.1.

The system that was tested during the experiment consisted of three application nodes, and three storage nodes. Each storage node interacted with two other storage nodes. Each application node can communicate with any storage node via gRPC. The application's client balancer is configured so that if an application fails to exchange messages with a storage node with a 503 (Unavailable) error, then the application switches to any other storage node. Each storage and application node is a separate container with its own operating system. Docker-tc controls all traffic on each of the containers.

It was necessary to identify the parameters that would be logged during the experiment and further analyzed. There are timestamps, durations and the sequence of calls to the key operations of the algorithms and payload. At the same time, this data must be collected and analyzed from all nodes in the aggregate.

Due to the fact that the entire experiment is performed on one physical device, there is no problem of time synchronization [10, 11]. The system does not execute the same payload in parallel, so in practice, the order of operations can be distinguished by timestamps, with nanosecond precision. If suddenly two operations were performed simultaneously, then in this case the order can be set according to the values in etcd. Because of this, it will be necessary to develop another additional application that will log the most interesting operations in etcd. This application is called Event Collector. In controversial moments, it will be possible to refer to it's log. Etcd allows you to set the channel on which it will report captured events, each event has a unique integer number. If the connection is interrupted, you can get missed events, because. Etcd keeps versions of all entries and keeps a history of keys.

For everything else, OpenTelemetry NuGet version 1.3 was used. Blocks of code important for analysis were marked up for telemetry collection. However, the usual telemetry export used in enterprises is not quite suitable for the current system. The fact is that telemetry export implies network interaction: either the application itself sends telemetry to the collector, or the collector requests telemetry from the application. Due to emulations on the network, this can affect the doing of the experiment: for example, the bandwidth is limited and the channel is clogged with telemetry instead of useful data. Therefore, it was decided to develop new telemetry exporter in the influx line protocol format, which exported all telemetry to files. These files were then uploaded to InfulxDb for further analysis. Actually, they are the output data.

The input data is the configuration files for another application, which is essentially an experiment runner. This application is called Runner. The configuration is passed in JSON format from the tests to be run. The configuration of one test consists of a name, duration, and a section with the configuration of nodes and their network settings for applications and storage. Before each test, all containers (except the Event Collector) are stopped and the Runner starts the configuration from the containers according to the JSON file. Containers work for a set time, then Runner completes their work and writes the date and time of the start and end of the test, the name of the test to a csv file. It then waits for a short, configurable interval and starts the next test (Fig. 1).

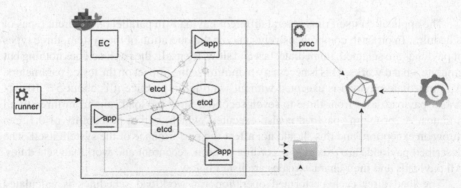

Fig. 1. Scheme of the experiment.

Tests can be classified into the following categories:

0. Test without any network interference

1. Tests that limit bandwidth on application nodes: 10 mbps, 7 mbps, 3 mbps, 1 mbps, 512 kbps, 128 kbps, 1 kbps, 512 bps
2. Tests that limit bandwidth on storage nodes: 10 mbps, 7 mbps, 3 mbps, 1 mbps, 512 kbps, 128 kbps, 1 kbps, 512 bps
3. Tests limiting bandwidth to 128 kbps on one and two application nodes.
4. Tests that create network delays on application nodes: 100 ms, 300 ms, 500 ms, 700 ms, 900 ms, 1100 ms, 1 kbps, 512 bps
5. Tests that create network delays on storage nodes: 100 ms, 300 ms, 500 ms, 700 ms, 900 ms, 1100 ms, 1 kbps, 512 bps
6. Tests creating network delays up to 1100 ms: on one application node, on two application nodes
7. Tests that create packages loss on application nodes with a probability of: 10%, 30%, 50%
8. Tests that create packages loss on storage nodes with a probability of: 10%, 30%, 50%
9. Tests that generate packages loss with 50% probability: on one application node, on two application nodes
10. Tests that create duplicate packages on application nodes with a probability of: 10%, 30%, 50%
11. Tests that create duplicate packages on storage nodes with a probability of: 10%, 30%, 50%
12. Tests that create duplicate packages with a 50% probability: on one application node, on two application nodes
13. Tests that create packages corruption on the application nodes, with a probability of: 10%, 30%, 50%
14. Tests that create packages corruption on storage nodes, with a probability of: 10%, 30%, 50%
15. Tests that create packages corruption with a probability of 50%: on one application node, on two application nodes

The application itself runs several different payloads in parallel on different types of schedules. In order to comprehensively analyze the operation of the system, three types of payloads are selected: immediate, fast and slow. By itself, the payload does nothing but emulate what it works. This is necessary to minimize the impact on the tested parameters. An immediate payload is executed without waiting, in practice it is about $5 * 10^3$ ns. A fast payload lasts from three to seven seconds. Slow payload runs from three to all minutes. A "problem" payload is also executed, which, with a probability of 0.1, can throw an exception, and this should not affect the performance of the system itself. The described payloads are executed according to cron, reccurent and workload schedules. All payloads and their characteristics are listed below.

The load after each performed operation for workload schedules is calculated randomly (Table 1).

When all the tests are done and the Runner has completed its work, all files with tracing are loaded into InfluxDb via the influx cli. Another application was developed to request the required data for further analysis. It consists of several modules, each of which analyzes and validates certain system behavior.

Table 1. Payloads executed by the application.

Load ID	Schedule type	Description
Cron-Immediate	Cron * * * * *	Runs an instant/fast/slow/problem payload every minute
Cron-Fast		
Cron-Slow		
Cron-Problem		
Recurrent-Immediate	Recurrent 0	Runs an instant payload as often as it can
Recurrent-Fast	Recurrent 1 s	Runs a fast/slow/problem payload with a period of 1 s
Recurrent-Slow		
Recurrent-Problem		
Workload-Immediate	Workload from 0 to 0	Runs an instant payload as often as it can
Workload-Fast	Workload from 1 s to 10 s, at load from 0 to 50% + 1 s, at load from 50% −1 s	Runs a fast/slow/problem payload on a specified schedule
Workload-Slow		
Workload-Problem		

All analyzer modules work according to a similar algorithm. The input to each of them is the time range in which a certain test was made and the type of the analyzed payload. For some analyzers, the period in which the payload should have been executed is transmitted. Based on the transmitted data, the analyzer generates a request in the flux query language to the InfluxDB database. The database contains a huge array of data, from which the analyzer selects only what is needed. Such a request takes several minutes, and for the convenience of debugging, the analyzer caches the received data in a file. As a rule, the data is an array of objects containing a unix timestamp, the duration of one or more parameters, and tracing service values. The data comes with nanosecond precision. The analyzer aggregates and validates the data, after which it forms an array of the resulting numerical values of the analyzed indicator. These numerical values are used to calculate statistical measures such as variance and standard deviation (σ). Gross errors (misses) are excluded from the resulting sample according to the "three sigma" criterion. The output data of the analyzer is either a boolean value of the validity of operations, or the average value of the analyzed indicator and the error. The standard deviation is taken as the error.

Analyzers. Analyzer of the duration of operations of algorithms. Its purpose is to find out how long the logic of algorithms takes, including interactions with the storage. The analyzer asks for each iteration the duration of the payload, lock duration, and the duration of entire iteration from its start. The final result does not take into account (subtract) the duration of the lock wait and the duration of the payload execution. In this way, it is possible to quantify the costs of non-payload operations.

Intersection analyzer of execution intervals of the same payload. This analyzer obtains the start timestamp and duration of each payload. Based on this data, the timestamp of the end of the operation is calculated. It checks that the time intervals do not intersect.

Fixed period operation analyzer. Its task is to evaluate the difference between the expected execution time and the actual one. Like the previous analyzer, it gets data about the timestamp and duration of a certain payload for cron and recurrent worker processes. These payloads must have a fixed period. Based on the timestamp, the duration of the previous iteration, and the period parameter, determines the expected timestamp of the current iteration. The resulting differences between expected and actual timestamps make up an array of resulting numeric values.

Analyzer of the duration of operations with storage. Gets data about all storage operations, such as: acquire a lock, release a lock, mark the iteration status as successful, etc. An array of durations is formed for each operation.

The entire project with all the implemented application logic and all the necessary data to reproduce the current experiment is in an open repository in GitHub [3]. In addition, there you can find all the received data. In the current work, they will only be visualized.

3   Results

The results of this experiment, as described above, are the output of all analyzer modules.

Intersection analyzer of execution intervals found no issues. However, during the debugging of the entire scheme of the experiment, it revealed intersections. They were caused by incorrect calculation of TTL (time to live) of keys. The formulas by which TTL was calculated were written with the aim of minimizing memory consumption in storage and deleting unused keys. At the same time, the coefficient by which the minimum TTL was multiplied was 3. In scenarios with a short period of operations, the TTL ended before the system could use the key again. The problem manifested itself only when emulating destabilizing factors on the network. The problem was solved by a configurable minimum TTL value.

The data obtained during the experiment are visualized on the graphs. Values are displayed on a logarithmic scale for easier perception. The unit of measure for values is seconds. All tests were described earlier, their names on the graphs are abbreviated. There are no data for some tests. This was caused by emulated network destabilizing factors that completely stopped the functionality of the system. For example, violations in the interaction of storage nodes lead to the storage nodes not responding to requests correctly. This is the reason why the payload cannot be executed.

Figure 2 shows the results of the work of two analyzers: the analyzer of operations with a fixed period and a period depending on the current load.

The difference value without emulations on the network, for all operations, on average, is 1.414 ± 0.423 s.

For application throughput tests, the difference value began to increase when the throughput was limited to 1 kbps. Previously, the average values for all payloads were

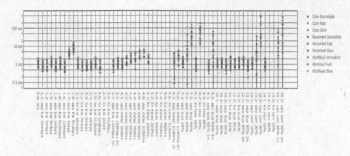

Fig. 2. Differences between expected and actual payload execution timestamps.

within 1.230 ± 0.332 s. For application throughput tests, the situation is similar, with the only difference that when the throughput is limited to 1 kbps, the storage stops responding, and timeout errors appear in the storage logs.

For network latency tests, there is an increase in values proportional to the latency value. At 300 ms. Storage stops responding with timeout errors. With network delays on one or two application nodes, the graph shows a noticeable spread of values, the maximum error is ± 1.810 s.

Packet loss tests show similar results to packet corruption tests. With a 10% probability of packet loss and corruption, the values are comparable to the control values. Starting at 30% losses/corruptions on the application, the values and scatter increase noticeably.

The average value for all operations at 30% losses/corruptions is 5.989 ± 9.946 s., and at 50% the average value is 56.558 ± 81.846 s.

When emulating losses and corruptions in storage, 50% of the system ceases to function, and 30% is close to this, with an average value equal to 69.554 ± 44.434 s. When emulating a loss of 50% on a single application node, the values are comparable to the control values, and when the packets are corrupted, the average value of all operations is 10.976 ± 19.865 s. When emulated on two application nodes, the values obtained are, on average, 12.133 ± 13.696 s. for losses and 68.984 ± 113.635 s. for corruption.

For tests with packet duplication emulation, no deviations from the control values are observed.

The minimum interval with which the system is able to execute the payload can be determined by the Recurrent Immediate, the value is 1.423 ± 0.732 s.

Figure 3 shows the results of the algorithm duration analyzer for each of the payloads. The duration of algorithms depends on the duration of storage operations.

There is a correlation here with previous measurements. Here is a distinguishing feature from previous changes. For different types of payload in these measurements, the spread of values is not so large.

Figure 4 shows the results of the Storage Activity Duration Analyzer for each type of activity.

These measurements also show a noticeable correlation with previous measurements. The most important are the values without emulating network factors. They are presented in the table below (Table 2).

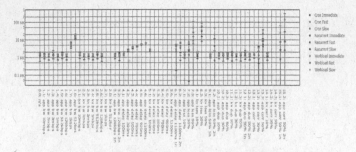

Fig. 3. Durations of algorithm operations, without payload.

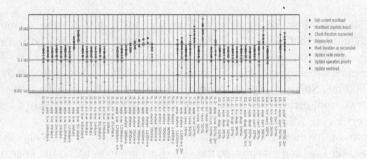

Fig. 4. Duration of operations of interaction with storage.

Table 2. Duration values for storage operations without emulating problems on the network.

Storage operation	Value (sec.)
Get current payload value	0.262 ± 0.192
Extend lease on node keys (heartbeat)	0.099 ± 0.09
Get the success status of an operation	0.274 ± 0.199
Release lock	0.276 ± 0.141
Mark operation as successful	0.552 ± 0.259
Update Node Priority	0.338 ± 0.148
Update Operation Priority	0.273 ± 0.153
Update load value when performing an operation	0.542 ± 0.26

The duration of the lock is excluded from the values, because when a lock is acquired, the process waits for the release of this lock from the process holding it. And how long the lock is held depends on the payload. Therefore, the lock capture duration values do not look representative.

Figure 5 shows the results of the priority delay analyzer. Reference value: 0.005 ± 0.003 s.

Fig. 5. Difference in receiving priorities

In this situation, the values do not in all cases correlate with previous measurements. In tests limited to 1 kbps and 512 bps, there is a noticeable increase in values.

In tests with network delays, the values turned out to be within the control value. Only values are highlighted in tests where the latency is emulated on one or two application nodes, and the resulting value is equal to the emulated latency value.

In tests with packet loss and packet corruption, the situation is the same as in previous measurements: at 10% loss/ corruption probability, the values differ slightly from the control, and average 0.035 ± 0.071 s. At 30% and 50% application loss probability, the values increase to 3.01 ± 11.083 s and 11.996 ± 24.785 s, respectively. And at 30% and 50% of the probability of corruption, the values are 0.707 ± 1.459 s and 12.173 ± 18.697 s, respectively. With losses of 30% probability in storage, the values differ slightly from the control. With a loss with 50% probability on one application node, the value is 0.01 ± 0.07 s, and on two nodes 10.004 ± 23.456 s. With corruption with 50% probability on one application node, the value is 6.017 ± 12.217 s, and on two 13.315 ± 35.531 s.

4 Discussion

The fact that the operations intersection analyzer did not detect problems after setting the minimum TTL threshold was due to the fact that the threshold was greater than the delays caused by emulated problems. It should be noted here that the TTL may expire earlier than expected, not only due to network problems, but also due to delays / freezes caused by CPU overload [4]. For these cases, you should provide a watchdog timer that will terminate the worker process when the lock is lost due to the expiration of the TTL. However, it was decided not to use the watchdog timer to exclude its influence on the analyzed results.

The lack of data for some tests is caused by errors in query processing by the etcd storage. There were timeout errors in the etcd logs. The experiment used the default configuration. The etcd documentation has a setting for the leader election timeout, which defaults to 1 s, and this timeout is sensitive to network latency [5]. During the experiment, the problems started from 300 ms. However, a delay of 300 ms was emulated on all three nodes, and leader election consists of several message exchanges [6]. The same explanation applies to tests for bandwidth limitation, packet loss, and packet corruption. With a bandwidth limit of up to 1 kbps, the difference between the expected execution time and the actual one increased to an average of 4.667 ± 1.045 s, and with packet loss and distortion with a probability of 30% or more, the difference was measured in tens of seconds.

An interesting result, which can be perceived as a characteristic of the evaluated developments in general, is the minimum possible payload execution interval. It turned out to be 1.423 ± 0.732 s. This value may depend on the number of storage nodes, but for minimum fault tolerance, a quorum of three storages is still required. What conclusions can be drawn from this value? If the load on the system has increased, then the worker process may need to process thousands of operations per second. In this case, the obtained value of delays between iterations seems unacceptable. However, the evaluated developments are primarily designed for the execution of business processes and the processing of workflow operations [1]. For this nature of operations, this value is acceptable. Moreover, it all depends on the payload. If it is acceptable to launch the payload at such an interval, then the payload can process those same thousands of operations, requesting them in batches. Next, it is a clear correlation between measurements of the difference between the expected and actual payload execution timestamps, the duration of algorithm operations, without payload, and the duration of operations of interaction with the storage. Such a correlation is explained by the fact that most of the operation time of all algorithms is occupied by operations of interaction with the storage. And the duration of storage operations depends on network factors. It makes sense to evaluate the results of the first three measurements in the aggregate.

With a throughput of 128 kbps, there is no significant impact on the performance of the system as a whole. From this we can conclude that an application with exactly these (previously specified) payloads and schedules will generate approximately this amount of traffic. The consumed traffic is influenced by many factors: the iteration frequency, the nature of the payload, the type of schedule. Therefore, it is difficult to do any extrapolated conclusions from the available data. Bandwidth limits further lead to longer storage operations.

When emulating network delays, you can see an increase in the duration of operations, in proportion to the emulated delays. In tests for network latency, the most interesting are tests where delays are emulated on one or two application nodes. There is always at least one application node running without network delays. It was expected that the values obtained in these tests for the difference between the expected and actual payload execution times would be comparable to the values without any network interference. However, in fact, there is an increase in indicators. This is due to the inner workings of locks in etcd: when a node holding a lock performs a lock release operation, the lock will be acquired by the node that first entered the lock pending state [2]. Therefore, operations are also performed on nodes with network interference.

Tests for emulating losses, corruptions and duplicate packets can be discussed at the same time. The results obtained are largely influenced by the operation of TCP. It is responsible for the correctness and delivery of packets. Duplicates can be detected and simply ignored on the recipient's side [7]. Moreover, a TCP segment can be duplicated due to its re-sending after the timeout expires, this is a regular situation for TCP. A similar situation with packet loss, if the sending side does not receive confirmation of the delivery of the segment, then the sending side, after the timeout expires, sends it again [7]. In a situation where the data in the TCP segment has been corrupted, the receiving side will notice this at the checksum verification stage. If the checksum does not match, then the segment is discarded, the sending side will have to send it again after the timeout expires [7]. From all this, we can conclude that corruptions and packet losses increase network delays. The situation here is the same as in tests with delay emulation.

When evaluating differences in receiving priorities, bandwidth limitations led to uneven data delivery times from storages to all application nodes. The opposite situation can be seen in latency tests. Regardless of the value of delays, if they are the same for all nodes, then they will receive information about priorities with a difference of 0.035 ± 0.071 s. However, if the delays for the application nodes are different, as is usually the case in practice, then the difference in receive times will be significant. Duplicate packages, as in other cases, do not affect the values. In cases with losses and curruptions, due to the variability in packet delivery time, the results are significantly different from normal operation, with a large scatter.

What can a discrepancy in priority data on all nodes do? This can lead to system locks on itself (deadlock): each node thinks it has a low priority and waits its turn before acquiring a lock that will never come. This is solved by timeout for prioritization [2].

5 Conclusion

In total, based on the results of the experiment and their analysis, it can be concluded that the proposed algorithms with a fixed iteration interval are more suitable for solving problems that do not involve high load. Or big batches of data processing tasks.

Answering the questions posed in the introduction, we can say that during the experiment, no payload execution was recorded more than once during the specified period or its parallel execution. The minimum intervals between iterations were also identified. The dependence of the duration of operations of interaction with the storage and the logic of the algorithm without payload on network factors was revealed.

References

1. Zeynally, T., Demidov, D.: Fault tolerance of distributed worker processes in corporate information systems and technologies. Communications in Computer and Information Science (2022)
2. Zeynally, T., Demidov, D., Dimitrov, L.: Prioritization of Distributed Worker Processes Based on Etcd Locks. Communications in Computer and Information Science (2022)
3. GitHub — Teymur Zeynally / Recurrent Worker Service. https://github.com/TeymurZeynally/RecurrentWorkerService. Accessed 12 Feb 2023
4. Brendan Burns: Designing Distributed Systems: Patterns and Paradigms for Scalable, Reliable Services (2018)
5. Etcd Tuning. https://etcd.io/docs/v3.3/tuning/. Accessed 20 Jan 2023
6. Ongaro, D., Ousterhout, J.: In Search of an Understandable Consensus Algorithm (2014)
7. RFC 793: Transmission Control Protocol. https://www.rfc-editor.org/rfc/rfc793. Accessed 20 Jan 2023
8. Bolfing, A.: Distributed Systems. Oxford University Press, Oxford (2020)

9. Śliwa, M., Pańczyk, B.: Performance comparison of programming interfaces on the example of REST API, GraphQL and gRPC. J. Comput. Sci. Inst. **21** (2021)
10. Lamport, L.: Specifying Systems (2003)
11. Tadayon, T.: Time Synchronization in Distributed Systems without a Central Clock (2019)

Investigation of the Possibility of Using Neural Networks to Predict the Concentration of Sodium in a Steam

O. V. Yegoshina and S. K. Lukutina[✉]

National Research University "MPEI", 14, Krasnokazarmennaya, Moscow 111250, Russia
sofi.zvonareva@yandex.ru

Abstract. Currently, two types of mathematical models are used at energy facilities: displaying current information and predicting. Since forecasting is a promising direction of research, this aspect is investigated in the work. Promising models for predicting the behavior of impurities along the energy block path are: mathematical models based on ion interactions, material balance and neural networks. Now an urgent question is whether it is possible to predict the onset of a violation of the water-chemical regime in the energy sector with the help of neural networks. Thus, the paper investigated the possibility of using the simplest logical regression of the sklearn library and the long-term short-term memory block LSTM of the keras library to predict the sodium concentration in saturated steam. For the construction of models, real industrial data measured on a steam power plant were used. Neural networks had one input and one output layer. The error of using the simplest logical regression is determined - about 65%, which makes it impossible to use this system at energy facilities for forecasting without algorithm adjustments. The error of using LSTM networks is 0.80 (absolute value), which proves the possibility of using this type of neural networks to predict impurities. It is assumed that in order to reduce the prediction error, it is necessary to use several features on which the target variable dependsцелевая.

Keywords: Thermal Power Plants · Forecasting · Neural Networks · Cycle Chemical · Impurity Concentration

1 Introduction

The reliability of power equipment operation largely depends on the level at which the chemical and technological monitoring system is located: improvement of measurement methods, development of new devices for sampling water and steam, and application of various forecasting and control methods at thermal power plants. Monitoring of the condition, diagnosis of violations and maintenance of the water-chemical regime are among the most difficult tasks, the solution of which should be sought in the direction of increasing the information content of devices and automatic chemical control systems based on simple and reliable measurements, as well as the development of new calculation methods adapted to the conditions of industrial operation [1, 2].

The development of monitoring systems is mainly carried out on the basis of the basic principles and requirements formulated in the guidance document [3], which focuses on the need to use mathematical models in monitoring systems.

The mathematical models currently used are divided into two groups: displaying current information about the state of the water-chemical regime and predicting the behavior of impurities along the energy block path. Among the promising models, one can single out the development and development of mathematical models based on ionic equilibria, material balance and neural networks [4–21]. The training of neural networks is based on the determination of a weighting factor that reflects the importance of a certain factor in the system.

The use of such methods for the analysis of physical and technological processes makes it possible to identify the importance of certain measurable indicators and predict their behavior. The authors of [12, 13] investigated the feasibility of using neural network modeling methods to control the pH values of the coolant at nuclear power plants, the results of the study were satisfactory, however, to date, verification on industrial data has not been carried out.

Currently, a promising direction is the use of neural networks to predict the behavior of impurities. The possibility of using mathematical models based on neural networks is investigated not only to display the current state of the concentration of impurities along the tract, but also for the purpose of forecasting.

2 Materials and Methods

It should be noted that neural networks and machine learning are similar in structure, but the main difference is that neural networks have the skill of self-learning. Machine learning uses methods that use mathematical statistics, probability theory, algebra, basic principles of mathematical analysis, working with matrices, but there are no principles by which this type of machine learning could be trained. However, the difficulty in working with neural networks is to choose a network architecture that will produce the correct results. Consider the structure of neural networks.

Neural networks, regardless of the types used, have a basic component - a neuron.

An artificial neuron is a weighted sum of vector values of input elements. This amount is transferred to the nonlinear activation function.

$$z = f(y) \tag{1}$$

$$y = W_0 X_0 + W_1 X_1 + \ldots + W_{m-1} X_{m-1} \tag{2}$$

where W_0, W_1, W_{m-1} – weight of each vector element; X_0, X_1, X_{m-1} – values of the input vector; y – weighted sum of elements X; z – result of the activation function application.

The training of neural networks is based on the determination of a weighting factor that reflects the importance of a certain factor in the system. Neural networks are classified by the number of layers used, by the direction of information distribution through synapses from one neuron to another, by the method of network training, by the type of input signals, by their designation. Unfortunately, at the moment there is a small number of articles in relation to energy, where neural networks are used for management, forecasting. A number of literature sources have been investigated to select the type of neural network suitable for predicting the behavior of impurities along the path of the power unit [22–28]. It is noted that despite the fact that neural networks are classified into a large number of groups: by the number of layers used (single-layer and multi-layer), by the direction of information distribution through synapses from one neuron to another (unidirectional and recurrent), by the method of network training (with and without a teacher), by the type of input signals (analog, binary, figurative), according to their purpose (classification, regression, prediction, clustering and generation), only a certain type of neural networks is suitable for forecasting. Thus, in the case under study, a neural network will be used to analyze a large amount of data with further prediction, therefore, a recurrent neural network was chosen. According to the neural network training method, a method of teaching with a teacher is chosen, since this algorithm will allow achieving a minimum error.

The choice in favor of recurrent neural networks was made due to a number of advantages over neural networks with direct communication. Neural networks with direct communication have several problems [29] [30]: they cannot process sequential data; they take into account only the current input information; it is impossible to remember the previous input.

Any time series problem, such as predicting a certain parameter in a certain time interval, can be solved using RNN.

An important property of recurrent models is that this network approximates the behavior of a dynamic system. RNN can work sequentially, accepting current and previously received input data, and also memorize thanks to its internal memory. The most popular RNN neurons are the Elman RNN, the LSTM long-term short-term memory block, and the GRU block. The operation of the GRU block is similar to the operation of LSTM type networks, but only a lightweight version. This network determines how much information needs to be saved from the final state and how much information is received from the previous level. One of the differences between the GRU block and LSTM is that GRU works a little faster and easier. This model is used when high performance is needed and where additional functions inherent only in LSTM networks are not required [31]. According to the study [32], LSTM shows the best performance in time series forecasting tasks. Because in our case, accuracy plays the greatest role compared to performance. In this paper, the LSTM network is chosen as one of the networks for the study.

The LSTM block of long–term short–term memory implements: forget gate - a residual memory valve that allows the network to store certain information and forget other information; save gate – an addition valve that allows filtering incoming information in order to either delete or add it to long-term memory; attention gate - an attention valve that allows use only the necessary information from the entire block of long-term memory. Next, we will consider the mathematical formulation of the principle of operation of the LSM block.

At a certain point in time (t), new input data (x_t) arrives at the input and comes from the previous time points long-term memory (ltm_{t-1}) and working memory (wm_{t-1}). Long-term and working memory are represented as n-dimensional vectors. Long-term memory should determine the residual memory gate in order to calculate which information should be remembered and which should be forgotten. This process uses input data and working memory. The residual memory gate is a vector that contains a certain number (n) of numbers in the range from zero to one. Each number specifies how much of a given element of long-term memory needs to be remembered. Thus, one is to continue to remember the element, zero is to completely forget. An example of calculating the residual memory gate is presented in Eq. 3 [33].

$$remember_t = \sigma(W_r x_t + U_r wm_{t-1}) \tag{3}$$

To determine the information that will be added to long-term memory from newly received data, the activation function $[\varphi]$ is used. An example of the calculation is presented in Eq. 4 [33].

$$ltm'_t = \varphi(W_l x_t + U_l wm_{t-1}) \tag{4}$$

To determine which elements of the filtered data will enter the long-term memory block, the addition gate is calculated. An example of calculating the addition valve is presented in Eq. 5 [33].

$$save_t = \sigma(W_s x_t + U_s wm_{t-1}) \tag{5}$$

Thus, it turns out to update long-term memory (adding useful elements of information and forgetting unnecessary) by combining all the steps described above by means of element multiplication (°). An example of the calculation is presented in Eq. 6 [33].

$$tm_t = remember_t \circ ltm_{t-1} + save_t \circ ltm'_t \tag{6}$$

After updating the long-term memory, the working memory should be updated, taking into account the fact that the model should be trained to extract information from its long-term memory that will be useful in the near future. To do this, it is necessary to calculate the attention valve, the operation of which is similar to the principle of the residual memory valve: one pays maximum attention to these elements, zero is ignored. An example of calculating the attention valve is presented in Eq. 7 [33].

$$focus_t = \sigma(W_f x_t + U_f wm_{t-1}) \tag{7}$$

After determining the attention valve, the working memory is updated. An example of working memory is presented in Eq. 8 [33].

$$wm_t = focus_t \circ \phi(ltm_t) \tag{8}$$

Thus, the LSTM network uses several equations to update its memory:

$$ltm_t = remember_t \circ ltm_{t-1} + save_t \circ ltm'_t \tag{9}$$

$$wm_t = focus_t \circ \tanh(ltm_t) \tag{10}$$

Currently, there are numerous Python libraries that are designed not only for the implementation of machine learning algorithms, but also for algorithms with neural networks. For the study, the Python Karas library was used, the advantage of which is an intuitive interface, extensibility, high integration speed, a large amount of documentation on working with this library.

The paper also compares the predicted values using LSTM networks and the simplest logical regression model from the sklearn library.

3 Results

The object of the study is the concentration of sodium in saturated steam. To build the model, we used two samples: training and test. The training sample is the sample that was submitted to the input of the neural network during its training. A test sample is a sample that was submitted to the input of the neural network after its training to verify compliance with real data. All data in the samples are valid industrial values measured at a combined cycle gas plant.

The first stage of the work was training a logical regression model from the Sklearn library. This algorithm is used to predict the probability of a categorically dependent variable.

To read the data, a method was used – conversion directly into the dataframe of the Pandas library.

```
import pandas as pd
train = pd.read_csv('/content/train.csv')
train.head()
test = pd.read_csv('/content/test.csv')
test.head()
```

Next, all the relationships between the independent and the target variable were analyzed. In this paper, it is assumed that the dependent (target) variable is the concentration of sodium in saturated steam.

There were missing rows in the industrial sample, so it was decided to identify and fill in the gaps with the average value of this column, which will reduce the likelihood of errors when training neural networks.

```
train[' Concentration'].fillna(train[' Concentration'].mean(), inplace = True)
```

The sodium concentration variables are expressed in numbers, not strings, so this variable was converted to the str type via the map() function.

```
train.columns = train.columns.map(str)
```

After data conversion, the training sample was divided into attributes of the target variable.

```
X_train = train.drop(' Concentration ', axis = 1)
y_train = train[' Concentration ']
X_train.head()
```

Thus, we put everything in X_trail except the column with the sodium concentration, which became our target variable.

The Sklearn library was used to train the logical regression model. After importing the logical regression from the linear_model module of the Sklearn library, an object of this class is created and written to the mod-el variable. Then the model was trained.

```
from sklearn.linear_model import LogisticRegression
model = LogisticRegression()
model.fit(X_train, y_train)
```

In this case, it remains to make a forecast and evaluate the quality of the model. A training sample was used to build the forecast. To begin with, a prediction of the class was made on a training sample.

```
y_pred_train = model.predict(X_train)
```

To compare the predicted values with the actual ones, an "error matrix" was constructed. This metric is used to evaluate the quality of the model. It shows how many parameters were classified correctly and incorrectly.

```
rom sklearn.metrics import confusion_matrix
conf_matrix = confusion_matrix(y_train, y_pred_train)
conf_matrix_df = pd.DataFrame(conf_matrix)
conf_matrix_df
```

However, since the "error matrix" does not show the proportion of correctly predicted values, the accuracy function was additionally used. This function takes only those values that are predicted correctly and divides by the total number of predictions.

```
rom sklearn.metrics import accuracy_score
model_accuracy = accuracy_score(y_test, y_pred)
round(model_accuracy, '')
```

Thus, it was found that in 35% the model predicted the correct result on the training sample. It should be noted that this error value is high for use for forecasting at energy facilities, therefore, this algorithm requires improvement.

The test sample was processed according to the principles of data separation, filled in the gaps with the arithmetic mean of variables and all columns were rotated into rows. After processing, a forecast was made and the result was output.

```
y_pred_test = model.predict(X_test)
y_pred_test[:'']
```

It was found that the training of the logical regression model gave very low prediction results, which is not applicable to energy facilities. To reduce the error, it is necessary to introduce more than one attribute on which the target variable depends, apply the reduction of quantitative variables to the same scale, use a training sample of more data and reduce the number of rows with empty values.

Then a similar work was carried out on the LSTM network of the Keras library. The training and test samples are identical to the samples with the logical model of the sklearn library.

The neural network under study had an input layer with one input, a hidden layer with eight LSTM blocks or neurons, and an output layer that gives a prediction of a single value. Activation function – sigmoid. The network was trained on 60 epochs.

Figure 1 shows the result of experimental testing of the existing neural network of the STM network for predicting sodium values in saturated steam. The initial data is represented by a blue line. The orange line shows the data predicted by the neural network from the source data. The green line is the predicted data for 200 values.

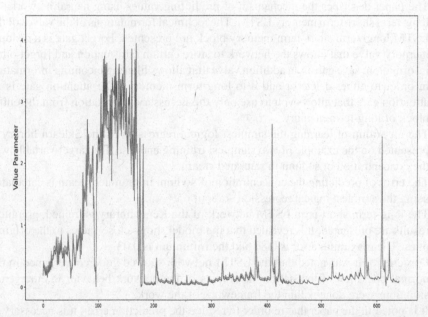

Fig. 1. Prediction of sodium values in saturated steam using a neural network of the LSTM type.

As can be seen from the graph, the model shows fairly close values to the original ones. The maximum error is 0.80 and the minimum is 0.03. Thus, the model works out the algorithm with minimal error, which makes it possible to use this algorithm for forecasting. To reduce the error in this case, it is necessary, similarly to the simplest logical model, to use a training sample of a larger amount of data, reduce the number of empty rows and introduce additional values that affect the value of the target variable.

4   Discussion

It was found that the simplest logical regression in the basic configuration gives only 35% of the actual values, which, if used on energy facilities, can lead to incorrect actions of operators. Therefore, it is necessary to refine the model in the form of adding influencing features to the target variable, a larger amount of training selection.

The study of long-term short-term memory LSTM confirmed the possibility of using this type of neural networks for forecasting. However, it should be noted that despite the low error value obtained, the model requires refinement in adding features that affect the target variable, since the work investigated a sample of values in the normal operation of the station and there is no data on the applicability of the model in the event of an accident yet.

5   Conclusion

1. The paper describes the mechanism of predicting values using neural networks of long-term short-term memory LSTM. The technical formulations of the valves of the LSTM long–term short–term memory block are presented. Forget gate is a residual memory valve that allows the network to store certain information and forget other information; save gate is an addition valve that allows filtering incoming information in order to either delete or add it to long-term memory.; The attention gate is an attention gate that allows you to use only the necessary information from the entire block of long-term memory.
2. The algorithm of learning the simplest logical regression of the Sklearn library is presented on the example of two samples: training and test. The target variable was the concentration of sodium in saturated steam.
3. The error of predicting the concentration of sodium in saturated steam is calculated using the simplest logical regression – about 65%.
4. The long-term short-term LSTM network of the Keras library is trained, graphical results are presented. It is revealed that the model shows close values to the original ones. The maximum error is 0.80 and the minimum is 0.03.
5. Отмечено, It was noted that the LSTM network showed good convergence in the normal operation of the station, no studies of the network behavior in emergency situations were done within the framework of the work.
6. It is noted in the paper that in order to reduce the prediction error, it is necessary to refine the models: to introduce more than one feature on which the target variable depends, apply the reduction of the number of variables to the same scale, use a training sample of more data and reduce the number of rows with empty values.

Acknowledgments. The research was carried out at the expense of a grant from the Russian Science Foundation No. 22–29-20314, https://rscf.ru/project/22-29-20314/.

References

1. Larin, A.B.: Monitoring of the water-chemical regime of TPP power units with PSU.: Bulletin of IGEU, vol. 3, pp.14-18 (2013)
2. Kolegov, A.B.: Larin, B.M., Larin, A.B., Kozyulina, E.V.: Introduction of the system of automatic chemical control over the water–chemical regime of TPP. Bulletin of IGEU, vol. 4, pp. 5–19 (2011)
3. RD 153–34.1–37.532.4–2001 General technical requirements for systems of chemical and technological monitoring of water and chemical modes of thermal power plants (2001)
4. Mostofin, A.A.: Calculation of pH values and specific electrical conductivity of aqueous solutions of NH3 and CO2 Water treatment, water regime and chemical control at steam power plants, vol. 2, pp.178–187 (1966)
5. Maurer, H.: On-Line pH-Measurement by Differential Cation and Specific Conductivity. Presented at the 1997 International Chemistry On-Line Process Instrumentation Seminar in Clearwater Beach, VGB-R 450 L (1998)
6. Sampling and Physic-Chemical Monitoring of Water and Steam Cycles (VGB Power Tech Service GmbH, Essen, Germany) VGB-006–00–2012–09-EN (2012)
7. Lendi, M., Peter, H.W.: Wuhrmann pH calculation by differential conductivity measurement in mixtures of alkalization agents. Power Plant Chem. **16**(1), 1–8 (2014)
8. Kozyulina, E.V., Larin, B.M., Oparin, M.: Industrial tests of methods for calculating condensate impurities and feed water of the SVD drum boiler Bulletin of IGEU, vol. 1, pp. 47–51 (2002)
9. Larin, A.B., Larin, B.M., Savinov, M.P.: Computational determination of steam quality at power plants boilers for measuring electrical conductivity and pH. Teploenergetika **5**, 63–71 (2021)
10. Kotenkov, V.N., Tyapkov, V.F.: Application of neural network modeling for continuous monitoring of the pH of the NPP coolant. Teploenergetika **7**, 36–40 (2004)
11. Gotovtsev, P.M., Voronov, V.N.: Analysis of the state of the coolant using artificial neural networks. Teploenergetika **7**, 15–20 (2008)
12. Smetanin, D.S.: Analysis of various types of algorithms for finding the causes of violations of the water-chemical regime of thermal power plants. Water Treatment, Water Treatment, Water Supply **1**, 57–65 (2008)
13. Voronov, V.N., Nazarenko, P.N., Shmelev, A.G.: Modeling of the dynamics of the development of violations of the water-chemical regime by ionogenic impurities for steam generators PGV-1000. Heat Power Eng. **11**, 37–42 (1993)
14. Voronov, V.N., Petrova, T.I., Nazarenko, P.N.: Mathematical models and their use in systems of chemical and technological monitoring of power plants. Heat power Engineering **4**, 51–53 (2005)
15. Voronov, V.N., Endrukhina, O.V.: Mathematical modeling of the water-chemical regime of thermal power plants in non-stationary conditions. Teploenergetika **7**, 63–66 (2003)
16. Endrukhina, O.V., Voronov, V.N., Nazarenko, P.N.: Analysis of the efficiency of using the chemical and technological monitoring system on the example of the Cherepetskaya GRES. Teploenergetika **8**, 17–20 (2006)
17. Voronov, V.N., Egoshina, O.V.: Mathematical model of impurity distribution along the power unit path for chemical and technological monitoring systems. New Russ. Electric Power Ind. **10**, 28–33 (2008)
18. Lukashov, M.: Electrolytic method of forecasting the zone of deposition of coolant admixtures in steam generators of thermal power plants and nuclear power plants. Safety of life. Environmental protection: Mezhvuz. sb. scientific. Tr, vol. 8, pp. 82–83 (2004)

19. Kokoshkin, I.A.: Determination of hydrogen dissolved in water for corrosion control of equipment of thermal power plants: Diss. for the degree of Candidate of Sciences (1968)
20. Kritsky, V.G., Berezina, I.G., Gavrilov, A.V.: Modeling of corrosion products migration in the II circuit of NPP with VVER-1200. Teploenergetika **4**, 72–81 (2016)
21. Gafarov, F.M., Galimyanov, A.F. Artificial neural networks and their applications, Nejron-GafGal.pdf (kpfu.ru). Accessed 23 Oct 2022
22. Classification of neural networks, studfile.net. Accessed 23 Oct 2022
23. Barsky, A.B.: Neural networks: recognition, management, decision-making. Moscow (2004)
24. Galushkin, A.I., Tsypkin, Ya.Z.: Neural networks: the history of theory development : a textbook for universities. Moscow (2001)
25. Osovsky, S.: Neural networks for information processing. Moscow (2004)
26. Recurrent Neural Network, helenkapatsa.ru. Accessed 23 Oct 2022
27. Introduction to RNN Recurrent Neural Networks for Beginners, bookflow.ru. Accessed 23 Oct 2022
28. Recurrent blocks of GRU. An example of their implementation in the sentimental analysis proproprogs.ru. Accessed 23 Oct 2022
29. Recurrent neural networks for time series forecasting: current state and directions for the future, arxiv.org. Accessed 23 Oct 2022

Using Ensemble Machine Learning Methods for Regional Forecasting of Geocryological Manifestations (on the Example of the European North-East of Russia)

Tatiana Zengina⑩, Vladimir Baranov⑩, Sergey Kirillov(✉)⑩, and Mikhail Slipenchuk⑩

Lomonosov Moscow State University, 1, Leninskie Gory, Moscow 119991, Russia
eco-msu@mail.ru

Abstract. An algorithm is proposed and the results of ensemble machine learning are presented for the purposes of spatiotemporal forecasting of thermokarst processes in the Bolshezemelskaya tundra. Open georeferenced data were used: the Arctic Circumpolar Distribution and Soil Carbon of Thermokarst Landscapes project of the Oak Ridge National Laboratory; bioclimatic current and predicted variables of the WorldClim database, digital elevation model. The GIS QGIS 3.16.4, Jupyter Notebook software, Python 3.9 programming language, R-Studio (R 4.1.1) development software with the Biomod2 platform installed were used in the work. An algorithm for pre-preparation of initial raster and vector data is described, the choice of modeling parameters that are most significant for the development of thermokarst is substantiated, and an SRC model is built. To train the model, out of the number of algorithms built into Biomod2, 4 algorithms were used: generalized linear model (GLM), generalized additive model (GAM), generalized boosting method (GBM), random forest (RF). Based on these algorithms, ensemble modeling was carried out. The results of predicting thermokarst activation for 2040 for ensemble models were visualized and prepared for further mapping. The predicted directions of changes in thermokarst manifestations by 2040 are determined and visualized based on the SRC (species range change) algorithm built into the BIOMOD_RangeSize function. This made it possible to distinguish 4 types of territories where: there are no thermokarst manifestations now and will not be in 2040; will proceed without changes in comparison with the current situation; will be activated; will fade away.

Keywords: Thermokarst Manifestations · Bolshezemelskaya Tundra · Spatio-Temporal Forecasting · Ensemble Methods of Machine Learning · Biomod2 Platform · Species Range Change (SRC) Algorithm

1 Introduction

At present, the economic development of the North, which is primarily associated with the development of raw materials, faces a number of geoecological problems, many

A. Gibadullin (Ed.): ITIDMS 2022, CCIS 1821, pp. 109–121, 2023.
https://doi.org/10.1007/978-3-031-31353-0_10

of which arise due to the specifics of the northern nature and are often exacerbated by modern climate trends, which, among other things, contribute to the activation of thermokarst processes.

Thermokarst is a cryogenic physical-mechanical thermal process of uneven subsidence of soils and underlying rocks, associated with the thawing of underground ice of various genesis and the formation of sinkholes and subsidence forms above emerging voids [1]. Thermokarst is caused by an increase in temperature, melting of ice-bearing rocks and subsequent subsidence of the day surface due to water extrusion and rock compaction [2]. The development of thermokarst is most often dangerous, since it can proceed at a rate of 10–30 cm/year under normal conditions and accelerate to 1 m/year under technogenic conditions [3]. The development of the process is often accompanied by thermal erosion and heaving, leading to gradual degradation of permafrost, changes in the area of frozen rocks, their temperature and thickness. This, in turn, creates serious problems for economic facilities due to changes in the engineering and geological conditions for the development of the territory [4]. Therefore, the study of regional features and trends in changes in geocryological conditions seems to be a very urgent task.

In this regard, the study of the modern dynamics of thermokarst processes, their speed and direction of development seems to be one of the most significant tasks, the solution of which can ensure the identification of potential zones of thermokarst activation in areas of economic development in order to make optimal and economically sound engineering solutions today when designing economic objects and objects of oil and gas infrastructure in the northern regions of the country [5]. These issues are especially relevant for the most actively developed regions of the European North-East of Russia, including the Bolshezemelskaya tundra.

Given the large areas occupied by permafrost and the need for spatial analysis and identification of places of possible manifestations of geocryological processes, the use of spatial analysis methods for these purposes, including those based on the use of geoinformation technologies in combination with computer modeling and geoinformation mapping methods, can be very effective.

The purpose of this study was to develop and test an algorithm for predictive geoinformation modeling of thermokarst manifestations by 2040 on the example of the territory of the Bolshezemelskaya tundra (BZT), located in the Nenets Autonomous Okrug and in the northern part of the Komi Republic. The cryolithozone of the BZT is characterized by a complete set of zonal types of permafrost distribution, where the development of cryogenic processes can create serious problems for oil and gas and transport infrastructure facilities.

In the course of the study, it was necessary to:

– Get acquainted with the existing experience and methods of computer modeling of thermokarst processes and choose the most optimal one based on the available data;
– Select and analyze possible modeling parameters from among the most significant for the development of thermokarst processes;
– On the basis of free access data, form an appropriate geospatial database;
– To test the chosen technique and develop an algorithm for training the model;
– To carry out modeling and spatial forecast of thermokarst development for the next 20 years.

2 Materials and Methods

Materials. To select the main modeling parameters, an analysis of literary sources was carried out, which showed that among the main natural factors affecting the development of thermokarst processes, the most significant are: rock ice content, as well as neotectonic movements and relief features [2, 3].

Only open Internet data were used in the work. In view of the fact that the modeling results should be suitable for further mapping, georeferenced spatial data were selected that are most significant for the development of the process under study - climatic, bioclimatic and hypsometric. They were three types of data:

- A dataset on the current distribution of thermokarst landscapes in the northern circumpolar permafrost zone;
- A set of bioclimatic variables presented in the WorldClim global weather and climate database;
- Digital elevation model SRTM. Let's consider them in more detail.

I. Data on the current distribution of thermokarst landscapes within the BZT were taken from the Arctic Circumpolar Distribution and Soil Carbon of Thermokarst Landscapes project [6]. Project materials are presented on the website of the Center for Distributed Active Archives of the Oak Ridge National Laboratory, which is part of the NASA Earth Observation System Data and Information System Center (https:// daac.ornl.gov/about/). The project defines thermokarst landscapes as "landscapes where thermokarst landforms are currently present or may develop." In addition to assessing the content of organic carbon in the soil, the set provides a territorial assessment of three types of thermokarst landscapes (lake, wetland, slope) as of 2015. In addition, all thermokarst landscapes were assessed by the level of regional coverage and divided into five classes from zero to very high:

- Very high (60–100% of regional coverage);
- High (30–60%);
- Medium (10–30%);
- Low (1–10%);
- Zero (0–1%).

An important argument in favor of choosing this particular dataset was the fact that the regional distribution of thermokarst landscapes within this project was obtained based on modeling using 6 layers of spatial circumpolar data describing key landscape characteristics: permafrost zoning (isolated, sporadic, discontinuous or continuous), ground ice content (<10%, 10–20%, or >20%), sediment thickness, terrestrial ecoregion (boreal or tundra), terrain (flat, hilly, hilly, or mountainous/ragged), and landscape coverage (<10%, 10–30% or >30%). As a result of the intersection of these layers, 1 polygonal layer was obtained in the form of a shape-file (.shp), containing more than 130 thousand polygons [6].

From the data set described above, we used only information on thermokarst lake landscapes corresponding to the column of the attribute table of the TKThLP (Lake thermokarst terrain coverage) layer. The abundance of thermokarst lakes is a characteristic landscape feature of the study area. Within the BZT, it is thermokarst lakes that predominate, which determine the specificity of the tundra and forest-tundra landscapes of the region [7].

II. The set of bioclimatic variables featured in the WorldClim global weather and climate database is a georeferenced, high-resolution raster mapping of weather and climate indicators around the world, provided by climate modeling groups and the Earth System Grid Federation (ESGF) on the worldclim website.org. 2 types of data are presented - for the so-called historical conditions (i.e. close to current) and for future (predicted) conditions.

The current (historical) climate data WorldClim version 2.1 (v2) refers to the years 1970–2000 and became available in January 2020. They were formed with the support of a grant from the Geospatial and Agricultural Systems Consortium of the Sustainable Intensification Innovation Laboratory Feed the Future [8].

Future (ie predicted) climate data are CMIP6 (Coupled Model Intercomparison Projects) forecasts of future climate. CMIP6 represents a significant expansion over CMIP5 in terms of the number of modeling teams involved and the number of future scenarios considered. For 23 global climate models, the lowest temperature, highest temperature, and precipitation variables for each month were processed. The calculation was also carried out for four general scenarios of socio-economic development of mankind SSP (socio economic pathways): 126, 245, 370 and 585. In our work, we used the SSP-126 scenario with low radiative forcing by the end of the century, which likely future paths and depicts the "best case" for the future in terms of sustainable development. Monthly values were calculated as average values over 20 years, for different periods: 2021–2040, 2041–2060, 2061–2080, 2081–2100.

The data sets provide 19 bioclimatic variables. However, since thermokarst is attributed to the processes of the summer period, out of all those proposed by us, 6 variables were selected, reflecting the climatic features, primarily of the summer period, as well as average annual indicators (Table 1). The data is available in four spatial resolutions ranging from 30 s to 10 min and is presented in GeoTiff (.tif) format. In our work, we used data with a resolution of 2.5 min for the period 2021–2040.

III. Publicly available SRTM data obtained by the Shuttle Radar Topography Mission (SRTM) and aggregated to 30 arcseconds were used as a digital elevation model (DEM).

Of course, the data set used in the work for modeling such a complex process as thermokarst is very limited. However, in the framework of our study, such an assumption is possible, since when creating the layer we used on the distribution of thermokarst landscapes, we used 6 layers of spatial data that describe the key characteristics of thermokarst landscapes. This partially compensates for the absence in our modeling of a number of parameters that determine the development of thermokarst processes.

Methods. In recent years, many works, both domestic and foreign, have been devoted to the issues of the possibility of using computer simulation to study and predict the development of thermokarst processes. At the same time, many authors point out the difficulty of implementing this type of research, since modeling of the thermokarst process is complicated by the lack of a single mathematical model of thermokarst,

Table 1. Bioclimatic variables of the WorldClim global weather and climate database selected for modeling.

Variable	Meaning
BIO1	Mean annual temperature
BIO5	Maximum temperature of the warmest month
BIO7	Annual temperature range (BIO5-BIO6)
BIO10	Average temperature of the warmest quarter
BIO12	Annual precipitation
BIO18	Precipitation of the warmest quarter

which describes the process from the moment of its inception to attenuation, as well as by the close relationship between engineering and geocryological processes [9].

The analysis of publications has shown that there are some differences between Russian and foreign methods for solving the problem. The Russian experience is largely based on the classical probabilistic approach to modeling [10–12]. In foreign countries, in addition to classical approaches, there is a tendency to use various software, in the structure of which the most popular computer modeling methods based on machine learning algorithms are implemented [13–15].

Thus, an interesting approach was used in 2021 by Chinese specialists [13] in a work devoted to machine learning modeling of the exposure to thermokarst landslides in the permafrost region on the Qinghai-Tibet Plateau. The authors solve the problem of assessing spatially appropriate environmental conditions for the development of thermokarst landslides based on the application of several machine learning algorithms and their combination for multiple ensemble modeling. The selected and mathematically justified machine learning algorithms were implemented by them in the R software environment based on the Biomod2 platform. The modeling results were then transferred to the ArcGIS GIS package, where forecast maps were further built.

The Biomod2 modeling computer platform is an updated version of the BIOMOD package, which was originally designed for ensemble prediction of species distribution, i.e. allows you to study and model the distribution of species using several methods in various environmental conditions. BIOMOD is implemented in the R environment and is a free and open source package. The updated version of Biomod2 offers the ability to run 10 state-of-the-art modeling techniques to describe and predict the relationship between a species and its habitat. Although it was mainly developed for solving problems in the field of ecology, Biomod2, like BIOMOD, can be used to model almost any data, depending on any associated and determining variables [13, 16]. Based on this information, it was decided to try out Biomod2 for our thermokarst problem.

In addition, taking into account the features of the set of materials used by us, which included both vector and raster data, it was also decided to use as the basic software:

– The free geographic information system QGIS 3.16.4 with GRASS 7.8.5 with open source, distributed under the GNU General Public License (Hannover), in which vector

and raster layers were prepared for further modeling, all calculations were carried out, and cartographic visualization of the modeling results was carried out;
- Jupyter Notebook software for interactive calculations using the Python 3.9 programming language;
- Software development environment R-Studio (R 4.1.1) with the Biomod2 platform installed, in which the simulation was carried out.

The proposed methodological approach for solving the problem in question includes two stages. The first one was the development of the technique on materials with a relatively low spatial resolution of 10 min, within which machine learning algorithms were mastered for processing heterogeneous data (vector, tabular, raster). The second stage is the process of the final predictive modeling of the dynamics of the development of thermokarst manifestations for 2040, which was carried out according to the already tested methodology on higher resolution data of 2.5 min.

3   Results

The implementation of the proposed predictive modeling algorithm began with the preparation of the initial data.

When preparing raster layers with bioclimatic data and a layer with relief data in the QGIS 3.16.4 GIS package, the layers were first cut along the boundary of the study area using the ClipMultipleLayers plugin.

The vector layer with data on the modern distribution of thermokarst landscapes Circumpolar_Thermokarst_Landscapes was also cut in the QGIS-3.16 program along the border of the study area. Then the geometry of the objects contained in it was corrected. Next, the layer objects were converted to centroids (Vector → Geometry Tools → Centroids), and the layer itself was saved in CSV (comma-separated values) format for presentation in a tabular format. It should be noted that when using data with a resolution of 10 min, the coverage of the study area by informative pixels immediately amounted to 99%. However, when working with data with a resolution of 2.5 min, additional steps were required to create additional points inside the polygons for more complete coverage, for which the Random points in polygons algorithm was used (Vector → Research Tools → Random points in polygons). This allowed, when loading data into R-studio, to increase the coverage of the territory up to 90% instead of 40–50%.

Next, the resulting table in CSV format was loaded into the Jupyter Notebook software, which made it possible to use the Python 3.9 programming language. With its help, all columns with unnecessary data were removed from the table and only information about the presence of thermokarst in lake thermokarst terrain coverage (TKThLP - Lake thermokarst terrain coverage), as well as data on coordinates (LATITUDE and LONGITUDE) was left. The following code was used for this:

```
data=data.loc[:,data.columns.intersection(['TKThLP','LATITUDE','LONGITUDE'])]
```

Then, since this work did not take into account the degree of activation of the development of thermokarst lakes in the landscape, but only the presence (presences) or absence (absences) of thermokarst lakes was taken into account, for further modeling it was necessary to convert the data to the boolean (true/false) format, i.e. e. into a format indicating whether a natural phenomenon is present or absent at a given point. For this, the values of the 'TKThLP' columns in the table were converted based on the five values presented - 'None', 'Low', 'Very High', 'Moderate', 'High'. If the value was 'None' it was set to zero, any other value was set to one. This was implemented with code:

```
data.loc[data['TKThLP'] == 'None', 'TKThLP'] = 0
data.loc[data['TKThLP'] == 'Low', 'TKThLP'] = 1
data.loc[data['TKThLP'] == 'Moderate', 'TKThLP'] = 1
data.loc[data['TKThLP'] == 'High', 'TKThLP'] = 1
data.loc[data['TKThLP'] == 'Very High', 'TKThLP'] = 1
```

After that, using the appropriate code, all values \u200b\u200bthat are not equal to one were removed:

```
data = data.drop(data[data['TKThLP'] !== 1].index)
```

Thus, a converted tabular file with data on the distribution of thermokarst lakes in CSV format was obtained and finally saved.

The next necessary stage of the work was to check the parameters selected for the modeling process for multicollinearity using the Pearson coefficient, which is measured on a scale from $+1$ (positive correlation - an increase in one factor on a par with another) to 0 and -1 (negative correlation - a decrease in one factor and an increase in another). Multicollinearity negatively affects simulation results and model training. Analysis of the Pearson correlation matrix between bioclimatic variables and elevation variable showed that there is a positive correlation $> = 0.9$ between bio_5 and bio_10, as well as between bio_18 and bio_12, which indicates the presence of multicollinearity. There are several methods to combat this phenomenon, one of which is the standard removal of one of the features. However, BIOMOD2, on the basis of which the simulation will be carried out, offers a choice of several machine learning algorithms, one of which is RF (random forest), which is considered a multicollinearity resistant algorithm. Ensemble modeling also solves this problem.

Next, the model was trained. The data of the current state of thermokarst manifestations were used as a training sample. First, the transformed layer of thermokarst lakes was loaded into R-Studio to select the machine learning algorithms built into Biomod2. Of all the possible methods, four machine learning methods were chosen: generalized linear model (GLM), generalized additive model (GAM), generalized boosting method (GBM), random forest (RF). The last two are ensemble modeling methods and combine multiple classification trees to form a single model with improved prediction accuracy. These machine learning algorithms work well with this kind of natural data, which is confirmed in the publications of many researchers [13, 15, 17–18].

Individual parameters were configured for each algorithm:

```
termo_opt <-
BIOMOD_ModelingOptions(
GLM = list(type = 'quadratic', interaction.level = 1),
GBM = list(n.trees = 1000),
GAM = list(algo = 'GAM_mgcv'))
```

For each individual algorithm, these parameters are standard. The value of the number of main runs was set to two. The training of the model took about 6 h.

4 Discussion

The calculation of the performance metrics for each of the four machine learning algorithms showed that the RF (random forest) algorithm worked best due to its resistance to multicollinearity.

The assessment of natural factors carried out after that showed that in most cases all of them really influence the modeling of the dynamics of the development of thermokarst processes (Table 2). For example, for most algorithms (except RF), such natural factors as bio 18 (precipitation of the warmest quarter) and elev (height) turned out to be influencing in >50% of cases.

Table 2. Estimates of the influence of natural factors for each individual algorithm.

	GLM	GBM	RF	GAM
BIO_1	0.4936667	0.01600000	0.14900000	0.4540000
BIO_5	0.3743333	0.00000000	0.08733333	0.2470000
BIO_7	0.7586667	0.03766667	0.10100000	0.5233333
BIO_10	0.6063333	0.23366667	0.16066667	0.7393333
BIO_12	0.4713333	0.02400000	0.14666667	0.2980000
BIO_18	0.8726667	0.07666667	0.28133333	0.5870000
ELEV	0.6370000	0.76033333	0.28266667	0.4526667

This was also confirmed by the analysis of the constructed response curves of variables (predictors) for the RF model. A detailed examination of each predictor revealed the following:

– For BIO_1 (average annual temperature) the highest percentage of response is in the range from −6 to −3°
– For BIO_7 (annual temperature range) the highest response percentage is between 37 and 45°

- When the BIO_10 predictor value (the average temperature of the warmest quarter) $>=$ 10°, the response value drops sharply
- With the predictor value BIO_18 (precipitation of the warmest quarter) $>=$ 195° the response value drops sharply
- The ELEVATION predictor shows that at an altitude of >200 m, the impact on the activation of the development of thermokarst lakes drops sharply.

To improve the results of all algorithms, ensemble learning was carried out. In statistics and machine learning, ensemble methods use several learning algorithms to obtain higher predictive performance than could be obtained using any of the constituent learning algorithms alone [19]. Empirically, ensembles tend to give better results when the models differ significantly. Thus, many ensemble methods take into account the advantages of each individual model learning algorithm that they combine [20]. In our case, all the models used were selected for ensemble learning, since all of them have TSS (true skill statistics) metric values greater than 0.6.

The next step in modeling the forecast of the activation of thermokarst processes was the creation of mathematical forecasts of the current situation and the situation for 2040.

The current situation was projected using BIOMOD_Projection for each of the 4 machine learning algorithms and using BIOMOD_EnsembleForecasting for the ensemble learning model.

To predict the situation in 2040, a raster layer was loaded containing selected bioclimatic variables (BIO5, BIO10, BIO 2, BIO18) corresponding to the future climate predicted in the CMIP6 project under the ssp126 scenario [21]. In R-studio, this layer was divided into 4 raster layers, each of which corresponded to its own bioclimatic variable. Further, the rasters corresponding to the hypsometric parameters of the territory (elevation_data) were selected.

The result of mathematical prediction of thermokarst manifestations for ensemble models is shown in Fig. 1, in which the color scale corresponds to the calculation of the probability of formation of thermokarst lakes, multiplied by 10. Then the results were visualized in the QGIS program in the form of a map.

The next step was to determine changes in the distribution of thermokarst manifestations by 2040 based on the SRC (species range change) algorithm built into the BIOMOD_RangeSize function, which is defined as a change in the limits of the distribution of a natural phenomenon, usually along vertical or latitudinal gradients [22]. To calculate this algorithm, we used forecasts of the dynamics of thermokarst lake landscapes for 2040, created based on the results of ensemble modeling (according to the characteristics ca - commute average and wm - weighted mean). After working out the algorithm, a bitmap file was obtained with the values: −2, −1, 0, 1.

This made it possible to distinguish 4 types of territories: 1) territories where there are no thermokarst manifestations now and will not be in 2040; 2) where they will proceed without changes in comparison with the current situation; 3) where they will be activated; 4) where they will fade away. The interpretation of these values for the studied natural phenomenon is presented in Table 3.

Next, a color palette was created and the result was visualized for both variants of ensemble modeling (ca, wm). An example of visualization for ensemble modeling ca

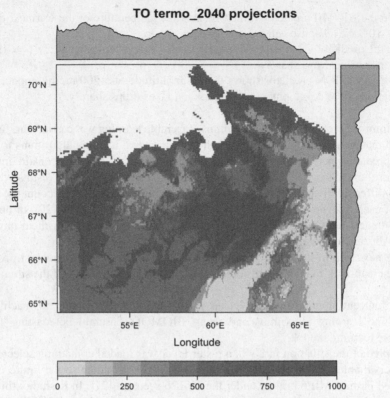

Fig. 1. Visualization of the results of mathematical prediction of thermokarst manifestations for an ensemble of models.

Table 3. Interpretation of the obtained results of the work of the SRC function to determine the change in the limits of the distribution of thermokarst manifestations.

Number	Meaning
−2	lost (draining and drying out)
−1	pres (stable state without change)
0	abs (absence before and in 2040)
1	gain (formation of new ones in 2040)

- commute average is shown in Fig. 2. The image obtained with further visualization in the QGIS GIS program makes it possible to compare the modeling results with the boundaries of the geocryological subzones of the BZT and the locations of areas of active economic development, for which the activation of thermokarst can pose a serious threat.

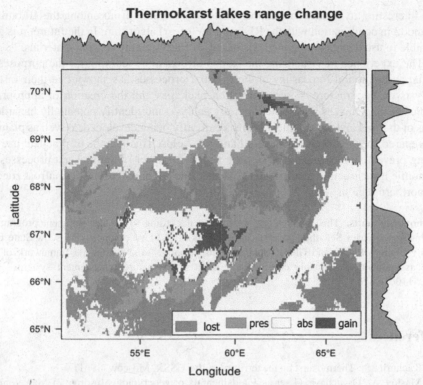

Fig. 2. Visualization of the results of the SRC algorithm based on Biomod2 (ca - commute average).

5 Conclusion

The use of the ensemble machine learning method based on the Biomod2 computer modeling platform for the purposes of spatial and temporal forecasting of geocryological manifestations on the example of the Bolshezemelskaya tundra showed that the proposed and tested algorithm can be used quite effectively, including for predicting the development of thermokarst manifestations.

However, it seems quite obvious that the obtained simulation results can be improved. This can be realized by improving the spatial resolution and expanding the number of bioclimatic variables used in the model, as well as by using a larger number of non-climatic series parameters, such as the background temperature of permafrost, the depth of seasonal thawing, soil ice content, vegetation cover features, etc. This will significantly optimize the model and increase the reliability of the results.

The machine learning algorithms we used in the R software environment based on the Biomod2 platform included four selected machine learning methods: GLM, GAM, GBM, and Random Forest (RF). The calculation of the efficiency metrics for each of the four algorithms showed that the RF (random forest) algorithm worked best due to its resistance to multicollinearity. The accuracy of the TSS and ROC metrics for the RF model was > 0.9, for the other tested algorithms this value reached a maximum of 0.7.

It is interesting to expand the number of used algorithms from among the 10 built-in Biomod2 in combination with the RF (random forest) algorithm. In the future, it is also possible to use deep learning methods based on Earth remote sensing materials.

The experience of visualizing the results of ensemble learning for the purposes of spatial and temporal forecasting of thermokarst processes has shown that their further analysis in the structure of geoinformation packages and the creation of appropriate predictive maps makes it possible to jointly analyze and identify potentially hazardous areas of thermokarst development in areas currently being developed, as well as planned or prepared for the development of oil and gas fields. This may be of practical use for taking preventive measures to reduce the negative impact of thermokarst processes on economic infrastructure facilities in the areas of development of the permafrost zone in the northern regions.

Acknowledgments. This research was performed according to the Development program of the Interdisciplinary Scientific and Educational School of M.V.Lomonosov Moscow State University "Future Planet and Global Environmental Change" and within the framework of the state assignment "Sustainable development of territorial nature management systems" (No 121051100162-6).

References

1. Kachurin, S.: Thermokarst on the territory of the USSR. Moscow (1961)
2. Maslov, A., Osadchaya, G., et al: Fundamentals of geocryology. Institute of Management, Information and Business, Ukhta (2005)
3. Tumel, N., Zotova, L.: Geoecology of permafrost. Faculty of Geography, Moscow State University, Moscow (2014)
4. Osadchaya, G., Zengina, T.: Opportunities for balanced use of the biosphere and resource potential of the Bolshezemelskaya tundra. Cryosphere Earth **16**(2), 43–51 (2012)
5. Zengina, T., Osadchaya, G., Parada, N.: Biospheric functions of the permafrost zone of the Timan-Pechora oil and gas province under conditions of industrial development. Bulletin of the Peoples' Friendship University of Russia. Ecol. Life Saf. Ser. **3**, 32–38 (2011)
6. Olefeldt, D., Goswami, G., Grosse, D., et al.: Arctic Circumpolar Distribution and Soil Carbon of Thermokarst Landscapes, 2015. ORNL DAAC, Oak Ridge, Tennessee, USA (2016)
7. Kravtsova, V.: Distribution of thermokarst lakes in Russia within the modern permafrost zone. Bull. Moscow Univ. Geogr. Ser. **3**, 33–42 (2009)
8. Fick, S., Hijmans, R.: WorldClim 2: new 1 km spatial resolution climate surfaces for global land areas. Int. J. Climatol. **37**(12), 4302–4315 (2017)
9. Khabibullin, I., Lobastova, S., et al.: Modeling the thermokarst process. Bull. Bashkir Univ. **1**, 21–24 (2007)
10. Viktorov, A., Kapralova, V., Arkhipova, M.: Modeling the development of the morphological structure of erosion-thermokarst plains using remote sensing data. Earth Explor. Space **2**, 55–64 (2019)
11. Polishchuk, V., Polishchuk, Y.: Geosimulation modeling of fields of thermokarst lakes in permafrost zones. Khanty-Mansiysk (2013)
12. Kapralova, V., Viktorov, A.: Quantitative patterns of changes in the size of thermokarst lakes and risk assessment. Sergeev Readings **15**, 437–442 (2013)

13. Yin, G., Luo, J., Niu, F., Lin, Z., Liu, M.: Machine learning-based thermokarst landslide susceptibility modeling across the permafrost region on the Qinghai-Tibet Plateau. Landslides **18**(7), 2639–2649 (2021). https://doi.org/10.1007/s10346-021-01669-7

14. Huang, L., Liu, L., Jiang, L., Zhang, T.: Automatic mapping of thermokarst landforms from remote sensing images using deep learning: a case study in the Northeastern Tibetan Plateau. Remote Sens. **10**, 2067 (2018)

15. Nitze, I., Cooley, S., Duguay, C., Jones, B., Grosse, G.: The catastrophic thermokarst lake drainage events of 2018 in North Western Alaska: fast-forward into the future. Cryosphere **14**, 4279–4297 (2020)

16. Thuiller, W., Lafourcade, B., Engler, R., Araujo, M.: BIOMOD-a platform for ensemble forecasting of species distributions. Ecography **32**, 369–373 (2009)

17. Guisan, A., Thuiller, W., Zimmermann, N.: The Biomod2 Modeling Package Examples. In: Habitat Suitability and Distribution Models: With Applications in R (Ecology, Biodiversity and Conservation), pp. 357–400. Cambridge University Press, Cambridge (2017).

18. Wood, S.: Fast stable restricted maximum likelihood and marginal likelihood estimation of semiparametric generalized linear models. J. R. Stat. Soc. B **73**, 3–36 (2011)

19. Opitz, D., Maclin, R.: Popular ensemble methods: an empirical study. J. Artif. Intell. Res. **11**, 169–198 (1999)

20. Kuncheva, L., Whitaker, C.: Measures of diversity in classifier ensembles. Mach. Learn. **51**, 181–207 (2003)

21. Ziehn, T., Chamberlain, M., Lenton, A., et al.: CSIRO ACCESS-ESM1.5 model output prepared for CMIP6 C4MIP. Earth System Grid Federation (2019)

22. Thuiller, W., Georges, D., Engler, R.: Biomod2: Ensemble platform for species distribution modelling (2014)

Deghosting Diffusion Model for Facial Attribute Editing via Differential Activations

Chongyu Gu$^{(\boxtimes)}$ and Maxim Gromov

Tomsk State University, Tomsk, Russia
chongyugu@gmail.com

Abstract. Deghosting networks aim to eliminate the unavoidable ghosting effect for facial attribute editing via differential activations. Existing deghosting networks are based on GAN priors that combine the features of a pretrained Style-GAN generator with a decoder to generate the target images. However, these methods cannot effectively remove the ghosting effect and may produce other artifacts. In order to solve the above problems, we suggest a novel deghosting diffusion model that employs a conditional diffusion model to restore ghosting images to the face distribution, effectively eliminating ghosting. Experimental results outperform state-of-the-art facial attribute editing methods at a resolution of 256×256 in both qualitative and quantitative evaluations.

Keywords: Deghosting Networks · Diffusion Models · Facial Attribute Editing

1 Introduction

Facial attribute editing seeks to change desired facial attributes in images while preserving other information. It has traditionally been a major focus of face generation. Recently, StyleGAN encoders [18, 28], have achieved promising results because their feature pyramid networks enable them to generate feature maps and style vectors at various feature levels. Alaluf et al. [1] propose using an iterative refinement process to improve the effectiveness of encoder-based inversion techniques for generating real images. To some extent, facial attribute editing demonstrates the ability of deep learning for face data augmentation.

Despite advances, such approaches rely on low-bit-rate latent codes, which make it hard to keep high-fidelity details in edited images. Since late last year, researchers have been trying to enable attribute editing with well-preserved image-specific details. Wang et al. [26] present a distortion consultation method that uses a distortion map to obtain a high-rate latent map and combines it with a basic low-rate latent code using consultation fusion in the generator. This process results in a high-fidelity reconstruction. To improve the alignment between the edited image and the inverted one, the authors introduce an adaptive distortion alignment (ADA) module, which is trained using a self-supervised scheme. Instead of creating a distortion map between the source image and the initial reconstruction, Dinh et al. [5] fuse the intermediate features of the input and the reconstruction into a single feature tensor, then use a set of hypernetworks to

A. Gibadullin (Ed.): ITIDMS 2022, CCIS 1821, pp. 122–133, 2023.
https://doi.org/10.1007/978-3-031-31353-0_11

generate residual weights for the convolutional layers in the generator. This process helps to recover information lost during inversion.

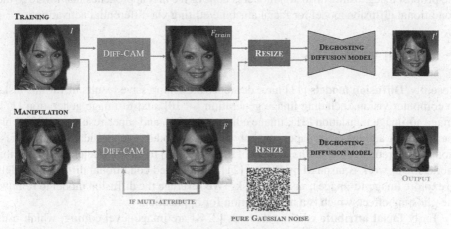

Fig. 1. The training and image manipulation pipeline of our model. During training, the original images and the ghost images are given to the deghosting diffusion model in pairs. During editing, the inputs are the ghosting images and pure Gaussian noise.

Even though the generator can recover some image-specific details, they become blurry and lose their original shape. Song et al. [25] suggest using a differential activation module to find the range of the editing-relevant region and combine the manipulated area with the original image. With the Diff-CAM mask, the parts that do not matter for editing can be saved, but there will always be a ghosting effect [25] around the edges of the editing area. In a way that is like earlier research, the authors use a deghosting network that combines an encoder-decoder network with a pretrained StyleGAN generator [13, 14]. The features of the pretrained StyleGAN generator are combined with the decoder to decompose the target image. There are three types of loss functions in the deghosting network: adversarial loss, MSE loss, and perceptual loss.

Although using the differential activation module is an effective strategy to preserve the non-editing areas, the aforementioned deghosting networks are prone to losing image-specific details that overlap the edge of the edited part. For example, (1) they are the ears and earrings when the upper face is activated; (2) they are the fingers and microphone when the lower face is activated. Moreover, the method based on feature map sharing with a pretrained StyleGAN generator has a certain probability of producing other artifacts in the background.

To address these issues, we propose a deghosting diffusion model to remove the ghosting effect for the methods via differential activations. As shown in Fig. 1, we adopt a pretrained Diff-CAM network to detect editing-related areas and combine the editing area of manipulation with the original images to generate the target images with the ghosting effect. After that, we utilize our deghosting diffusion model to remove artifacts and generate target images that conform to the face distribution.

The experimental results on the first 1,000 images from CelebA-HQ show that our method achieves the best results in both qualitative and quantitative analysis of facial attribute editing at 256×256 pixel resolution. In particular, our model can remove more artifacts and preserve more details than previous methods. To the best of our knowledge, the proposed deghosting diffusion model is among the first approaches that leverage the conditional diffusion model for facial attribute editing via differential activations.

2 Related Work

Recently, **Diffusion models** [11] have demonstrated impressive results in various tasks in computer vision, including image generation [4, 10], text-to-image generation [17], image-to-image translation [21], image editing [16, 24], and super-resolution [22]. Furthermore, the authors of the paper [7] apply diffusion models to classification and regression. In theoretical research, the authors of the paper [15] focus on accelerating diffusion models. Our work is inspired by Palette [21], which used conditional diffusion models to explore image-to-image translation tasks. We leverage the diffusion model to remove the ghosting effect, which is a new direction for application.

Early **facial attribute editing** methods [3, 8] are image-level editing, which uses adversarial loss to train the generator and discriminator from scratch for each attribute. Since attributes are differentiated by 0 or 1, they cannot offer continuous attribute editing.

Latent-level editing refers to GAN inversion approaches that first invert an original image into a latent vector z and then edit the vector to change the attribute. Lastly, they add the latent vector to a pretrained StyleGAN generator to reconstruct the image. These methods can be grouped into three categories: optimization-based [27, 30], learning-based [1, 5, 18, 26, 28], and hybrid [2, 19]. The optimization-based approaches are slow due to the need to optimize the reconstruction loss on each image, but they ensure good image reconstruction quality. The learning-based methods, in contrast, use datasets to train an encoder network. The encoder makes it possible to convert any image into a latent code to offer fast inversion. Hybrid methods combine the two methods mentioned above.

Richardson, Elad, et al. [18] introduce a feature pyramid pSp encoder that embeds images into an extended W^+ space. Alaluf et al. [1] suggest an iterative refinement process for image inversion. To better preserve image details, Wang et al. [26] propose using a distortion consultation inversion method to recover ignored image details. Instead of making a distortion map, Dinh et al. [5] suggest fusing the intermediate features. However, these methods make details blurry and lose their original shape due to the combination of feature maps and pretrained StyleGAN generators.

Song et al. [25] suggest using a differential activation module to find the editing-relevant region and combining the manipulated area with the original image, then using an encoder-decoder-like network to remove unavailable ghosting. Their deghosting network is also a way to share weights between the pre-trained generator and decoder that cannot effectively remove the ghosting effect and may produce other artifacts in the preserved content. We aim to solve this problem by using a conditional diffusion model.

Diffusion models and generative adversarial networks (GANs) [6] are both powerful techniques in the field of generative modeling, but there are several advantages of diffusion models over GANs:

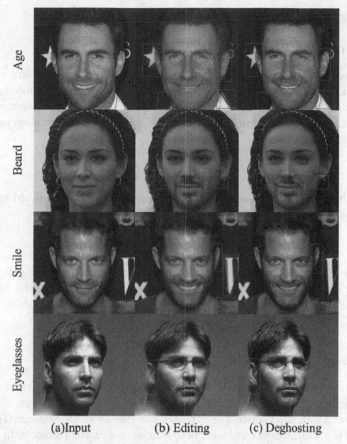

Fig. 2. Deghosting diffusion model effectively removes the ghosting effect while preserving image-specific details.

- No need for a discriminator: GANs require a discriminator network to distinguish between real and generated samples, which can be computationally expensive and difficult to train. Diffusion models do not require a discriminator, which simplifies the training process.
- Improved stability: GANs are notorious for their instability during training, which can make them difficult to work with. Diffusion models, on the other hand, have been shown to be much more stable and reliable.
- More interpretable: Diffusion models are based on well-understood physical processes, which makes them more interpretable than GANs. This can be important in applications where interpretability is critical, such as scientific simulations or medical imaging.

3   Deghosting Diffusion Model

3.1   Prepare the Training Dataset

As mentioned in Sect. 1, the differential activation module is an efficient method for detecting editing-relevant regions. However, when the edited area is combined with the original image, there will be an unavoidable ghosting effect. To begin with, we utilized the pretrained Diff-CAM to generate a ghosting image dataset. The training image F_{train} is generated using the formula:

$$F_{\text{train}} = T \odot M_{\text{train}} + I \odot (1 - M_{\text{train}}),$$ (1)

where I is the original image and T is the edited inversion. The Diff-CAM mask M_{train} is defined using the following formula, as outlined in [25]:

$$M_{\text{train}}(i, j) = 1 - M_{\text{Diff-CAM}}(i, j), \text{ if } M_{\text{Diff-CAM}}(i, j) > 0.5.$$ (2)

The goal is to preserve the ghosting part of the combined image to the greatest extent, while other parts use the original image as the dominant. So far, we have our training dataset, a dataset of image pairs—the original images and their corresponding ones with ghosting.

3.2   Deghosting Network

Diffusion models involve two processes: forward diffusion and reverse denoising. Our proposed method is a conditional diffusion model, which not only performs denoising on samples from a standard Gaussian distribution but also on an input image. The form of our method is $p(y|x)$, where x and y are both images, e.g., x is an image with a ghosting effect, and y is a ghosting-free image. We utilize conditional diffusion models to restore the input image to the distribution of the face dataset, thus removing the ghosting effect.

Training: Following [10], given a ghosting-free image y_0, we generate a noisy target $\tilde{y}$ in one step by the following formula:

$$\tilde{y} = \sqrt{\gamma}y_0 + \sqrt{1 - \gamma}\epsilon, \epsilon \sim \mathcal{N}(0, I),$$ (3)

where $\gamma = \prod_{i=1}^{t} \alpha_i$, α_i are hyper-parameters of the noise schedule, and $t \sim \{0, ..., T\}$.

To reconstruct the target image y_0 from $\tilde{y}$. We use a U-Net structure f_θ [20] to predict the added noise vector ϵ. The denoising model $f_\theta(x, \tilde{y}, \gamma)$ takes as input the source image x, the noisy target image $\tilde{y}$, and a noise level indicator γ. The loss function is defined using the following formula:

$$E_{(x,y)}E_{\epsilon,\gamma} \|f_\theta(x, \underbrace{\sqrt{\gamma}y_0 + \sqrt{1 - \gamma}\epsilon}_{\tilde{y}}, \gamma) - \epsilon\|,$$ (4)

where $\epsilon \sim N(0, I)$, $\gamma \sim p(\gamma)$, and (x, y) is sampled from the training dataset. Following [21], to improve the stability of the model and reduce diversity, we use L_1 loss instead of L_2.

Inference: Since we set the prior distribution $p_{(y_T)}$ to approximate a normal distribution, the inference begins with pure Gaussian noise and the ghosting images, followed by T steps of iterative refinement. We use the trained network f_θ to fit the noise for extracting the target image from the concatenation of the noise and the ghosting image, so Eq. 3 can be rewritten as:

$$\hat{y}_0 = \frac{1}{\sqrt{\gamma_t}}\left(y_t - \sqrt{1 - \gamma_t}f_\theta(x, y_t, \gamma_t)\right). \tag{5}$$

Following [22], the parameterized mean and variance of $p_\theta(y_t - 1|y_t, x)$ is defined respectively as follows:

$$\mu_\theta(x, y_t, \gamma_t) = \frac{1}{\sqrt{\alpha_t}}\left(y_t - \frac{1 - \alpha_t}{\sqrt{1 - \gamma_t}}f_\theta(x, y_t, \gamma_t)\right), \tag{6}$$

$$\sigma^2 = 1 - \alpha_t. \tag{7}$$

With Eq. 6 and 7, each iteration of the reverse process is given by,

$$y_{t-1} \leftarrow \frac{1}{\sqrt{\alpha_t}}\left(y_t - \frac{1 - \alpha_t}{\sqrt{1 - \gamma_t}}f_\theta(x, y_t, \gamma_t)\right) + \sqrt{1 - \alpha_t}\epsilon_t, \tag{8}$$

where $\epsilon_t \sim N(0, I)$.

Architecture and Noise Schedule: Our model is like the U-Net found in [10]. We redesigned the network structure to suit our task at 256×256 resolution. We use a linear noise schedule. Our model randomly chooses a time step $t \sim 0, \ldots, T$ during the training process, then calculates γ_{t-1} and γ_t. (See Experiment 4.2 for all details.)

4 Experiment

4.1 Datasets and Evaluation Metrics

Flickr-Faces-HQ (FFHQ) [13] is a collection of 70,000 high-quality PNG images at 1024×1024 resolution, with a wide range of age, race, and image background. It also covers a broad range of accessories such as eyeglasses, sunglasses, and hats.

CelebA-HQ [12] is a well-known dataset of face attributes that includes 30,000 images at 1024×1024 resolution.

We train our model on full FFHQ. To assess the performance of our model in comparison to the existing works listed in Table 1. Quantitative comparison with state-of-the-art methods, we used the first 1,000 images from CelebA-HQ and applied standard metrics to evaluate them.

Following [25], we evaluate our model using two metrics: Fréchet inception distance (FID) [9] and Learned perceptual image patch similarity (LPIPS) [29]. The FID metric computes the distribution distance between the original and generated images, while the LPIPS metric calculates the perceptual similarity between the activations of two image patches. For both metrics, lower values indicate better performance.

Fig. 3. Qualitative evaluation using state-of-the-art facial attribute editing models. Our proposed model ensures efficient manipulation and preserves unedited image details.

4.2 Experimental Settings

Training Details: All experiments are performed using PyTorch on a PC with a Nvidia GeForce RTX 3090. Inputs and outputs of the deghosting diffusion model are represented as 256×256 RGB images. We train our model with a batch size of 8 for 3M training steps and use the checkpoint from 3M steps to report the final results. We use Adam as the optimizer, and fix the learning rate at $5e - 5$, $1e - 5$, and $5e - 6$ per 1M training steps, respectively. The dropout rate is set to 0.2.

Diffusion Hyper-Parameters: About the U-Net structure, we use a dimension of 64 for the first layer. The depth multipliers are $\{1, 2, 4, 8, 16\}$. The number of residual blocks is 2. The model's total parameters are 242M. $T = 2,000$ was set for both training and validation. In all our experiments, we use a linear noise schedule increasing from $\beta_1 = 1e - 6$ to $\beta_T = 1e - 2$.

Generating Ghosting Images: We follow [25], and generate the ghosting images dataset using pretrained Diff-CAM, then resize it to 256×256. The data consists of 70,000 images generated from FFHQ. The editing direction is randomly selected from 7 directions, i.e., "Beard", "Bushy eye- brows", "Eyeglasses", "Mouth open", "Narrow eyes", "Old", and "Smile". The mixing coefficient is set to 20.

(a) Input (b) Age (c) Beard (d) Eyebrows (e) Eyeglasses (f) Smile

Fig. 4. In comparison to the state-of-the-art model that uses a deghosting network, our method is better able to preserve the details of the same ghosting image.

4.3 Effect of Deghosting Diffusion Mode

In Fig. 1. The training and image manipulation pipeline of our model. During training, the original images and the ghost images are given to the deghosting diffusion model in pairs. During editing, the inputs are the ghosting images and pure Gaussian noise., we show the images before and after deghosting. Our deghosting diffusion model effectively removes ghosting produced by facial attribute editing via differential activations, while preserving background and image-specific details.

4.4 Compare to SOTA

We compare our model with the state-of-the-art methods mentioned in Sect. 1, i.e., Restyle [1], HFGI [26], and Editing out-of-domain GAN inversion [25]. Note that these methods all use the StyleGAN generator as the output module or part of it, so their outputs are all at 1024×1024 resolution. Except that the inference output of the HFGI official code is 256×256 pixels, we use official codes from GitHub and resize the output images to 256×256 using Bicubic with no other editing.

Table 1. Quantitative comparison with state-of-the-art methods

	Restyle	HFGI	EODGI	Ours
FID↓	51.08	46.66	25.89	**15.58**
LPIPS↓	0.253	0.179	0.096	**0.048**

Quantitative Evaluation. We employ FID and LPIPS to measure the quality of the output images. For HFGI and Restyle, we select two attributes ("age" and "smile"). We choose five attributes for Editing out-of-domain GAN inversion ("age", "smile", "bushy eyebrows", "eyeglasses", and "beard").

Quantitative results are shown in Table 1. Quantitative comparison with state-of-the-art methods. As shown, the suggested model outperforms state-of-the-art methods in terms of FID and LPIPS scores, indicating that our method is able to more effectively generate images that belong to the face distribution.

Qualitative Evaluation. We perform a qualitative analysis by comparing the outputs of several models. The results of editing are shown in Fig. 3. Qualitative evaluation using state-of-the-art facial attribute editing models. Our proposed model ensures efficient manipulation and preserves unedited image details. We can observe that our model produces the highest quality results compared to the other methods. Our output is particularly effective at altering the attribute while preserving other details. The background and details in the HFGI and Restyle outputs are blurry, indicating that the lost data cannot be accurately recovered through the insertion of features into the StyleGAN generator. Specifically, when editing face images toward "old" with the editing direction of InterfaceGAN [23], the resulting images also include glasses. EODGI performs well in preserving non-edited areas, but still loses significant detail and fails to accurately remove redundant ghosting. Furthermore, the brightness of their output images may differ from the original image. Figure 4. In comparison to the state-of-the-art model that uses a deghosting network, our method is better able to preserve the details of the same ghosting image. Illustrates additional deghosting results using the same ghosting images. Our method significantly improves upon the results obtained by EODGI, which uses facial prior knowledge from pretrained StyleGAN models for deghosting.

4.5 Multi-attribute Editing

Similar to other methods, our model also supports multi-attribute editing. The multi-attribute editing procedure is performed by changing the attributes one by one. First, the original image examines multiple sequential edits via differential activations. After that, the image only needs the deghosting process once. Examples of editing two attributes "bushy eyebrows" and "beard" are presented in Fig. 5. Examples of multi-attribute editing. First, the original image examines multiple sequential edits via differential activations. After that, they only need one deghosting process. Our model's final outputs correctly incorporate the modifications needed in the two editing steps while still keeping image-specific information like backgrounds.

4.6 Limitation

Although our model achieves the best results in both qualitative and quantitative analysis of facial attribute editing and demonstrates the effectiveness of our method, it still suffers from various shortcomings. To begin with, our model is only able to process images with a resolution of 256×256. In addition, the inversion process of the diffusion model is slow, e.g., about 63 s for 2,000 steps. Last, when deghosting, the deghosting diffusion model treats unreasonable changes to attributes as artifacts, like beards on women. To ensure the editing effect, we increase the editing multiplication coefficient. The above content is also our future improvement direction.

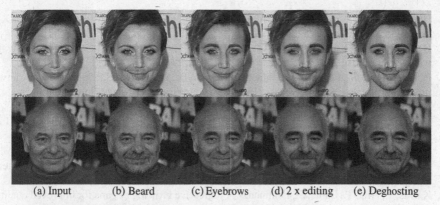

| (a) Input | (b) Beard | (c) Eyebrows | (d) 2 x editing | (e) Deghosting |

Fig. 5. Examples of multi-attribute editing. First, the original image examines multiple sequential edits via differential activations. After that, they only need one deghosting process.

5 Conclusion

We present a deghosting diffusion model, a novel approach to deghosting after facial attribute editing via differential activations. Our method yields impressive results compared to state-of-the-art facial attribute editing methods. Our model better preserves the unedited features while ensuring the editing effect. This paper fully demonstrates the potential of our model. Improving the problems mentioned in Sect. 4.6 is a promising route for future work.

Acknowledgement. This work was supported by China Scholarship Council (CSC) Grant No. 201908090255.

References

1. Alaluf, Y., Patashnik, O., Cohen-Or, D.: Restyle: A residual-based stylegan encoder via iterative refinement. CoRR abs/2104.02699 (2021). https://arxiv.org/abs/2104.02699
2. Alaluf, Y., Tov, O., Mokady, R., Gal, R., Bermano, A.: Hyperstyle: Stylegan inversion with hypernetworks for real image editing. In: Proceedings of the IEEE/CVF Conference on Computer Vision and Pattern Recognition, pp. 18511–18521 (2022)
3. Choi, Y., Choi, M., Kim, M., Ha, J.W., Kim, S., Choo, J.: Stargan: Unified generative adversarial networks for multi-domain image-to-image translation. In: Proceedings of the IEEE conference on computer vision and pattern recognition, pp. 8789–8797 (2018)
4. Dhariwal, P., Nichol, A.: Diffusion models beat gans on image synthesis. Adv. Neural. Inf. Process. Syst. **34**, 8780–8794 (2021)
5. Dinh, T.M., Tran, A.T., Nguyen, R., Hua, B.S.: Hyperinverter: Improving stylegan inversion via hypernetwork. In: Proceedings of the IEEE/CVF Conference on Computer Vision and Pattern Recognition (CVPR) (2022)
6. Goodfellow, I., Pouget-Abadie, J., Mirza, M., Xu, B., Warde-Farley, D., Ozair, S., Courville, A., Bengio, Y.: Generative adversarial nets. Advances in neural information processing systems. 27, (2014)

7. Han, X., Zheng, H., Zhou, M.: Card: Classification and regression diffusion models. arXiv preprint arXiv:2206.07275 (2022)
8. He, Z., Zuo, W., Kan, M., Shan, S., Chen, X.: Attgan: Facial attribute editing by only changing what you want. IEEE Trans. Image Process. **28**(11), 5464–5478 (2019)
9. Heusel, M., Ramsauer, H., Unterthiner, T., Nessler, B., Hochreiter, S.: Gans trained by a two time-scale update rule converge to a local nash equilibrium. Advances in neural information processing systems 30 (2017)
10. Ho, J., Jain, A., Abbeel, P.: Denoising diffusion probabilistic models. Adv. Neural. Inf. Process. Syst. **33**, 6840–6851 (2020)
11. Isola, P., Zhu, J.Y., Zhou, T., Efros, A.A.: Image-toimage translation with conditional adversarial networks. In: Proceedings of the IEEE conference on computer vision and pattern recognition. pp. 1125–1134 (2017)
12. Karras, T., Aila, T., Laine, S., Lehtinen, J.: Progressive growing of gans for improved quality, stability, and variation. arXiv preprint arXiv:1710.10196 (2017)
13. Karras, T., Laine, S., Aila, T.: A style-based generator architecture for generative adversarial networks. In: Proceedings of the IEEE/CVF conference on computer vision and pattern recognition, pp. 4401–4410 (2019)
14. Karras, T., Laine, S., Aittala, M., Hellsten, J., Lehtinen, J., Aila, T.: Analyzing and improving the image quality of stylegan. In: Proceedings of the IEEE/CVF conference on computer vision and pattern recognition, pp. 8110–8119 (2020)
15. Lu, C., Zhou, Y., Bao, F., Chen, J., Li, C., Zhu, J.: Dpmsolver++: Fast solver for guided sampling of diffusion probabilistic models. arXiv preprint arXiv:2211.01095 (2022)
16. Meng, C., Song, Y., Song, J., Wu, J., Zhu, J.Y., Ermon, S.: Sdedit: Image synthesis and editing with stochastic differential equations. arXiv preprint arXiv:2108.01073 (2021)
17. Ramesh, A., Dhariwal, P., Nichol, A., Chu, C., Chen, M.: Hierarchical text-conditional image generation with clip latents. arXiv preprint arXiv:2204.06125 (2022)
18. Richardson, E., Alaluf, Y., Patashnik, O., Nitzan, Y., Azar, Y., Shapiro, S., Cohen-Or, D.: Encoding in style: a stylegan encoder for image-to-image translation. In: IEEE/CVF Conference on Computer Vision and Pattern Recognition (CVPR) (June 2021)
19. Roich, D., Mokady, R., Bermano, A.H., Cohen-Or, D.: Pivotal tuning for latent-based editing of real images. ACM Transactions on Graphics (TOG) **42**(1), 1–13 (2022)
20. Ronneberger, O., Fischer, P., Brox, T.: U-net: Convolutional networks for biomedical image segmentation. In: International Conference on Medical image computing and computer-assisted intervention, pp. 234–241, Springer (2015)
21. Saharia, C., Chan, W., Chang, H., Lee, C., Ho, J., Salimans, T., Fleet, D., Norouzi, M.: Palette: Image-toimage diffusion models. In: ACM SIGGRAPH 2022 Conference Proceedings, pp. 1–10 (2022)
22. Saharia, C., Ho, J., Chan, W., Salimans, T., Fleet, D.J., Norouzi, M.: Image super-resolution via iterative refinement. IEEE Transactions on Pattern Analysis and Machine Intelligence (2022)
23. Shen, Y., Yang, C., Tang, X., Zhou, B.: Interfacegan: Interpreting the disentangled face representation learned by gans. TPAMI (2020)
24. Sinha, A., Song, J., Meng, C., Ermon, S.: D2c: Diffusion-decoding models for few-shot conditional generation. Adv. Neural. Inf. Process. Syst. **34**, 12533–12548 (2021)
25. Song, H., Du, Y., Xiang, T., Dong, J., Qin, J., He, S.: Editing out-of-domain gan inversion via differential activations. In: European Conference on Computer Vision, pp. 1–17. Springer (2022)
26. Wang, T., Zhang, Y., Fan, Y., Wang, J., Chen, Q.: Highfidelity gan inversion for image attribute editing. In: Proceedings of the IEEE/CVF Conference on Computer Vision and Pattern Recognition (CVPR) (2022)

27. Wu, Z., Lischinski, D., Shechtman, E.: Stylespace analysis: Disentangled controls for stylegan image generation. In: Proceedings of the IEEE/CVF Conference on Computer Vision and Pattern Recognition, pp. 12863– 12872 (2021)
28. Xu, Y., Shen, Y., Zhu, J., Yang, C., Zhou, B.: Generative hierarchical features from synthesizing images. CoRR abs/2007.10379 (2020), https://arxiv.org/abs/2007.10379.
29. Zhang, R., Isola, P., Efros, A.A., Shechtman, E., Wang, O.: The unreasonable effectiveness of deep features as a perceptual metric. In: Proceedings of the IEEE conference on computer vision and pattern recognition, pp. 586–595 (2018)
30. Zhu, P., Abdal, R., Qin, Y., Femiani, J., Wonka, P.: Improved stylegan embedding: Where are the good latents? arXiv preprint arXiv:2012.09036 (2020)

Minimizing Defaultation in Lending Using Blockchain-Based Loan Management System

Saha Reno[1]([⊠]) [iD], Sheikh Tasfia[2] [iD], Mehedi Manav[1] [iD], and Marzia Khan Turna[1] [iD]

[1] Bangladesh Army International University of Science and Technology, Cumilla 3501, Bangladesh
reno.saha39@gmail.com
[2] Military Institute of Science and Technology, Dhaka, Bangladesh

Abstract. The use of Blockchain and smart contracts ensures a safe and reliable transaction by preventing untrustworthy or malicious lending. Regular lending systems put lenders at risk of loan defaultation. However, in cryptocurrency lending, the value of the currency can fluctuate, resulting in the lender receiving less than the original lent amount when calculated in fiat or real-life currency. This research proposes using ERC-20 tokens as collateral to mitigate the risk for the lender. Our lending administration system based on the Ethereum blockchain is autonomous, making it a safe and reliable transaction option for users. The system tracks the fluctuation of the cryptocurrency lent and increases the value of the ERC-20 token accordingly. At the end of this paper, the effectiveness of the system is shown through tests conducted and presented in charts. The proposed system can prevent economic loss for lenders by addressing the decline in Ether's exchange rate and incrementing collateral price.

Keywords: Blockchain · Collateral · Smart Contract · Non-performing Loan · Ethereum · ERC-20

1 Introduction

Financial institutions in the United States provide borrowers with various loan types to facilitate the launch and maintenance of small enterprises. Customers earn money in the market to repay the loan plus interest. Financial firms can keep their credit lines flowing by reinvesting the cash from repaid loans into new loans. As long as this pattern persists, a country's economy will be relatively secure however a loan default occurs when this one is not repaid. Non-performing and default loans disrupt the banking system's normal monetary cycle, making it difficult for banks to extend credit and deliver other financial services to their customers [7]. In the long run, collapsing of these institutions will have devastating effects on the economy.

Any loan made by a bank that has been defaulted on or is unlikely to be repaid in full by the borrower is considered a non-performing loan (NPL). Since non-performing loans reduce banks' profitability and, in some cases, discourage banks from lending more money to firms and individuals, they pose a serious threat to economic growth. Banks

A. Gibadullin (Ed.): ITIDMS 2022, CCIS 1821, pp. 134–152, 2023.
https://doi.org/10.1007/978-3-031-31353-0_12

generate revenue primarily through interest payments from borrowers. Since NPLs make it harder for banks to give fresh loans to existing customers and new customers, they reduce the amount of money available for investment or lending. The bank's CAMELS (Capital adequacy, Asset quality, Management, Earnings, Liquidity, and Sensitivity) and credit rating decline as a result of loan defaulting scams, which also damage the bank's reputation [8]. Large amounts of non-performing loans (NPLs) have the potential to damage the confidence of depositors and foreign investors, leading those parties to take unusual measures against banks, which in turn creates a negative signal and a liquidity problem. For several years, loan money worth thousands of crores of taka has been stolen from these institutions.

These authors hoped to demonstrate the feasibility of a blockchain-based automated collateral management system (ACMS) for lending in their paper titled "P2P Loan Management Scheme Using Public Blockchain in 6G Network." The metrics used to gauge the success of the developed system are throughput, packet loss, bandwidth, storage costs, and lending rates. However, it must be improved so that the most advanced deep learning-based algorithms can handle enhanced credit checks and detect peer anomalies [10]. For financial banking, the paper "Bank Loan Sanction (BLS) Using Blockchain" relied on a digital loan processing system using blockchain technology, where users' data is collected and validated, determining loan eligibility, and making referrals. As users' identities are hidden from public sight, this approach makes it more difficult to validate paperwork in the financial sector [9]. To guarantee the automatic evaluation and execution of LoC transactions, the new financial loan management system LoC uses smart contracts to implement a locking and unlocking mechanism for smart semantic contracts (chain code) and to use an oracle and signature in smart contracts to protect the legitimacy of poverty relief loans and personal information. But the whole industry still needs to agree on the best way to match up centralized and distributed ledgers [13].

Considering the fact that the regular lending system has some potential risks, blockchain technology would be a lifesaver. By using smart contracts and storing the rules and regulations in the smart contracts, the necessity of a third party can be minimalized [14]. In this research, we propose a more secure and risk-free transaction system for both the lenders and the borrower using a smart contract system which makes sure of the fact that the lent money is repaid correctly in time mitigating any risk of loan defaulting. To protect the lenders' interests, all transactions will be performed in regular fiat money rather than the system's cryptocurrency. This is due to the fact that the value of bitcoin fluctuates over time, altering its exchange rate. If the borrower fails to repay the lender (either intentionally or unintentionally), the smart contract automatically transfers the ERC-20 token, which is utilized as the collateral in our system, to the lender also leaving the lender the ability to maintain the ownership of the tokens.

Table 1. Related Works: Contributions and Limitations.

Authors	Contribution	Limitations
Hartmann and Hasan (2021) [5]	They created a decentralized Ethereum financing platform based on a user's social network data. This technology might let customers get loans without collateral or enough income	There are a number of issues that need to be fixed on the platform, including the number of linked accounts, the number of photographs shared, the date an account was created, the incentive for joining five accounts, and user privacy
Hang and Kim (2021) [4]	In an effort to boost Hyperledger Fabric's functionality, this study suggests a new approach to building blockchain networks. Hyperledger Fabric is an open blockchain platform that can be scaled to fit a wide range of business use cases, from finance to governance	The efficiency of a blockchain network may be affected by its underlying physical environment. Increasing a peer's vCPU allocation is one way to boost performance. Disk space and memory are two other areas that should be investigated. The blockchain infrastructure is also put on an inappropriate LAN for a live service
Firdayati et al. (2021) [2]	Blockchain technology is implemented, with its attention to the construction of Hyperledger Fabric. A node's location on the Hyperledger Fabric is only relevant while processing transactions on that network. The findings of this research apply a design to a blockchain system based on a Hyperledger, which helps to address issues with throughput, scalability, and interoperability inherent to blockchains and improves the effectiveness of buying plans	Incorporating the Hyperledger fabric design into the procurement strategy necessitates making sure the hardware/network employed can handle data loads with bigger quantities in the future since the database created will grow steadily as the number of channels increases. Therefore, lesser-capacity hardware systems may not benefit from this study's findings about scalability

(*continued*)

Table 1. (*continued*)

Authors	Contribution	Limitations
Uriawan et al. (2021) [12]	Explained the fundamentals of a DApp-based personal loan platform that operates without a central server. The dashboard, applications, smart contracts, Metamask wallet, front end, and back end of the system. Detailed diagram of the lending platform's infrastructure, including the DApp environment, use cases, functional and non-functional needs	The vulnerabilities include being susceptible to security breaches because transactions are uncontrollable, as well as the potential for bad software to get access and engage in transactions as users or miners
Sriman et al. (2022) [11]	Put forward the theoretical and practical consequences of developing an app for financially trading bitcoins (Crypto-coins) through the compound protocol, which makes the app extremely protected and secret in exchanging the Crypto-coins directly to borrowers. The role player who is playing the borrower can set up a regulated account by filling out a form and getting a username and password	The ability to transfer funds between network nodes, apply for and receive loans, and obtain comptroller approval are all subject to a number of restrictions

2 Literature Review

As the problem of students not repaying their student loans becomes more widespread, The National Higher Education Fund Corporation (PTPTN) is hurting as it becomes harder to fund new students. The PTPTN and other organizations will be able to track their creditors' progress thanks to a blockchain and smart contract-based system that addresses these issues. There are three types of smart contracts that ensure the system's members continually re-balance their loans: Customer-Provider Relationships (CPR) are accountable for the maintenance and management of all education loan records, while Summary Contracts (SC) are used to maintain the debtor's transaction records in the system. Because the loans are disbursed by PTPTN and other centralized government agencies, the system cannot be deemed totally decentralized until it has been reconstructed utilizing blockchain technology [3].

Poverty Relief Loans are difficult to keep transparent and managed when a central service delivery node is responsible for them. Therefore, it is advocated that smart contracts be used to construct this system for handling loans for the impoverished [1]. The suggested system depends on (i) Chaincode, a smart contract defining all the prerequisites that must be fulfilled in order to carry out certain actions, and (ii) Unlocking Code, a coding unit that satisfies the conditions mentioned in Chaincode to facilitate the execution of any particular transaction. Those with low incomes in China are the only ones who can apply for a loan through a new program designed to reduce poverty [13].

Popular online lending platform Dharma was created by Nathan Hollander to facilitate direct meetings between potential borrowers and lenders. An Underwriter is a neutral third party who researches a borrower's reliability to reduce risk. Lenders appreciate the system because borrowers are expected to provide the collateral equivalent to the amount loaned multiplied by 1.5 to ensure repayment of the principle plus 8% interest, which is plainly not practicable for the borrowers [6].

Lastly, Table 1 includes the contributions and limitations of a few more recent blockchain-based debt administration platforms.

3   Methodology

Cryptocurrencies are used for all exchanges, while fiat currency is used in all calculations to hedge against fluctuations in the ether price. In order to secure loans made on the network, borrowers put up the network's native tokens, which adhere to the ERC-20 standard. These tokens can be purchased from the system and then resold to the platform. Two smart contracts govern the system's operation. An associated smart contract is used to create tokens and governs how they can be traded among users. The second one is responsible for managing the repayment of loans, the accrual of interest, and the increase in collateral value. The main ideas of the proposed system are depicted in Fig. 1, and its core concepts and operations can be split down into the subsequent subsections.

3.1   Adjusting the Value of Tokens to Paper Currency

The high volatility of Ether necessitates those tokens be paid in physical cash rather than using Ether. The volatility of cryptocurrency markets results in a wide range of values for tokens and losses for token holders who sell or borrow against their tokens when the value of Ether falls. The values of the tokens and the Ether changes to the currency rate and other dynamic factors. To do this, the "cheerio" and "request" JavaScript modules get the relevant information from the CoinGecko website. The request will inquire about the current USD value of Ether. In case of a successful request, the service will grant "cheerio" access and pay out the equivalent of $1 USD in Ether. Since 1018 Wei is equivalent to 1 Ether, the current USD value of one Ether is obtained via Cheerio and entered into the smart contract. This number is inverted to get the amount of Ether that may be bought for 1 USD since that information is not provided by CoinGecko. In light of the dynamic nature of cryptocurrency markets, this value is regularly revised. When converted to Wei, this figure is obtained by multiplying the sum by the token price (in USD). To compensate for the fluctuation in the value of Ether, the platform or its holder may ask for a larger amount of Ether from buyers in exchange for tokens. By doing so, the token price will be protected from dropping in parallel with the value of Ether. The internal smart contract value of one Wei to one US Dollar is dynamic and is adjusted frequently. Because the system and token holders will have tokens of varying values, the value of certain tokens held as collateral for the duration of a loan will fluctuate over time. As a result, not only will cheap tokens be made accessible, but so will expensive ones. A mapping data structure in the programming language Solidity that accepts the address of the user/contract and rate fluctuations may be used to handle tokens with dynamic pricing (many price changes and the amount of tokens under a given price).

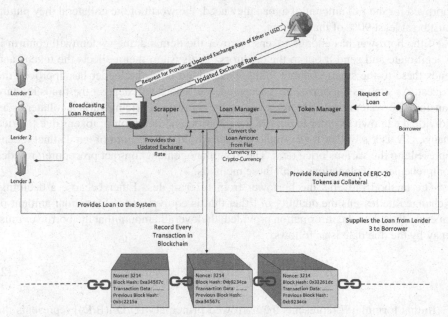

Fig. 1. Smart-Contract Based Loan Default Prevention System Mechanism.

3.2 Procedure for Providing Finances to Borrower and Securing It for Lenders

After taking into account that the borrower is in possession of enough number of tokens that have been taken as collateral, the smart contract accepts the loan request. In this case, ERC-20 standardized tokens are used of which prices (prices that vary depending on the fluctuation of the cryptocurrency) are stored in the system and those prices keep increasing or decreasing depending on the difference of that cryptocurrency. This act reduces the risk for the lender. As per the process, a huge amount of prices gets considered as possible implementation for the tokens. The system gives the user the ability to keep track of the tokens held in their wallet as their prices may differ from each other. Statistics depicting the total number of tokens for trade and their pricing are displayed when a user submits a token sale or borrowing request. Loan applicants must demonstrate that they have access to a minimum of 90% of the full token supply comparable to the loan amount.

From among a wide range of tokens with different costs, it is the borrower's responsibility to choose a bundle that meets the following requirement:

$$\sum_{i=1}^{n} (TN_i \times P_i) \geq 0.9E \tag{1}$$

In this equation, TN represents the total token supply, P is the collateral cost, I is the user's token alternatives, and E is the total Ether borrowed. If a borrower wants to get approved for the full amount of a loan they need, the worth of the collateral they put up must be at least 90% of that amount.

If the borrower has enough tokens to cover the demand, the system will confirm it as legitimate and send it out to the creditors. The system then collects the tokens and sends these to the smart contract in the background once the lender has approved the request. As soon as the borrower is accepted, the lender will deposit the funds by wire transfer. The system could enforce a cap on the number of pricing variant collaterals an individual can own in order to control the inflation and deflation of tokens due to price changes. A user's wallet, for example, can only hold a maximum of ten distinct tokens representing the various price tiers. The loan management contract procedure provides comprehensive explanations of all these methods.

The method prevents the borrower from offering less Ether because a declining exchange rate lessens the quantity of Ether that is equivalent to a particular amount of fiat cash. Based on the information provided, the overall amount that the borrower must repay by the due date is as follows:

$$E + \left(\frac{D}{D'} - \frac{B}{D}\right) + (E \times 2\% \times N)Ether \tag{2}$$

In this formula, E represents the borrowed principal, $[(D/D')(B/D)]$ represents the additional Ether owing in the event of a decline in the currency rate, $(E \times 2\% \times N)$ represents the total interest accrued over the loan period, and N denotes the elapsed days. If the borrower can pay the sum derived from the aforementioned formula, then Debtor's request to repay the loan and obtain all tokens back will be granted. If the borrower fails to make their loan repayments as agreed, the contract will automatically send the borrower's escalating amount of tokens to the lender. Figure 2 depicts the repayment process as outlined by the smart contract in order to reimburse the lender.

In our system, the smart contract itself acts as the validator, as it automates the validation process and therefore, the requirement of any third-party intervention is eliminated. Also, automated validation by the smart contract does not charge any fee from the system as no remuneration is required by this computer program.

Nonetheless, at the time of lending money, the creditor must provide a transaction fee while submitting the amount to the system. As there is no procedure to this transaction fee on behalf of any Ethereum users, the system cannot waive this fee even if it wants to. Therefore, any users executing any kind of transaction must pay this fee by themselves, whether they are borrowers or lenders.

```
                          Borrower's Payback Procedure

JavaScript Segment

INITIALIZE VARIABLE onPayment =
    ARROW FUNCTION(event): async
        event.preventDefault()

        INITIALIZE VARIABLE loanStatus AND STORE AWAIT
        moneyLending.methods.getLoanStatus(this.state.loanID).call()
        INITIALIZE VARIABLE deadlineStatus AND STORE AWAIT
        moneyLending.methods.getDeadlineStatus(this.state.loanID).call()
        IF loanStatus IS True AND deadlineStatus IS False:
            THEN:
                INITIALIZE VARIABLE lender AND STORE AWAIT
                moneyLending.methods.getLender(this.state.loanID).call()
                AWAIT tokenContract.methods.transfer(this.state.contractAddress,l
ender, this.state.priceVariants).send({
                    from: this.state.contractAddress, gas:'1000000'}
                })
            END IF
        END IF




Solidity Segment

FUNCTION payback(unit256 loanID, unit256 currentRate, unit256[] pricing): public
payable BOOLEAN
    IF msg.value IS EQUAL TO MULTIPLICATION OF dollarBorrowed[loanID] AND current
Rate , ether + interest[loanID] ether:
        THEN:
            CALL FUNCTION transfer ON tokenContract AND PASS ARGUMENTS: this, msg
.sender,pricing
            CALL FUNCTION lenders[loanID] AND PASS ARGUMENT: msg.value
            SET statusOfLoan[loanID] TO False
            deadline[loanID] TO NULL
            RETURN True
    ELSE:
        RETURN False
    END IF
END
```

Fig. 2. Smart Contract Payback System (Automated).

3.3 Evaluating the Potential Dangers

The blockchain is an immutable public ledger that records all Ethereum network transactions. Every single payback transaction, regardless of whether it was successful or not, is recorded on the blockchain, and this information may be used to evaluate possible dangers. The user's unique risk profile determines the degree to which you should exercise caution before giving money to any particular user. The following formula may be used to estimate the level of danger that the user is exposed to:

$$1 - \frac{Total\ Number\ of\ Successful\ Paybacks}{Total\ Number\ Of\ Loans\ Taken}. \tag{3}$$

The loan servicing agreement maintains a record of the one-of-a-kind block address for each individual borrower. This deal makes advantage of the address of the block in order to determine the degree of risk involved before ever posting a debtor's loan

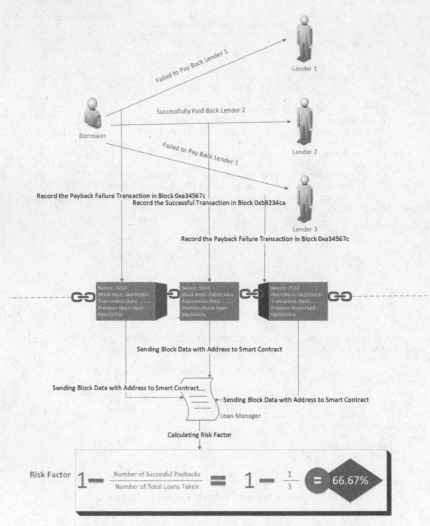

Fig. 3. Data Being Accessed from a Block for Ensuring the Security.

request. The deal makes use of both the individual borrowers' addresses as well as the block address at which the loan data is kept. Both of these addresses are required. After that, the computer retrieves the information it needs from the storage places that have been designated for that purpose. This smart contract does an analysis of the information it has acquired subject to the terms the phrase "success" and counts the number of blocks it discovers after all blocks with the appropriate transaction state have been discovered. The level of risk that is connected with a debtor may then be determined by taking the total number of loans obtained and deducting the number of loans that have been repaid on time. When a potential borrower asks for a loan, the system immediately communicates information about the potential borrower's risk profile to the lender. For example, a risk factor of 50% might be indicated if a borrower asked for and was granted ten loans from a variety of lenders, of which they successfully repaid five of them, but they still owed the other five lenders money. Figure 3 is a diagram that illustrates, in a schematic format, the process of analyzing the dangers that the system faces.

3.4   Raising Token Price and Determining Interest Rates to Reduce Credit Risk

To benefit the lender and reduce credit risk, the cost of tokens offered as collateral is raised as follows: Considering a daily rise of 2% in token price, an initial exchange rate of TP for each token in terms of Ether, and a maturity time of R days, the increase in the price of each token during the life of the loan would appear as follows:

$$\sum_{i=1}^{R} TP_i \times 2\% \tag{4}$$

This increase in cost can be seen in the token's price. The interest on the borrowed amount is computed as follows: If daily interest is computed at 2% per day, the number of Ethers borrowed is E, and the minimum interest to be paid is M, then the total interest owing at any given moment is:

$$\sum_{i=1}^{R} (E \times 2\%) \geqslant M \tag{5}$$

However, this interest rate is not fixed and can be regulated via the smart contract. A higher interest rate guarantees financial safety and greater profit for lenders while a low-interest rate makes it easier and more convenient for the debtor to borrow money from the semi-decentralized system.

The token's value is incremented once every day using a smart contract invoked from a JavaScript part of the front end with the loan ID and a variety of cost variation tokens (which will be collected as collateral) as parameters. Contracts for debt management often have deadlines. If the loan is ongoing and the due date is not extended beyond that point, any token price fluctuation for a certain loan ID will increase by 2%. This increase will continue until either the loan issue is resolved or the due date is reached. When the time limit has passed, the smart contract will send all the seized collateral to the creditor's address. This occurs regardless of whether or not the value of the collateral has increased or decreased since the deadline. Interest that was earned before security was put into active status. The memory of the smart contract stores the values of the incremental cost variations associated with a particular user wallet. These variables will be utilized in the future to construct any security arrangement that is required for obtaining loans. Again, the loan's interest is calculated by the JavaScript front-end calling the contract back-end with the loan's status, due date, and the number of days passed as inputs. If the loan remains open, the due date has not been overlooked, and one day has passed, the system will compute interest for fifteen days (according to the system rule given below), and the interest amount will be stored against a distinctive loan ID; however, the increment will stop after fifteen days. If the loan is still active, the due date has not been missed, and one day has passed, the scheme will calculate interest for fifteen days. After a period of fifteen days during which there has been no rise in the rate, it will go back to being 2% per day. The aforementioned procedures are laid down in an official manner in Fig. 4.

Increment Token Price

```
FUNCTION incrementTokenPrice(unit256 loanID, unit256[] pricing): public
    IF statusOfLoan[loanID] IS True AND deadline[loanID] IS False:
        THEN:
            WHILE prcing[i] IS NOT NULL:
                INCREMENT tokenPriceVariants[loanID][pricing[i]] BY tokenPriceVa
riants[loanID][pricing[i]] * 0.02
            END WHILE
    ELSE IF statusOfLoan[loanID] IS True AND deadline[loanID] IS True:
        THEN:
            WHILE pricing[i] IS NOT NULL:
                SET tokenContract.balanceOf[lender[loanID]][tokenPriceVariants[l
oanID][pricing][i]] TO tokenContract.balanceOf[this][tokenPriceVariants[loanID][
pricing[i]]]
                SET tokenContract.balanceOf[this][tokenPriceVariants[loanID][pri
cing[i]]] TO NULL
                CALL FUNCTION push ON userTokenPriceVariants[lender[loanID]] and
 PASS ARGUMENT: tokenPriceVariants[loanID][pricing[i]]
            END WHILE
    END IF
END
```

Calculating Interest

```
FUNCTION generateInterest(unit256 baseAmount, unit256 loanID): public
    IF statusOfLoan[loanID] IS True AND deadline[loanID] IS FALSE AND firstDay
    EQUAL TO daysPassed EQUAL TO 1:
        THEN:
            SET interest[loanID] TO amountBorrowed[loanID] * 0.02 * 15
            IF statusOfLoan[loanID] IS True AND deadline[loanID] IS False AND
daysPassed IS LESS THAN 15:
                THEN:
                    CONTINUE
            ELSE:
                INCREMENT interest[loanID] BY interest[loanID] * 0.02
            END IF
    END IF
END
```

Fig. 4. Token Price Fluctuation Process Depending on the Internet.

4   Result Analysis

Borrowers and lenders are able to communicate with one another and the system via a user interface that was created with the help of the JavaScript framework React, which was used by the suggested architecture. This program for decentralized lending requires a back-end architecture called Infura in order to connect to the Ethereum network. Web3 and Metamask are used in this scenario because it is necessary for smart contracts to be able to connect with the front end. The efficiency of our system may be gauged by seeing how it performs on the test scenarios presented in Table 2.

As can be seen in Table 2, the rate of exchange for Ether went down on the day that the debt was repaid as compared to the day that the loan was issued. This was the case in Tests 1, 2, 3, 4 and 5. If the borrower were to pay back the very same principal amount that was loaned on the date the debt was issued, the lender would get less fiat currency

Table 2. Case Study Analysis: Additional Return Amount Due to Currency Exchange Rate Variations.

Number of Test Cases in Serial Order	Date of the Loan's Initial Issue	Date while Payment on the Loan Is Due	Quantity of Loan	Date of Ether's exchange rate on loan issuance	Date of Ether's Rate on Loan Repayment	Payback (Ether)	Payment of Additional Ether
01	19 Feb, 2021	28 Mar, 2021	$502/1.923 Ether	$272.06	$146.00 (-)	4.695	+2.81
02	20 Feb, 2021	13 Mar, 2021	$301/1.573 Ether	$285.93	$194.26 (-)	2.695	+1.490
03	25 Feb, 2021	20 Mar, 2021	$355/1.976 Ether	$280.69	$122.73 (-)	3.989	+2.700
04	02 May, 2021	13 May, 2021	$399/1.986 Ether	$215.85	$184.89 (-)	3.178	+1.297
05	12 Mar, 2021	18 Mar, 2021	$704/3.548 Ether	$205.79	$119.99 (-)	7.318	+3.86
06	25 May, 2021	29 May, 2021	$835/3.989 Ether	$209.89	$238.59 (+)	4.582	N/A

due to the fall in the exchange rate. This scenario would occur if the borrower repaid the same with which that was loaned here on the date the debt was approved. Because of this, the possibility exists that the lender will really suffer a loss of funds. To demonstrate, let's assume a lender in the initial scenario lends a borrower $502; assuming an exchange rate of 1.923 Ether on February 19, 2021, this is the same as giving the borrower $502 due to the equal value of the Ether at that time. On March 28, 2021, 39 days later, the borrower returned the loan; however, because of the reduction in the exchange rate, the value of 1.923 Ether had reduced to $272.06 USD at the time of the repayment. Because of this, if the borrower paid back the entire 1.923 Ether on the due date, the creditor would get 146.00 USD less because of the volatility in exchange rates between the two currencies from the borrowers. The beginning of the loan. This loan has a payback requirement of 4.695 ETH, which is equivalent to around $502 USD.

This loan comes with a payback requirement of 2.81 ETH, which is equivalent to around $502 USD. Even if the converting rate is higher and it appears that the debtor may consider giving the lenders a lower amount of Ether in instance 6, the protocol requires the borrower to pay back the very same fundamental amount of Ether that he or she loaned. This is the case even if it appears that the debtor may give less Ether to the lenders.

For instance, during the most recent case, the debtor was forced to make a repayment of 5.577 Ether, which, regardless of the fact that the exchange rate had dropped on April 30th, is still comparable to $989 in US currency. The protocol of our system, on the other hand, insisted that the debtor make payments of 7.498 Ether, which resulted in a gain of

$425 USD for the lender. This chart compares our protocol with other Blockchain-based lending protocols that are currently in use (which only require the principal value of the loan to be repaid, in addition to the accrued interest). The purpose of this chart is to illustrate the possibility of a loss of remuneration due to a drop in the exchange rate. As can be seen in Fig. 5, according to our technique, which is represented by the orange line, the borrower is required to economically compensate the lender by supplying more Ether six out of nine times when the exchange rate declines on the day of the payback. When we consider the other three scenarios, each of which involves a rise in the rate of exchange, we see that the effectiveness of the system is comparable to that of existing Blockchain-based lending Protocols (e.g., Dharma). The six case studies are summed up in Table 3, which provides information on the current status of the collateral that was taken in order to safeguard the loans. In addition to this, it illustrates how the value of something like the collateral might be regularly reassessed in order to compensate for losses incurred in the event that the borrower defaults on their payments.

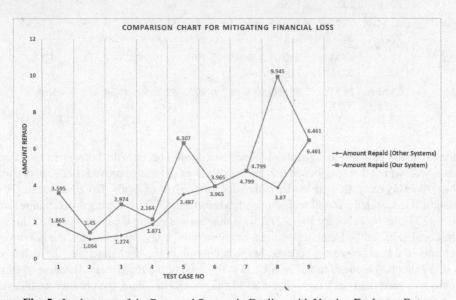

Fig. 5. Inadequacy of the Proposed System in Dealing with Varying Exchange Rates.

Let's assume that on February 19, 2021, a borrower takes out a loan in the sum of $502 USD at an exchange rate that converts that sum of money into 1.853 Ether. As an illustration of how the increase in the price of the collateral reduces the lender's exposure to financial risk, let's pretend that this scenario actually occurred. To secure the loan, the borrower put up tokens for collateral, and those tokens were kept in escrow until the debt was paid back in full. Tokens with a total value of almost 90 percent of the original amount were provided by the borrower as repayment for the loan (1.70564 Ether; 102 tokens purchased at a price of 0.003598 Ether, 76 tokens purchased at a price of 0.00800 Ether, and 46 tokens purchased at a price of 0.01369 Ether). The value of such tokens grew by 2% on a daily basis in the days running up to the deadline for making the payback.

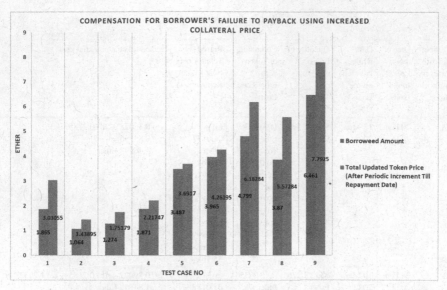

Fig. 6. Price of Security Increase Due to Default in Payment.

Table 3. Case Study Analysis: Raising ERC-20 Token Prices.

Number of Test Cases in Serial Order	Date of the Loan's Initial Issue	Date while Payment on the Loan Is Due	Quantity of Loan	Combining of Tokens with Ether-Based Costs	Raised Token Cost (Until Loan Repayment)	Seized token's potential cost
01	19 Feb, 2021	28 Mar, 2021	$502/1.923 Ether	(a) 0.00386 Ether: 105 Tok (b) 0.00822 Ether: 79 Tok (c) 0.01838 Ether: 56 Tok	(a) + 0.00298 Ether: 107 Tok (b) + 0.00635 Ether: 78 Tok (c) + 0.01273 Ether: 52 Tok	(a) 0.67801 + (b) 1.07753 + (c)1.31019 = 3.04089 Ether

(*continued*)

Table 3. (*continued*)

Number of Test Cases in Serial Order	Date of the Loan's Initial Issue	Date while Payment on the Loan Is Due	Quantity of Loan	Combining of Tokens with Ether-Based Costs	Raised Token Cost (Until Loan Repayment)	Seized token's potential cost
02	20 Feb, 2021	13 Mar, 2021	$301/1.573 Ether	(a) 0.00367 Ether: 66 Tok (b) 0.00425 Ether: 46 Tok (c) 0.01967 Ether: 38 Tok	(a) + 0.00177 Ether: 67 Tok (b) + 0.00199 Ether: 48 Tok (c) + 0.00899 Ether: 35 Tok	(a) 0.33038 + (b) 0.28857 + (c) 0.85596 = 1.46998 Ether
03	24 Feb, 2022	19 Mar, 2022	$352/2.276 Ether	(a) 0.00356 Ether: 78 Tok (b) 0.00467 Ether: 42 Tok (c) 0.0512 Ether: 19 Tok	(a) + 0.00188 Ether: 78 Tok (b) + 0.00233 Ether: 38 Tok (c) + 0.02556 Ether: 19 Tok	(a) 0.39222 + (b) 0.2185 + (c) 1.24577 = 1.84152 Ether
04	02 May, 2021	13 May, 2021	$399/1.986 Ether	(a) 0.00475 Ether: 87 Tok (b) 0.00687 Ether: 52 Tok (c) 0.06492 Ether: 24 Tok	(a) + 0.00099 Ether: 86 Tok (b) + 0.00137 Ether: 47 Tok (c) + 0.01308 Ether: 22 Tok	(a) 0.45981 + (b) 0.47678 + (c) 1.40613 = 2.31950 Ether

(*continued*)

Table 3. (*continued*)

Number of Test Cases in Serial Order	Date of the Loan's Initial Issue	Date while Payment on the Loan Is Due	Quantity of Loan	Combining of Tokens with Ether-Based Costs	Raised Token Cost (Until Loan Repayment)	Seized token's potential cost
05	12 Mar, 2021	18 Mar, 2021	$704/3.548 Ether	(a) 0.00499 Ether: 71 Tok (b) 0.00726 Ether: 51 Tok (c) 0.08424 Ether: 31 Tok	(a) + 0.00075 Ether: 76 Tok (b) + 0.00106 Ether: 56 Tok (c) + 0.01198 Ether: 37 Tok	(a) 0.48761 + (b) 0.56351 + (c) 2.98461 = 3.59573 Ether
06	25 May, 2021	29 May, 2021	$835/3.989 Ether	(a) 0.004836 Ether: 91 Tok (b) 0.04237 Ether: 76 Tok	(a) + 0.00088 Ether: 95 Tok (b) + 0.00776 Ether: 79 Tok	(a) 0.56346 + (b) 3.85851 = 4.26197 Ether

If somehow the borrower doesn't really return the loan by the date that was previously agreed upon, the lender will get an amount of Ether that is more than the basic value of 1.923 Ether for each of the tokens that have been confiscated. After a failed effort to recuperate the original investment, the price of tokens continues to progressively grow, as can be seen from the bar graph in Fig. 6. The fact that the current value of the surrendered collateral is higher than the original base amount in each of the 9 instances demonstrates that now the lender would not experience a loss regardless of the possibility that the borrower was unable to repay the loan.

Table 4 provides a concise summary of the testing conditions that were applied to the loan processing system. (This includes the interest as well as the total amount that is due).

Table 4. Case Study Analysis: Using Extra Ether to Pay Interest for Preventing Losses in the Event of a Declining Exchange Rate.

Number of Test Cases in Serial Order	Date of the Loan's Initial Issue	Date while Payment on the Loan Is Due	Quantity of Loan	Date of Ether's Exchange Rate on Loan Issuance	Date of Ether's Rate on Loan Repayment	Combining of Tokens with Ether-Based Costs	Increased Token Cost (Until Loan Repayment)	Interest that was Generated (Two Percent Daily, Minimum of 15 Days)	Payback (Ether)	Ether Paid (Interest + Principal)	Financial Loss
01.	19 Feb, 2021	28 Mar, 2021	$502/1.923 Ether	$272.06	$146.00 (-)	(a) 0.00386 Ether: 105 Tok (b) 0.00822 Ether: 79 Tok (c) 0.01838 Ether: 56 Tok	4.04646 Ether	2.46465 Ether	4.586 Ether	7.0567 Ether	NO
02.	20 Feb, 2021	13 Mar, 2021	$301/1.573 Ether	$285.93	$194.26 (-)	(a) 0.00367 Ether: 66 Tok (b) 0.00425 Ether: 46 Tok (c) 0.01967 Ether: 38 Tok	2.48535 Ether	1.43267 Ether	2.598 Ether	4.045523 Ether	NO
06	25 Feb, 2021	20 Mar, 2021	$355/1.976 Ether	$280.69	$122.73 (-)	(a) 0.00356 Ether: 78 Tok (b) 0.00467 Ether: 42 Tok (c) 0.0512 Ether: 19 Tok	2.78590 Ether	1.68529 Ether	3.989 Ether	5.67476 Ether	NO
04.	02 May, 2021	13 May, 2021	$399/1.986 Ether	$215.85	$184.89 (-)	(a) 0.00475 Ether: 87 Tok (b) 0.00687 Ether: 52 Tok (c) 0.06492 Ether: 24 Tok	3.26743 Ether	1.56786 Ether	3.198 Ether	4.53572 Ether	NO
05.	12 Mar, 2021	18 Mar, 2021	$704/3.548 Ether	$205.79	$119.99 (-)	(a) 0.00499 Ether: 71 Tok (b) 0.00726 Ether: 51 Tok (c) 0.08424 Ether: 31 Tok	4.63456 Ether	2.056421 Ether	7.378 Ether	8.969845 Ether	NO
06.	25 May, 2021	29 May, 2021	$835/3.989 Ether	$209.89	$238.59 (+)	(a) 0.004836 Ether: 91 Tok (b) 0.04237 Ether: 76 Tok	5.22349 Ether	2.178842 Ether	4.999 Ether	6.67246 Ether	NO

5   Conclusion

Our approach guarantees accurate risk assessment and keeps everything open and honest as a result. To lessen the blow of Ether's declining exchange rate, the fiat amount will be used instead of the cryptocurrency amount for processing refunds. We predict that a reduction in loan defaults will result from the increased value of tokens and the protocol's approach to dealing with currency rate changes, provided that the protocol is properly implemented. Countries, where trading in cryptocurrencies is allowed, can adopt the proposed system as a digital micro-finance network. As the collaterals are applicable and usable only inside this network of lenders and debtors, these become invalid outside the system. Therefore, any financial fraudulent activities can be considered useless. Moreover, as the smart contract is responsible for the management of every activity of the lending procedure and no third party gets involved with it, it can be considered safe and reliable. Considering the aforementioned aspects, it is safe to state that using the introduced system does not break the law.

Tokens with changing prices may generate Utilizing Ethereum-Based Lending System to Prevent Defaulting on Loans 15 confusion if the collateral price is adjusted to match the cost of repaying the loan plus interest. Moreover, the execution of transactions in Ethereum is not free and requires a transaction fee in the form of Gas. The concept of utilizing ERC-20 tokens as collateral is not feasible as transacting the digital tokens with the system users can turn out to be a failed solution due to (i) the reluctance, incuriosity and less trustability in purchasing a completely new type of assets and (ii) failure of normalizing the trading of these pseudo-cryptocurrencies. Without a doubt, these are some of the issues which can be resolved once the researchers have a better grasp of the underlying principle of the system and have found a way to optimize it.

References

1. Firdaus, A.H., Nugraha, I.G.B.B.: Saving and loan transaction system in cooperative using blockchain. In: 2019 International Conference on ICT for Smart Society (ICISS), vol. 7, pp. 1–4. IEEE (2019)
2. Firdayati, D., Ranggadara, I., Afrianto, I., Kurnianda, N.R.: Designing architecture blockchain of hyperledger fabric for purchasing strategy. Int. J. 10(2) (2021)
3. Gazali, H.M., Hassan, R., Nor, R.M., Rahman, H.M.: Re-inventing ptptn study loan with blockchain and smart contracts. In: 2017 8th International Conference on Information Technology (ICIT), pp. 751–754. IEEE (2017)
4. Hang, L., Kim, D.H.: Optimal blockchain network construction methodology based on analysis of configurable components for enhancing hyperledger fabric performance. Blockchain Res. Appl. 2(1), 100009 (2021)
5. Hartmann, J., Hasan, O.: A social-capital based approach to blockchain-enabled peer-to-peer lending. In: 2021 Third International Conference on Blockchain Computing and Applications (BCCA), pp. 105–110. IEEE (2021)
6. Hollander, N.: Dharma: a generic protocol for tokenized debt issuance (2017)
7. Khairi, A., Bahri, B., Artha, B.: A literature review of non-performing loan. J. Bus. Manag. Rev. 2(5), 366–373 (2021)
8. Okoye, M.C., Clark, J.: Toward cryptocurrency lending. In: Zohar, A., Eyal, I., Teague, V., Clark, J., Bracciali, A., Pintore, F., Sala, M. (eds.) FC 2018. LNCS, vol. 10958, pp. 367–380. Springer, Heidelberg (2019). https://doi.org/10.1007/978-3-662-58820-8_25
9. Rabbi, M., Hradoy, P.M., Islam, M.M., Islam, M.H., Akter, M.Y., Biswas, M.: Bls: bank loan sanction using blockchain authenticity, transparency and reliability. In: 2021 International Conference on Electronics, Communications and Information Technology (ICECIT), pp. 1–5. IEEE (2021)
10. Shukla, A., Nankani, M., Tanwar, S., Kumar, N., Piran, M.J.: Delend: A p2p loan management scheme using public blockchain in 6g network. In: ICC 2021-IEEE International Conference on Communications, pp. 1–6. IEEE (2021)
11. Sriman, B., Kumar, S.G.: Decentralized finance (defi): the future of finance and defi application for Ethereum blockchain based finance market. In: 2022 International Conference on Advances in Computing, Communication and Applied Informatics (ACCAI), pp. 1–9 (2022)
12. Uriawan, W., Wahana, A., Slamet, C., Suci Asih, V.: A dapp architecture for personal lending on blockchain. In: 2021 7th International Conference on Wireless and Telematics (ICWT), pp. 1–6 (2021)

13. Wang, H., Guo, C., Cheng, S.: Loc—a new financial loan management system based on smart contracts. Futur. Gener. Comput. Syst. **100**, 648–655 (2019)
14. Yang, X., Chen, Y., Chen, X.: Effective scheme against 51% attack on proof-of-work blockchain with history weighted information. In: 2019 IEEE International Conference on Blockchain (Blockchain), pp. 261–265. IEEE (2019)

An Intelligent-Safe Network Traffic Distribution System in Cluster Mesh-Formations of Thermal-Technology Complexes

Alexey Lazarev[1](✉) , Elizabeth Vereykina[2] , and Viktor Sinyavskiy[1]

[1] National Research University "Moscow Power Engineering Institute" in Smolensk, 1, Energy Passage, Smolensk 214013, Russia
anonymous.prodject@gmail.com
[2] National Research University "Moscow Power Engineering Institute", 14, Krasnokazarmennaya, Moscow 111250, Russia

Abstract. Nowadays, means of communication development exchange affects the vast majority of industries in the world, in particular, data exchange in thermal technology systems. The rapid development of communications makes it possible to solve a number of automated exchange problems. However, insufficient development of intellectual separation cluster formations means and flexible traffic redirection leaves the safe management problem of technological complexes relevant. The proposed solution to the highlighted problem is the software, based on a universal flexible topology of network segments, the usage of which, in the aggregate with an intelligent model for predicting network traffic loads in thermal technology complexes, would allow to implement a secure remote network interaction and critical information exchange to ensure stable operation of complex technical equipment. An essential feature of this system is the secure access to the required information due to direct p2p exchange between clients using a secure tunnel. Among other features of the system there is the encryption data approach using dynamic binary comparison in combination with methods of generating one-time pairs without an active internet connection to initiate a local p2p connection is highlighted.

Keywords: Intelligent forecasting · Client-server IP Topologies · Fuzzy Logic · Security · Cluster Management

1 Introduction

The various means of communication development and information exchange is important for correct operation in many infrastructures in the world. Most of the trends in this area are aimed at automating the processes of information transfer between clients and the response server. At the same time, the conditions for encrypting transmitted messages are also taken into account to prevent data leaks and ensure the operation of critical infrastructures [1]. One of those areas is the data process exchange between heat technology blocks represented by heat technology, transport and energy subsystems of information exchange in order to produce good means and support the work of various enterprises. In these subsystems, information exchange can be carried out both in the framework of interaction with the server, and through peer-to-peer (P2P) data transfer technologies between clients [2, 3]. A number of existing software and hardware tools allow to automate the information exchange, both with the various data transfer protocols usage, and with remote access to various parts of complexes through a VPN tunnel [4–7]. However, these means do not allow to fully meet the requirements of critical data safe transmission, which can lead to catastrophic problems in production [8, 9].

To solve this problem, it is proposed to develop a unique system for the initial secure connexion initialization between customers of the heat and technology complex with subsequent support for work through a secure virtual tunnel. As the main topology for the implementation of the specified system, it is proposed to use a universal IP-device segmentation topology with subsequent predictive client traffic loads determination to support secure data exchange. The usage of this approach will provide the initial initialization of a secure connection and subsequent support for data exchange by deploying a virtual tunnel. Among the main features of such a system is the network data transmission intelligent choice method with support for p2p connexion with clients, which allows to use the implemented system in highly specialized network topologies of industrial installations to support the critical infrastructures operation.

2   Materials and Methods

Nowadays, the usual corporate interaction TCP/IP topologies between the organisation's entities represent the reliable equipment typed operation with the presence of a DHCP server for assigning addresses to clients [10]. This topology is commonly used in most organisations, but it has a number of disadvantages that do not allow its integration into thermal technology complexes (for example, the difficulty in tracking customer traffic with a link to a real identifier). Another problem of a standardized DHCP server is the relative difficulty in assigning server rights to the client to support flexible data clustering. As an alternative methodology for address allocation, the physical adapter supports static assignment of addresses to network clients. However, the static pool of a IP addresses use is not appropriate for organisations with partial/full employees outsourcing.

Considering TCP/IP technology, on the other hand, its multifaceted branch also supports wireless WiFi 4/5/6 operation on most portable devices – often, such a topology on the average scale of an organization is a router with amplifiers in remote network outlets locations. However, at the moment, the adaptive implementation of such a topology is applicable due to the use of mesh networks, which allow network wireless segment implementation limited only by the mesh clients range.

Mesh systems, are a decentralised network where each device is a client and a server – using such a topology is a universal method to distribute internet access for 3 both clients and IoT devices. Among other things, the usage of mesh allows to segment the network into separate sections with a dedicated IP addresses pool – as can be seen from the figure below, the formation of the network is carried out both with a crossover connexion (direct line) and via a WiFi connexion (dotted lines) (see Fig. 1).

Thus, the mesh topology usage in the proposed system allows to implement the same flexibility as in the presence of specialised hardware devices, which also confirms the

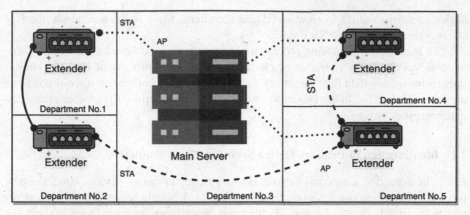

Fig. 1. The scheme of using the mesh system in the organization

proposed solution relevance. As a result, at the initial stage of address assignment, it is assumed to initialise its own DHCP server based on the *isc-dhcp-server* package with the virtual mesh allocation technology use (see Fig. 2).

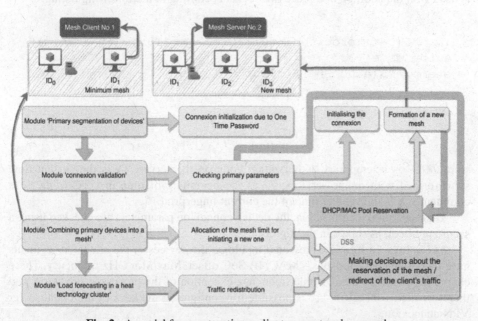

Fig. 2. A model for constructing a client-server topology mesh

As shown in Fig. 2, the tunnel initialization between the clients of the thermal-logical complex appears to be a relationships flexible system due to the fact that each client in dynamic mode can act as a server for the another client network segment (mesh) – in this case, the primary devices combination submodule in the mesh performs the subsequent limitation of the devices available segment, as a result, due to the decision-making system, a new mesh is allocated for the device segment. Thus, the initial mesh of two devices controls the ID_0 server, and ID_1 is the client, while in the new mesh, the ID_1 client is the server for the No.1 mesh.

The main decision-making process in this case is divided into the use of two components via the fuzzy character-by-character comparison process of both the digital fingerprint and the data flow variability – using this approach allows to use one software module, which in the future minimises the use of limited hardware resources of devices in the network.

2.1   Identification of Primary Device Segmentation Parameters

At the first creating a minimal mesh of devices stage, a primary devices bundle is performed by installing two autonomous agents that work both in server and client mode to search for friendly mesh elements. As the main dependency for the primary assignment of devices over the https protocol, the use a module for generating a unique temporary TOTP-AUTH code using a technology that converts a static identifier of the hardware device component and adding a time offset with subsequent encoding into a binary sequence (see Eq. 1). As a dependent hardware component, the processor system offset is used with the addition of a processor socket according to the following listing:

```
id ="$(cat /proc/cpuinfo | grep 'model name' | uniq)"
auth="date +%s"
stamp ="$(echo -n "$id$auth" | xxd)"
```

$$TOTP = \left[\frac{T_1 - T_0}{T} \right] \cdot X \qquad (1)$$

were *TOTP* is a temporary authorization code on the server; T_1 is the current time synchronised with online services; T_0 is the beginning of time in UTC (*date +%s* command); X is the validity time of the current fingerprint.

After the initial identification, the device connexion parameters are checked using a secure protocol, as shown in the Fig. 3.

As can be seen from the presented topology, the devices of the allocated segments have their own characteristics – MAC, IP, SoC offset, Max/Min GHz frequency. These characteristics, with the dynamic frequency exception of the processor, are static, and therefore their subsequent use is possible for configuring the keys of the client/server VPN connexion.

The main implemented software model of the VPN topology is OpenVPN (OVPN), which allows flexible virtual dedicated tunnel deployment [11, 12]. The main parameters used for tunnel initialization are:

- Pool of allocated addresses for the mesh – this parameter assumes the presence of an array/starting IPv4 address for assigning a network segment to clients;
- Redundancy limits – this parameter allows to set a limited number of connected devices;

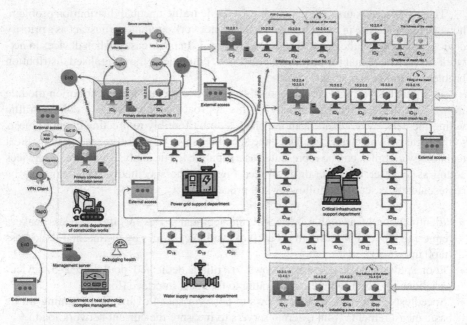

Fig. 3. Model of organisation of mesh segments in a heat technology system

- The server's open/private key is a unique sequence generated as an RSA key for client authorization;
- Password authorization is an optional parameter that allows to use a single client certificate for login/password authorization.

As the values of the parameters described above, it is assumed to use a dynamic counter for an addresses pool with 2 bytes of the address change, starting from the second cell (for example – *10.X.0.1*). For device redundancy restrictions, it is assumed to use a standard value of 10 devices, and as a server public/private key, the use of 2054-bit RSA encryption with support for a login/password connexion.

Thus, as clients of the dynamic system, it is assumed to use a single certificate with a dynamic password generation system by TOTP-time offset.

2.2 Traffic Load Forecasting

After passing the connexion initialization stages, as well as the several network segments creation, an important next process component of ensuring stable data transmission between the heat technology complex subjects is the optimising network traffic loads stage. Existing software solutions for optimised data delivery are integrated solutions, an example of which is the IntelliQoS technology from Keenetic. This technology allows to set priorities for traffic distribution through a classification service (for example, VoIP, IoT). The alternative Quality of Service (QoS) technology is also used in Cisco devices – this service uses the capabilities of the request-response system to select the traffic bandwidth.

These tools, of course, allow to solve available traffic unequal distribution problem, however, for their use in the presented topology, network equipment must act as a priority device or repeater in the network topology of Fig. 1. In other cases, when devices in network segments are managed from other network equipment, the centralised distribution problem of traffic is relevant.

To solve this problem, it is proposed to use a proprietary load distribution module from client devices. The peculiarity of this approach is the ability to control traffic within the network segment from the client side by forcibly redirecting client requests to the local network interface. Thus, the specified stage of load forecasting in the heat technology complex can be represented as a separate traffic analysis module for devices acting as a server for the n-th mesh (see Fig. 4). The specified module can also be represented by a set of the following sub-processes:

- "Identification of available devices in the segment". The specified process make a request to the OVPN server to get a list of available devices by the internal IP address (tap0 interface).
- "Pool splitting". This process allows to split a dedicated pool into 2–5 devices variations for point redirection of traffic to the local interface (lo).
- "Speedtest API". This process allows to perform speed of loading/returning traffic basic measurements from external servers to measure the current network load.
- The "Test Device shutdown" process is aimed at disabling the selected array of devices, followed by calling the "Speedtest API" to measure network load.
- The "Decision-making" process uses the results of several Speedtest API outputs for analytical changes during test disconnections devices comparison for subsequent decision-making on the continuation of operation or selected device deauthentication in the network segment.

As can be seen from Fig. 4 the process of predicting traffic changes is reduced to preliminary devices partitioning into segments of 2 IP addresses, as a result of which the traffic is measured current download/return rate, followed by temporary redirection each of devices to the local interface and repeated measurements. Then, after the entries are entered into the database, a predictive determination of traffic consumption in the future is carried out by using a trained LSTM-XGBoost model [13].

The Long short-term memory (LSTM) model applicability of the familiar is typical in most cases for obtaining a short-term forecast for a limited amount of data – such a methodology allows using a standardised neural network structure to predict the traffic changes processes within a network segment [14]. Together with these advantages, the solution to the traffic forecasting problem is isolated by the strong randomness of its consumption due to many different end-user factors – for example, viewing video content in between work, conducting planned/unplanned broadcasts, etc. The LSTM model allows to fix the correlation of the time interval, but does not allow to set external signs to influence on the output predictive vector [15, 16].

Due to this disadvantage, in order to increase the traffic forecasting accuracy, it is proposed to use a combined model with grandient boost, the input of which is data on the current traffic consumption by the user (vector g_i), and data on previous traffic consumption for this user (vector x_i) – vector data collectively represent the input matrix

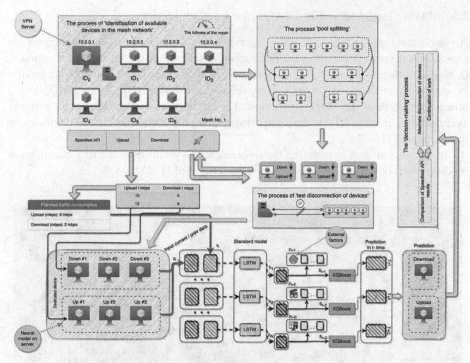

Fig. 4. The process of forecasting changes in the monitored traffic

X_i (See Eq. 2). So, after initialization of the LSTM layer, the PReLU activation function is performed, followed by the output of the predicted values of $\tilde{y}_{t+i}$ [17].

$$\tilde{y}_{t+i} = PReLU\left(\omega_i \cdot h_i + b_h\right) \tag{2}$$

were $\tilde{y}_{t+i}$ is the function of returning forecast values; $PReLU$ is the activation function of Parametric rectified linear unit.

At the stage of the output of the primary vectors S_{t+Q} from the LSTM model, the values are predicted due to the XGBoost model in an identical time interval $t+$, taking into account external factors affecting traffic, designated F_{t+Q} (See Eq. 3).

$$\hat{y}_{t+i} = \sum_{n=1}^{n} f_n(S_{t+Q}) \tag{3}$$

were $\hat{y}_{t+i}$ is the return function of the predicted values of XGBoost; S_{t+Q} is the output values of vectors from the neural network.

Thus, at this stage, the forecast values are obtained from the LSTM model, followed by refinement through gradient boosting – this approach made it possible to more accurately obtain the output values of the possible network load from a specific device for making decisions on optimising the network segment operation.

2.3 Making Decisions to Ensure Optimal Load and Safety

An important stage in the work of the described system is the decision-making process to optimise the network traffic load. For the organisation of this control, it is assumed to use initial authenticated sequence fuzzy comparison process of: Eq. 1 output data and the processor id glues at the output are a binary sequence of the form "0011010...01001010", however, by default, the TOTP generation of the time value updates the output variable every second, respectively, when comparing the values, there may be discrepancies in the sequences [18–20].

In connexion with the above, the implemented system uses a fuzzy comparison module based on the Fuzzy Wuzzy library (see Fig. 5) [21–23].

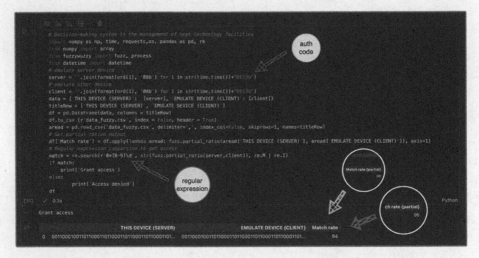

Fig. 5. The process of comparing the identified code at the primary authentication stage

The basis of the implemented decision-making module is a Python module that uses the pandas dataframe formation for primary saving of results to a csv file for subsequent loading and comparison through the library [24–26]. According to the illustration in Fig. 5 the process of comparing the source code is represented by comparing two authenticated server and the client sequences (in this case, the client is emulated on the server). First, a unique temporary fingerprint is generated, and then a unique agent identifier is superimposed. The output is a set of binary code, which is compared due to the partial match rate function integrated in the Fuzzy Wuzzy library [27]. The figure also shows different variations of the comparison output percentage (94, 95, 98%), which allowed to set the percentage of coincidence by 80%+ due to a regular expression to confirm the initialised connexion validity.

3 Results

Thus, as a development result of the software product, it is possible to create both a unique client-server thermal logic complexes interaction topology, and a separate system of predictive decision-making about customer access to network segments due to the implemented access verification algorithm. An important component of the presented system is the decentralised interchange approach based on mesh topology, which in the future will allow using this algorithm to implement full-fledged automated data management platforms in corporate organisations.

Special attention should be paid to the implemented traffic control module inside the network due to the cyclic request function for speed Internet connexion changes with an external server and excess predictive identification of the limit to optimise the operation of the heat technology network due to the ARP traffic.

4 Discussions

An integrated algorithm for predicting changes in the monitored users traffic of the thermal technology complex can be indicated as the main result of the research. The presented neural network model changes forecasting allows to get the values of possible differences in loading/return speeds at the output. The basis of the presented neural network is represented by the LSTM-XGBoost model, which differs from the LSTM by the possibility of taking into account data in the past and present time lines - the totality of the resulting ensemble allows minimising the each previous model losses based on the current nth model. Among the additional promising this model development areas, it is possible to highlight the possibility of preserving and resuming the trained network state to optimise work in multiple network segments of thermal technology complexes.

However, for changes in the structure of the presented topology, a decision-making module is required that allows to analytically calculate the difference between the allow-able traffic flow and the predicted one. In this case, a decision-making module based on the FuzzyWuzzy library is also used to track changes, followed by the interaction of the temporary/permanent client deauthentication module by using the ARP function of redirecting traffic from the network subject to the local interface using the scapy library (see Fig. 6) [28–30].

To cheque for speeding, a simple conditional expression is used, according to which the scrapy library is called: in this case, the "scrapy.arp" method is used, the input of which is supplied with the parameters receiving the device's mac address by ip, gateway and the client's ip address [31]. So, the implementation of this method allows to use the forced packets redirection, as well as to perform traffic tracking at the expense of the "man in the middle" [32, 33].

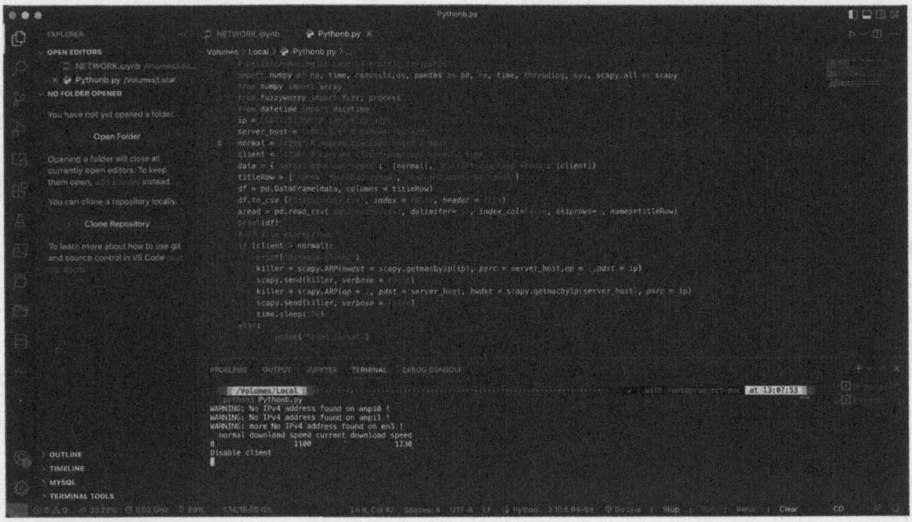

Fig. 6. The process of deauthenticating a client from a network segment

5   Conclusion

In conclusion, the main problem of traffic distribution systems in the corporate network was identified in this article. The solution to the specified safe-management problem of cluster formations and flexible traffic redirection is implemented software, which is based on a unique segmentation based on a mesh-decentralised topology. The implemented topology, due to its multimodularity, allowed both the primary implementation of the connexion process between the network entities and the information exchange support with the devices expansion in the network by deploying a VPN server reliable component on the client. An important component is the process of tracking traffic congestion, which made it possible, due to the combined use of an LSTM network with gradient boosting, to predictively identify traffic congestion and make a decision to exclude devices from the network segment.

In the future, this paper may have a significant impact on the systems development for building flexible network topologies of corporate solutions, as well as contribute to the traffic tunnelling systems development to ensure the transmitted data safety. In addition, the study can have a direct impact on the interaction system process automation in the thermal technology complex.

Acknowledgments. The research was supported by RSF (project No. 22-21-00487).

References

1. Solomon, M.G., Kim, D.: Fundamentals of Communications and Networking (ISSA: Information Systems Security & Assurance), 3rd edn. Jones & Bartlett Learning, Burlington (2021)

2. Sasabe, M., Kiyomitsu, M.: Analysis of minimum distribution time of two-class tit-for-tat-based P2P file distribution. Comput. Netw. **214**, 109142 (2022)
3. Djafri, L.: Dynamic distributed and parallel machine learning algorithms for big data mining processing. Data Technol. Appl. **56**(4), 558–601 (2022)
4. Nandhini, S., Vaishnav, S., Vikas, V.S.: VPN blocker and recognizing the pattern of IP address. In: AIP Conference Proceedings, vol. 2405, p. 030019 (2022)
5. Zakaria, M.I., Norizan, M.N., Isa, M.M., Jamlos, M.F., Mustapa, M.: Comparative analysis on virtual private network in the internet of things gateways. Indonesian J. Electr. Eng. Comput. Sci. **28**(1), 488–497 (2022)
6. Gentile, A.F., Macrì, D., De Rango, F., Tropea, M., Greco, E.: A VPN performances analysis of constrained hardware open source infrastructure deploy in IoT environment. Future Internet **14**(9) (2022)
7. Roy, S., Shapira, T., Shavitt, Y.: Fast and lean encrypted internet traffic classification. Comput. Commun. **186**, 166–173 (2022)
8. Haga, S., Esmaeily, A., Kralevska, K., Gligoroski, D.: 5G network slice isolation with WireGuard and open source MANO: a VPNaaS proof-of-concept. In: 2020 IEEE Conference on Network Function Virtualization and Software Defined Networks, NFV-SDN 2020 – Proceedings, pp. 181–187 (2020)
9. Cruz De La Cruz, J.E., Romero Goyzueta, C.A., Cahuana, C.D.: Open VProxy: low cost squid proxy based teleworking environment with OpenVPN encrypted tunnels to provide confidentiality, integrity and availability. In: Proceedings of the 2020 IEEE Engineering International Research Conference, EIRCON 2020, pp. 1–4 (2020)
10. Jain, A., Bhullar, S.: Network performance evaluation of smart distribution systems using smart meters with TCP/IP communication protocol. Energy Rep. **8**, 19–34 (2022)
11. Romero Goyzueta, C.A., Cruz De La Cruz, J.E., Cahuana C.D.: VPNoT: end to end encrypted tunnel based on OpenVPN and Raspberry Pi for IoT security. In: 2021 International Conference on Electrical, Computer, Communications and Mechatronics Engineering (ICECCME), Mauritius, pp. 1–5. IEEE (2021)
12. Vilakazi, M., Sebopetse, N., Khutsoane, O.: LCSM node based on geo location spectrum database for cooperative dynamic spectrum access. In: 2021 IEEE AFRICON, Arusha, pp. 1–6. IEEE (2021)
13. Dai, Y., Zhou, Q., Leng, M., Yang, X., Wang, Y.: Improving the bi-LSTM model with XGBoost and attention mechanism: a combined approach for short-term power load prediction. Appl. Soft Comput. **130** (2022)
14. Korstanje, J.: Advanced Forecasting with Python: With State-of-the-Art-Models Including LSTMs, Facebook's Prophet, and Amazon's DeepAR, 1st edn. Apress (2021)
15. Babcock, J., Bali, R.: Generative AI with Python and TensorFlow 2: Create Images, Text, and Music with VAEs, GANs, LSTMs, Transformer Models, 1st edn. Packt Publishing, Birmingham (2021)
16. Lee, N., Kim, H., Jung, J., Park, K., Linga, P., Seo, Y.: Time series prediction of hydrate dynamics on flow assurance using PCA and recurrent neural networks with iterative transfer learning. Chem. Eng. Sci. **263** (2022)
17. Chen, H., Ihnatsyeva, S., Bohush, R., Ablameyko, S.: Choice of activation function in convolutional neural networks for person re-identification in video surveillance systems. Program. Comput. Softw. **48**(5), 312–321 (2022)
18. Mendes, T.P.G., et al.: A new Takagi-Sugeno-Kang model-based stabilizing explicit MPC formulation: an experimental case study with implementation embedded in a PLC. Expert Syst. Appl. **210** (2022)
19. Peng, J., Xia, G., Li, Y., Song, Y., Hao, M.: Knowledge-based prognostics and health management of a pumping system under the linguistic decision-making context. Expert Syst. Appl. **209** (2022)

20. Sree, V.S., Srinivasa Rao, C.: Distributed power flow controller based on fuzzy-logic controller for solar-wind energy hybrid system. Int. J. Power Electron. Drive Syst. **13**(4), 2148–2158 (2022)

21. Aldrees, A., Awan, H.H., Javed, M.F., Mohamed, A.M.: Prediction of water quality indexes with ensemble learners: bagging and boosting. Process Saf. Environ. Prot. **168**, 344–361 (2022)

22. Pattewar, T., Jain, D.: Stock prediction analysis by customers opinion in twitter data using an optimized intelligent model. Soc. Netw. Anal. Min. **12**(1) (2022)

23. Tuli, P., Patra, J.P.: Symbol question conversion in structured query language using fuzzy with deep attention based rain LSTM. Multimed. Tools Appl. **81**(22), 32323–32349 (2022)

24. Kumar, A.: Mastering Pandas: A Complete Guide to Pandas, from Installation to Advanced Data Analysis Techniques, 2nd edn. Packt Publishing, Birmingham (2019)

25. Molin, S., Jee, K.: Hands-on Data Analysis with Pandas: A Python Data Science Handbook for Data Collection, Wrangling, Analysis, and Visualization, 2nd edn. Packt Publishing, Birmingham (2021)

26. Chen, D.Y.: Pandas for Everyone: Python Data Analysis (Addison-Wesley Data & Analytics Series), 2nd edn. Addison-Wesley Professional, New York (2022)

27. Karim, B.T., Allali, A., Boulouiha, H.M., Denai, M.: Voltage profile and power quality improvement using multicell dynamic voltage restorer. Int. J. Power Electron. Drive Syst. **13**(4), 2216–2225 (2022)

28. Muttair, K.S., Mosleh, M.F., Shareef, O.A.: Optimal transmitter location using multi-scale algorithm based on real measurement for outdoor communication. IAES Int. J. Artif. Intell. **11**(4), 1384–1394 (2022)

29. Hussein, A.M., Idrees, A.K., Couturier, R.: Distributed energy-efficient data reduction approach based on prediction and compression to reduce data transmission in IoT networks. Int. J. Commun. Syst. **35**(15) (2022)

30. Romano, F., Kruger, H.: Learn Python Programming: An In-depth Introduction to the Fundamentals of Python, 3rd edn. Packt Publishing, Birmingham (2021)

31. Smart, G.: Practical Python Programming for IoT: Build Advanced IoT Projects Using a Raspberry Pi 4, MQTT, RESTful APIs, WebSockets, and Python 3. Packt Publishing, Birmingham (2020)

32. Nasser, H.I., Hussain, M.A.: Provably curb man-in-the-middle attack-based ARP spoofing in a local network. Bull. Electr. Eng. Inform. **11**(4), 2280–2291 (2022)

33. Thankappan, M., Rifà-Pous, H., Garrigues, C.: Multi-channel man-in-the-middle attacks against protected Wi-Fi networks: a state of the art review. Expert Syst. Appl. **210** (2022)

Computer Research and Stabilization
of Dynamic Models of Conveyor Systems

Olga N. Masina[1]([✉]) [iD], Olga V. Druzhinina[1,2] [iD], and Alexey A. Petrov[1] [iD]

[1] Bunin Yelets State University, 28, Kommunarov St., Yelets 399770, Russia
olga121@inbox.ru
[2] Federal Research Center "Computer Science and Control" of Russian Academy of Science,
Building 2, 44, Vavilov St., Moscow 119333, Russia

Abstract. This paper discusses a model of a belt conveyor with a dynamic change in the angle between the horizontal plane and the plane of the conveyor belt. The model is given by a nonlinear system of four ordinary differential equations. The model takes into account switching, which are set by the factors of smooth loading and instant unloading of cargo. The proposed modification of the model makes it possible to take into account the use of such a damper-type conveyor support, which keeps the conveyor inclination angle close to zero in the absence of additional forces. A number of computational experiments are carried out to reveal the properties of the modified model equilibrium states. To study the constructed model, methods of stability theory, the theory of systems with switching, as well as numerical methods for solving differential equations are used. Motion trajectories are obtained taking into account the parameters variability. The qualitative effects that arise as a result of changing the model parameters are studied. The software is developed in the Julia language using the Differential Equations and Plots libraries. The results of the article can be used in the problems of designing new control systems for production lines, as well as in the problems of stability analysis and stabilization of multidimensional dynamic models.

Keywords: Switchable Dynamic Models · Differential Equations · Conveyor Belt · Trajectory Dynamics · Stabilization · Computational Experiments · Software

1 Introduction

The problems of designing and implementing continuous machines are among the important and topical scientific and technical problems [1–4]. Conveyor transport has such advantages as relative simplicity of design, high productivity, low operating costs.

Design, automation and monitoring of conveyor transport are closely related to the use of modern methods of applied mathematics, computer modeling, stability theory and reliability theory. In [5–12], various issues of modeling conveyor systems are studied. The results of these articles demonstrate a wide range of studied models, methods and approaches to modeling.

A. Gibadullin (Ed.): ITIDMS 2022, CCIS 1821, pp. 165–176, 2023.
https://doi.org/10.1007/978-3-031-31353-0_14

It should be noted that many models of conveyor systems are models with switching. Important aspects of the switched systems theory and their application to obtaining stabilization conditions for discrete systems are described in [13, 14] and in other articles. The application of the switched systems methodology to the modeling of production lines is considered in [15]. Sufficiently high efficiency for studying switched systems is demonstrated by numerical optimization and artificial intelligence methods [16–19]. Intelligent control of conveyor transport systems is considered in [20–25] and other articles.

The construction of belt conveyor models in present article is based on a generalization of the models considered in [24, 25]. In [24], a description of the basic model of a belt conveyor with a dynamic change in the angle between the horizontal plane and the plane of the conveyor belt is presented. This description contains a number of assumptions, in connection with which further improvement of this basic model is of theoretical and applied interest. In [25], such a modified mathematical model of a belt conveyor is proposed, in which axial friction is taken into account.

As an actual direction in refining the model of a belt conveyor with a dynamic change in the angle of elevation, it should be noted the addition of factors related to the stabilization of the system. In this article, we consider three types of generalized belt conveyor models and study the stabilization conditions for these models.

Here is a summary of the article by sections. Section 2 describes the model of a single-drive conveyor with a dynamic change in the angle of elevation. Modifications of this model are proposed, taking into account the smooth unloading and loading of cargo, as well as the conditions for the existence of an equilibrium state. Section 3 proposes a description of the developed software and presents the results of computational experiments to study the stability of modified models. Section 4 discusses the results of constructing and studying models.

2   Models and Methods

We investigate a model of a belt conveyor with a dynamic change in the angle between the horizontal plane and the plane of the belt. This model is generally given by an ordinary differential equation of the form:

$$
\begin{aligned}
\dot{x} &= \frac{p}{m}, \\
\dot{p} &= u_p(t) - k\frac{p}{m} - (m - m_0)g\sin(\alpha_0), \\
\dot{\alpha}_0 &= \alpha_1, \\
\dot{\alpha}_1 &= \frac{u_\alpha(t)}{mc\varepsilon^2} - \frac{g\cos(\alpha_0)}{\varepsilon}, \\
u_p, \ u_\alpha &\in U, \quad \varepsilon \in E, \quad m \in M,
\end{aligned}
\tag{1}
$$

where the designations are given in Table 1.

Table 1. Model designations (1).

Designation	Description
x	linear movement of the conveyor belt
p	system momentum
α_0	lifting angle of the conveyor relative to the zero position
α_1	conveyor angular rotation speed
m	total system weight
m_0	total mass of cargo on the conveyor
$u_p(t)$	conveyor traction control function
$u_\alpha(t)$	belt angle control function
ε	position of the center of mass of the conveyor relative to the lower roller
c	coefficient determining the moment of inertia of the conveyor
k	rolling friction coefficient

The sets M, E, U include all possible values of the total loads mass, center of mass and controls, respectively. Changes in the modes of operation in model (1) correspond to the choice of m and ε from the sets M, E according to a given law. System (1) refers to systems with switching.

We study the dynamics of system (1) with $u_p = u_\alpha = 0$. Let us assume that there is a stable equilibrium state in system (1). Let for (1) the restriction is valid:

$$\alpha_0 \in \left(0, \frac{\pi}{2}\right).$$

As a result of equating the right-hand sides in system (1) to zero, we obtain

$$\frac{p}{m} = 0,$$
$$u_p(t) - k\frac{p}{m} - (m - m_0)g\sin(\alpha_0) = 0,$$
$$\alpha_1 = 0,$$
$$\frac{u_\alpha(t)}{mc\varepsilon^2} - \frac{g\cos(\alpha_0)}{\varepsilon} = 0.$$

Taking into account $u_p(t) = 0$, $u_\alpha(t) = 0$, $m > 0$, $m > m_0$, $c > 0$, $\varepsilon > 0$, $g > 0$ the equations will take the form

$$\begin{aligned}
p &= 0, \\
\sin(\alpha_0) &= 0, \\
\alpha_1 &= 0, \\
\cos(\alpha_0) &= 0.
\end{aligned} \tag{2}$$

Obviously, system (2) has no solutions on the set of real numbers. Based on this, for system (1) there are no equilibrium states. This fact is associated with such features of the construction of system (1), which make the system unbalanced. From a geometric point of view, the phase planes in hyperspace do not intersect. In order to obtain a balanced system for at least some limited set of parameters, we propose to refine model (1) as follows. The modification consists in adding a new term to the fourth equation of model (1). The physical sense of this modification is to use damper-type conveyor supports that keep the conveyor tilt angle close to zero in the absence of additional forces. Figure 1 shows a diagram of a conveyor with a variable angle of inclination and dampers for fixing the angular position.

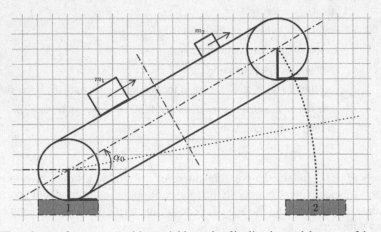

Fig. 1. The scheme of a conveyor with a variable angle of inclination and dampers of the minimum angle.

In Fig. 1, the following designations are introduced: m_1, m_2 are the masses of the first and second cargo, respectively, the numbers 1 and 2 represent the numbers of damper units, α_0 is the angle of elevation of the conveyor belt. It should be noted that the possible number of loads on the tape is not limited.

We modify model (1) to take into account an additional condition. Let the conveyor encounter support resistance when approaching "from above" to $\alpha_0 = 0$. Then the model will take the form:

$$\dot{x} = \frac{p}{m},$$

$$\dot{p} = u_p(t) - k\frac{p}{m} - (m - m_0)g\sin(\alpha_0),$$

$$\dot{\alpha}_0 = \alpha_1, \tag{3}$$

$$\dot{\alpha}_1 = \frac{u_\alpha(t)}{mc\varepsilon^2} - \frac{g\cos(\alpha_0)}{\varepsilon} + \frac{1}{(\alpha_0 + b)^\gamma},$$

$$u_p, u_\alpha \in U, \quad \varepsilon \in E, \quad m \in M,$$

where b, γ are the coefficients that determine the characteristics of the damper.

The construction of a generalized model (3) makes it possible to reveal the existence of a "near-zero" equilibrium state and obtain conditions for the stabilization of the conveyor model. Stabilization conditions impose restrictions on the parameters appearing in the right parts of the differential equations of the model. We note that the parameter ϵ from the fourth equation of the model plays a special role, since with its «small perturbation» the equilibrium state shifts. In addition, the assumption is made in model (3) which means that we neglect the influence of the conveyor mass on the damper.

According to the physical sense, for some values there is an equilibrium state $(p, \alpha_0, \alpha_1) = (0, 0, 0)$. Then the characteristics of the damper can be determined by solving the equations:

$$-\frac{g\cos(\alpha_0)}{\varepsilon} + \frac{1}{(\alpha_0 + b)^\gamma} = 0,$$

$$\alpha_0 = 0.$$

These equations make it possible to obtain the equality $b = \frac{\varepsilon}{g}^{\frac{1}{\gamma}}$. Taking into account the indicated equality, system (3) takes the form

$$\dot{x} = \frac{p}{m},$$

$$\dot{p} = u_p(t) - k\frac{p}{m} - (m - m_0)g\sin(\alpha_0),$$

$$\dot{\alpha}_0 = \alpha_1,$$

$$\dot{\alpha}_1 = \frac{u_\alpha(t)}{mc\varepsilon^2} - \frac{g\cos(\alpha_0)}{\varepsilon} + \frac{1}{\left(\alpha_0 + \left(\frac{\varepsilon_0}{g}\right)^{\frac{1}{\gamma}}\right)^\gamma},$$

$$u_p, u_\alpha \in U, \quad \varepsilon \in E, \quad m \in M,$$

(4)

where ε_0 is the average position of the mass center.

We study the dynamics of model (4) taking into account the certain set of parameters. To conduct computational experiments, a program is developed in the Julia language using the libraries DifferentialEquations, Plots, Printf. The trajectories of system (4) for $u_\alpha = u_p = 0$ are shown in Fig. 2. Note that it is expedient not to take into account the phase variable x in the process of stability analysis, since this variable corresponds to the linear movement of the conveyor belt.

According to Fig. 2, the system has an equilibrium state close to $(p, \alpha_0, \alpha_1) = (0, 0, 0)$.

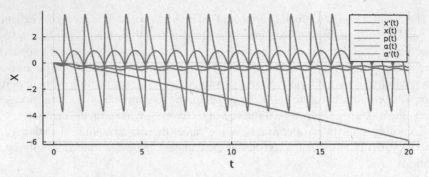

Fig. 2. Trajectory dynamics of the system (4).

However, oscillations occur in system (4), which is not consistent with the expected movement of the conveyor in the absence of control. This circumstance is due to the fact that the system is not dissipative with respect to angular momenta. In connection with this circumstance, model (4) requires clarification. It should be noted that the paper [25] considers a dissipative model of a conveyor with axial friction. Taking into account nonzero axial friction, model (4) takes the form:

$$\dot{x} = \frac{p}{m},$$
$$\dot{p} = u_p(t) - k\frac{p}{m} - (m - m_0)g\sin(\alpha_0),$$
$$\dot{\alpha}_0 = \alpha_1,$$
$$\dot{\alpha}_1 = \frac{u_\alpha(t) - l\alpha_1}{mc\varepsilon^2} - \frac{g\cos(\alpha_0)}{\varepsilon} + \frac{1}{\left(\alpha_0 + \left(\frac{\varepsilon_0}{g}\right)^{\frac{1}{\gamma}}\right)^\gamma},$$

$$u_p, u_\alpha \in U, \quad \varepsilon \in E, \quad m \in M,$$

(5)

where l is the coefficient of axial friction. The trajectories of system (5) for $u_\alpha = u_p = 0$ are shown in Fig. 3.

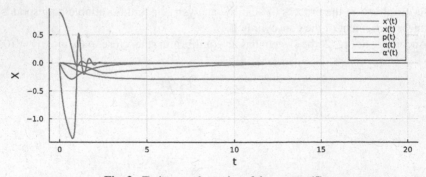

Fig. 3. Trajectory dynamics of the system (5).

According to Fig. 3, in the absence of load for model (5), there is a stable equilibrium state $(p, \alpha_0, \alpha_1) = (0, 0, 0)$. However, it should be noted that the equilibrium state of system (5), taking into account changes in the conveyor load, will vary.

Next, for system (5) with $u_\alpha = u_p = 0$, we propose a description of the load switching algorithm. The switching mode of loading is determined by the algorithm:

$$\text{if } t_i \notin \mathrm{T} : m(t_i) = m(t_{i-1});$$

$$\text{else} : m(t_i) = m(t_i) + (t_i - t_{i-1})(m_e - m_b)(t_e - t_b)^{-1} \tag{6}$$

In the description of the algorithm, the notation presented in Table 2 is adopted.

Table 2. Designations adopted in (6).

Designation	Description
T	loading intervals set
I	step number of the algorithm for solving ordinary differential equations
m_b	mass of cargo on the belt at the beginning of loading
m_e	mass of cargo on the conveyor at the end of loading
t_e	loading start time
t_b	loading end time

We will also assume that the unloading process occurs instantly. Taking this assumption into account, we introduce a switching mode, which determines the change in the mass and momentum of the system. This switching mode is determined by the algorithm:

$$\text{if } t_i \notin \mathrm{T} : m(t_i) = m(t_{i-1}), p(t_i) = p(t_{i-1});$$

$$\text{else} : m(t_i) = m(t_i) - \mu, p(t_i) = p(t_{i-1}) - \Delta x \mu. \tag{7}$$

In the description of the algorithm, the notation presented in Table 3 is adopted.

Table 3. Notation for (7).

Designation	Description
T_u	cargo unloading intervals
Δx	conveyor belt speed at the time of unloading
μ	weight of unloaded cargo

It should be noted that, in contrast to model (1), model (5) describes the momentum of the system, since m is given by a continuous piecewise linear function. Besides, we additionally assume that the position of the mass center at the moments of loading and unloading changes according to the Markov process:

$$\varepsilon(t_{l+1}) = f(\mu_1, \mu_2) + \varepsilon(t_i), \tag{8}$$

f is a random variable with a uniform distribution between the values μ_1, μ_2.

3   Results of Computational Experiments

We conduct a computer study of the model (5) taking into account switching modes (6)–(8). Loading and unloading of cargo is carried out in the time interval $t \in [0, 10]$. We assume that the loading and unloading of cargo occur regardless of the linear speed of the conveyor belt. Model parameters (5) are determined by the program structure shown in Listing 1.

Listing 1. Code snippet that defines the structure of the parameters.

```
mutable struct mParameters
    load_times::Vector{Float64}
    x::Vector{Float64}
    m_storage::Vector{Float64}
    load_intervals::Vector{Interval}
    mass_load::Vector{Float64}
    unload_times::Vector{Float64}
    mass_unload::Vector{Float64}
end

function mParameters(a::Vector{Float64})
    load_times = a
    x = Float64[]
    m_storage = Float64[]
    load_intervals = Interval.(load_times)
    mass_load = rand(range(.075,.5,10),
                     size(load_intervals))
    unload_times = load_times .+ 3.
    mass_unload = copy(mass_load)
    mParameters(load_times, x, m_storage, load_intervals,
                mass_load, unload_times, mass_unload)
end

loadParameters = mParameters([1., 2.5, 3., 4., 6., 6.5,
7., 8.])
systemParameters = [.1, 1.5, 1.5, 9.8, .5, .0, 0., 1.]
#                   mc,   mb,   k,    g,   c,  up,  u,  ε
```

The results of computational experiments for the selected parameters are shown in Fig. 4, 5, 6, 7 and 8.

Taking into account the one illustrated in Fig. 4, 5, 6, 7 and 8 of the trajectory dynamics of system (5), we can conclude that the system under consideration has the character of a stable system with an equilibrium state close to zero (under corresponding parameters set). Next, we present an interpretation of computational experiments and a description of the obtained results.

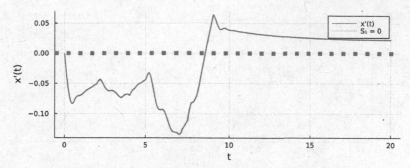

Fig. 4. Conveyor belt speed graph for model (5).

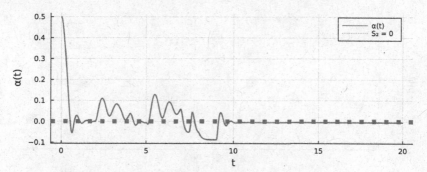

Fig. 5. Conveyor belt angular position graph for model (5).

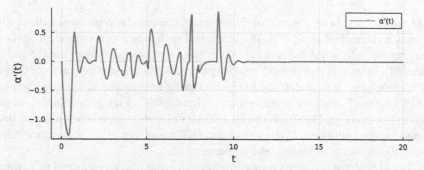

Fig. 6. Conveyor belt angular velocity graph for model (5).

4 Discussion

The computational experiments made it possible to obtain a linear velocity graph, an angular position graph, an angular velocity graph, a projection of the phase curve onto the plane (α_0, α_1), as well as a graph of the system momentum. According to Fig. 4, the linear velocity of the conveyor changes slightly as a result of changing loading modes and stabilizes when it reaches a value close to zero. It follows from Fig. 5 that the angular position of the conveyor during loading and unloading deviates from zero by up

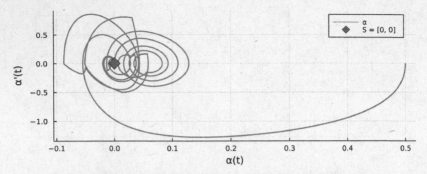

Fig. 7. Phase curve projection for the angular position of the model (5).

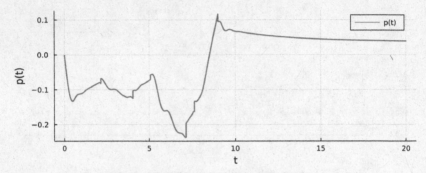

Fig. 8. Momentum graph for the model (5).

to 0.15 radians, and in the absence of disturbances, the angular position stabilizes when it reaches a value close to $\alpha_0 = 0$. The graph in Fig. 6 indicates a significant deviation of the angular velocity of the conveyor from the zero position (more than 0.5 radians per second). In the absence of loading change modes, the angular velocity stabilizes at a value close to $\alpha_1 = 0$. According to Fig. 7, during loading and unloading, the phase curve of system (7) does not leave the "attraction region" of the zero equilibrium state $(p, \alpha_0, \alpha_1) = (0, 0, 0)$. The graph in Fig. 8 indicates that momentum (similar to linear velocity) has an equilibrium state close to $p = 0$. We note that in Fig. 8 there are "teeth" showing the moments of loading and unloading cargo.

It should be noted that the obtained graphs as a result of computational experiments are consistent with the theoretical constructions of the proposed modifications and generalizations of the belt conveyor models with a dynamically changing elevation angle. The developed software demonstrates high performance due to the efficiency of using the Julia language to implement the constructed algorithms.

5 Conclusion

In this paper, we propose an approach to computer research of a number of models of conveyor transport technical systems and to the development of appropriate software. When creating software, algorithms for solving ordinary differential equations are implemented, as well as algorithms for generating switchings.

The proposed generalizations of switched dynamic models make it possible to take into account an extended range of the belt conveyor with a varying elevation angle operation features. These features include, in particular, the ability to take into account the smooth loading and instant unloading on the conveyor, as well as the presence of an angular position damper and the effect of axial resistance. The proposed approach to computer research allows study in detail the dynamics in relation to each of the three constructed models and obtain stabilization conditions. As part of the dynamics study, graphs are constructed that characterize changes in the state of phase variables and clearly demonstrate the behavior of systems for the considered sets of parameters. Based on the graphs obtained, the results are interpreted and a number of new qualitative effects are identified.

The results of the paper can be used in the problems of designing and improving systems of continuous transport, in the problems of analyzing the stability of multidimensional dynamic models with switching, as well as in the problems of finding conditions for stabilizing production line control systems.

As prospects for research, it should be noted the directions associated with the construction and study of the conveyor model "smooth loading – smooth unloading", as well as with the generalization of models for the controlled case. To study models in these directions, it is advisable to use the methods of intelligent control and optimization theory in addition to the methods of stability theory, the theory of switched systems, and the methods of differential equations numerical solution.

References

1. Subba Rao, D.V.: The Belt Conveyor: A Concise Basic Course. CRC Press, New York (2020)
2. Dmitriev, V.G., Verzhanskiy, A.P.: Grounds of the Belt Conveyor Theory. Gornaya kniga, Moscow (2017)
3. Rachkov, E.V.: Machines of Continuous Transport. Altair-MGAVT, Moscow (2014)
4. Fedorko, G., Komenskeho, P.: Implementation of industry conveyor transport. In: MATEC Web of Conferences, vol. 263, p. 01001 (2019)
5. He, D., Pang, Y., Lodewijks, G., Liu, X.: Healthy speed control of belt conveyors on conveying bulk materials. Powder Technol. **327**, 408–419 (2018)
6. Zhang, S., Xia, X.: Modeling and energy efficiency optimization of belt conveyors. Appl. Energy **88**(9), 3061–3071 (2011)
7. Karolewski, B., Ligocki, P.: Modelling of long belt conveyors. Maintenance Reliab. **16**(2), 179–187 (2014)
8. He, D., Pang, Y., Lodewijks, G.: Belt conveyor dynamics in transient operation for speed control. Int. J. Civil Environ. Struct. Constr. Architectural Eng. **10**(7), 865–870 (2016)
9. Zhao, L., Lyn, Y.: Typical failure analysis and processing of belt conveyor. Procedia Eng. **26**, 942–946 (2011)

10. Grincova, A., Marasova, D.: Experimental research and mathematical modelling as an effective tool of assessing failure of conveyor belts. Maintenance Reliab. **16**(2), 229–235 (2014)
11. Andrejiova, M., Grincova, A., Marasova, D.: Monitoring dynamic loading of conveyer belts by measuring local peak impact forces. Measurement **158**, 107690 (2020)
12. Listova, M.A. Dmitrieva, V.V., Sizin, PE.: Reliability of the belt conveyor bed when restoring failed roller supports. In: IOP Conference Series: Earth and Environmental Science, vol. 942, pp. 012002 (2021)
13. Liberzon, D.: Switching in Systems and Control. Springer Science & Business Media, Cham (2012)
14. Geromel, J.C., Colaneri, P.: Stability and stabilization of discrete time switched systems. Int. J. Control **79**(7), 719–728 (2006)
15. Malloci, I., Daafouz, J., Iung, C., Szczepanski, P.: Switched system modeling and robust steering control of the tail end phase in a hot strip mill. In: IFAC Proceedings, vol. 42, no. 17, pp. 386 391 (2009)
16. Druzhinina, O.V., Masina, O.N., Petrov, A.A.: The synthesis of the switching systems optimal parameters search algorithms. Commun. Comput. Inf. Sci. **974**, 306–320 (2019)
17. Kumar, R., Singh, V.P., Mathur, A.: Intelligent Algorithms for Analysis and Control of Dynamical Systems. Springer, Singapore (2021)
18. Yu, W.: Recent Advances in Intelligent Control Systems. Springer, Cham (2009)
19. Kim, H.: Intelligent control of vehicle dynamic systems by artificial neural network. Ph. D. Thesis, North Carolina State University (1995)
20. Khalid, H.: Implementation of artificial neural network to achieve speed control and power saving of a belt conveyor system. East.-Eur. J. Enterp. Technol. **2**, 44–53 (2021)
21. Žvirblis, T., et al.: Investigation of deep learning models on identification of minimum signal length for precise classification of conveyor rubber belt loads. Adv. Mech. Eng. **14**(6) (2022)
22. Kozhubaev, Y.N., Semenov, I.M.: Belt conveyor control systems. Sci. Tech. Bull. St. Petersburg State Polytech. Univ. **2**(195), 181–186 (2014)
23. Lutfy, O.F., Selamat, H., Mohd Noor, S.B.: Intelligent modeling and control of a conveyor belt grain dryer using a simplified type 2 neuro-fuzzy controller. Drying Technol. **33**, 1210–1222 (2015)
24. Druzhinina, O.V., Masina, O.N., Petrov, A.A.: Modeling of the belt conveyor control system using artificial intelligence methods. J. Phys: Conf. Ser. **2001**, 012011 (2021)
25. Masina, O.N., Druzhinina, O.V., Petrov, A.A.: Controllers synthesis for computer research of dynamic conveyor belt model using intelligent algorithms. In: Silhavy, R. (ed.) Artificial Intelligence Trends in Systems: Proceedings of 11th Computer Science On-line Conference 2022, Vol. 2, pp. 462–473. Springer International Publishing, Cham (2022). https://doi.org/10.1007/978-3-031-09076-9_41
26. Bezanson, J., Edelman, A., Karpinski, S., Shah, V.B.: Julia: a fresh approach to numerical computing. SIAM Rev. **59**(1), 65–98 (2017)

Author Index

A. Gibadullin (Ed.): ITIDMS 2022, CCIS 1821, p. 177, 2023.
https://doi.org/10.1007/978-3-031-31353-0

Printed in the United States
by Baker & Taylor Publisher Services